Praise for *Inside Delta Force*:

"A non-stop, page-turning drama [of] the formation of the elite group in 1978 . . . brilliant . . . exciting . . . chilling detail."   —*USA Today*

"A vivid portrait of the first decade of the elite counterterrorist unit, Delta Force [that is] so secret that even the Army does not officially confirm its existence . . . [Haney] writes well and details the gruesomeness of war with great honesty. . . . as exciting a description of counterterrorism operations as you can get."   —*Indianapolis Star*

"Nuanced, often disgusted description of the human cost of war."
—*Publishers Weekly*

"Details for the first time the [Delta] force's grueling selection process, designed to break the strongest of men, and describes the terrifying situations he has endured . . . particularly timely."   —*New York Daily News*

"A heart-pounding section on Haney's action as a sniper in Beirut and a you-were-there account of the debacle at Desert One [the failed Iran hostage rescue operation]. . . . Haney is a gung-ho soldier's soldier, to be sure, but all readers will be struck by Haney's sensitivity, depth, and skepticism. . . . [E]minently readable . . . the retired warrior also has a touch of the poet in him."   —*The Oregonian*

"Move over *Mission Impossible* . . . thrilling and disturbing . . . chilling . . . gives us the hope that, if deployed properly, these are the type of force and the kind of men of which we will all be proud."
—*The Tampa Tribune*

BEYOND SHOCK AND AWE

WARFARE IN THE 21ST CENTURY

Edited by Eric L. Haney
with Brian M. Thomsen

BERKLEY CALIBER, NEW YORK

THE BERKLEY PUBLISHING GROUP
Published by the Penguin Group
Penguin Group (USA) Inc.
375 Hudson Street, New York, New York 10014, USA
Penguin Group (Canada), 90 Eglinton Avenue East, Suite 700, Toronto, Ontario M4P 2Y3, Canada
(a division of Pearson Penguin Canada Inc.)
Penguin Books Ltd., 80 Strand, London WC2R 0RL, England
Penguin Group Ireland, 25 St. Stephen's Green, Dublin 2, Ireland (a division of Penguin Books Ltd.)
Penguin Group (Australia), 250 Camberwell Road, Camberwell, Victoria 3124, Australia
(a division of Pearson Australia Group Pty. Ltd.)
Penguin Books India Pvt. Ltd., 11 Community Centre, Panchsheel Park, New Delhi—110 017, India
Penguin Group (NZ), Cnr. Airborne and Rosedale Roads, Albany, Auckland 1310, New Zealand
(a division of Pearson New Zealand Ltd.)
Penguin Books (South Africa) (Pty.) Ltd., 24 Sturdee Avenue, Rosebank, Johannesburg 2196,
South Africa

Penguin Books Ltd., Registered Offices: 80 Strand, London WC2R 0RL, England

This book is an original publication of The Berkley Publishing Group.

Copyright © 2006 by Eric L. Haney and Brian M. Thomsen
Cover design by Steven Ferlauto
Cover photo courtesy of Reuters/CORBIS

PRINTING HISTORY
Caliber hardcover edition / April 2006
ISBN: 0:425-20798-6

This book has been cataloged by the Library of Congress

PRINTED IN THE UNITED STATES OF AMERICA

10   9   8   7   6   5   4   3   2   1

Contents

Beyond Shock and Awe— Military Operational Strategies for the New Century

As Operation Iraq Freedom has shown, military strategy has drastically changed, not just since World War II, but since Operation Desert Storm.

In just over ten years, our attack strategy has become more mechanized, targeted, and mobile, with brigades functioning in the place where armored division used to be deployed.

In a 2001 interview on CNN, Eric Haney, author of *Inside Delta Force*, explained some of the tactics that were being used in Afghanistan in terms of Special Forces strategy:

"The war being prosecuted in Afghanistan is the first war ever that could be characterized as a special operations war. Now, all conflicts are unique, and the generals of all militaries are always accused, and often rightly so, of planning the next war as a mirror image of the last one they conducted. That's not the case here. Since the time of the U.S. operation in Granada, every time we've deployed military forces, the coordination between conventional military forces and the special operations forces has evolved and improved. In Panama, that coordination was just about perfect. In the Gulf War, that perfection as much as is humanly possible, had been achieved. But the Gulf War was principally the classic clash of field armies, big units, masses of men wielding heavy equipment. The special operations missions were adjuncts to the main campaign.

"In this instance, it's just the opposite. The employment of special operations forces is the principal method of prosecuting the campaign. Periodically there still will be some limited use of conventional American forces when, to influence a specific battle, we need to bring in some real muscle. But at the conclusion of that battle, those forces will be withdrawn again, back out of Afghanistan. We cannot afford to have American forces fighting the war in Afghanistan. The country will have to be retaken by its own people. American forces will need to help them do that. In some instances against very specialized targets, those will principally be missions undertaken by Delta Force. We will go in to eliminate specific leaders, as we've discussed earlier. Delta Force by its very nature operates by going in, accomplishing its mission, and coming back out again."

Indeed, Haney's prescient analysis of the Afghanistan game plan casts a revealing light on the evolution of major military tactics by the United States, particularly now in respect to the recent "Shock & Awe" strategy that was utilized in the Spring 2003 invasion of Iraq.

The Shock and Awe strategy that had formerly been employed primarily by special forces units on a small scale were now being utilized on a city-sized target, yielding faster and more effective disruptive results that allowed the coalition forces to attack, seize, and occupy on a time line that formerly would have been allocated for an initial assault. With the appointment of General Peter Schoomaker, a special forces veteran, to the DoD, one can only assume that our tactics will continue to become lighter, faster, and more efficient in the tradition of the Seals, Delta Force, and other special forces units.

Consider the following questions:

- What does this mean to the evolution of military warfare?

- What is the next step?

- How does today's strategies vis a vis technology measure up in comparison with previous generations?

- How did we get here?

- What are the alternatives?

Essentially, what are the next necessary steps of our military evolution in terms of history, our changing times, technology, and adversaries? From the pinpoint analysis of lone and/or limited adversaries to the evaluation of future large-scale campaigns such as an invasion into Syria or Iran or even a major military stand-down with North Korea, *Beyond Shock and Awe* will be seen as the new provocative peek at America's army of the future.

The World War II method of prosecuting war is finally obsolete. The reasons for that are mainly cultural, but they happen to mesh with political reality and technical capability. There also is, and will be, a great dichotomy here. We will see the use of astonishingly effective smart hardware being used and directed by men on the ground, fighting under astoundingly brutal conditions. America is now in a position analogous to that of the British Empire in the last quarter of the nineteenth century. We will find ourselves fighting the brush wars of the world, engaging relatively primitive opponents with a combination of superior tools and a superior warrior force.

CHAPTER 1

War by Deception and Wishful Thinking

ERIC L. HANEY, COMMAND SERGEANT MAJOR, USA (RET.)

Know yourself and know your enemy, and you need not fear the result of a hundred battles. Know yourself but not the enemy, and for every victory gained you will suffer a defeat. Know neither the enemy nor yourself, and you will succumb in every battle. . . .

—From *The Art of War*, by the great military strategist of ancient China, Sun Tzu.

Even if it's not quite true, for the sake of argument, let's pretend we know ourselves. Or more precisely, let's pretend our government, knows *ourselves*: the American public. The next question then becomes, who is our enemy? Who or what is it that is opposed to us and our existence? Who is it that flies airplanes into tall buildings, blows up embassies, attacks and murders tourists, captures and beheads innocent people, blows themselves to smithereens, just for the chance of killing someone else? The ready answer comes back: Islamic terrorists. Right answer, but now comes the hard part; who the hell are they and what do they want?

Terrorism is a tactic of warfare usually employed by the weaker side in a confrontation, and it's been with mankind for a long, long time. But the sort of thing seen today is a relatively new phenomena, one that goes back about one generation.

I was one of the original operational members of the nation's counterterrorist organization, Delta Force and have lived and worked in the Arab and Islamic world for the last twenty-five years or so—and not in the Peace Corps. In 1980, I was part of the ill-fated force that attempted the rescue of our hostages in Tehran. I have guarded American ambassadors in the "Dodge City" of 1980s Beirut. Hunted terrorists around the eastern and southern rim of the Mediterranean. Lived in the tents of Bedouin tribesmen in North Africa while executing counterguerilla operations. Worked for a senior Saudi prince as bodyguard and trainer of security forces, and protected other American interests in the Middle East.

I've been intimately involved with what we face and believe I have achieved a certain level of understanding of both *Us* and *Them*. Let's start with *Us*, and shift to *Them*.

Each society and every individual in it is the end result of everyone and everything that has gone before them. I am who I am because of every ancestor I ever had. I look the way I do because most of my ancestors came from the northern parts of the British Isles. I speak English the way I do because I come from a rural working-class background in northern Georgia. My beliefs are based on the ideas of Western civilization because I am fruit from that branch of mankind's development. I view democratic participative self-government as necessary to the social compact because of its long development in Europe and eventual transition to the American shore.

In short, we in America are the result of innumerable social changes and developments that originated in the Greco-Roman world; through the relative intellectual stagnation of the Dark Ages; the flowering thought of the Renaissance; a maturing growth during the Age of Reason; the vast changes of the Industrial Age; and hence to our modern time. But the Arab/Islamic world has experienced almost none of that.

The halcyon days of Islam as a political force were relatively short and took place during that period of history when the Christian church held political sway in Europe; an era commonly referred to as the Dark Ages. By the time European thinkers were starting to liberate the West from the stultifying social dogma of the Holy Church, Islam had spent itself as a dynamic force. And it has been in a calcified state ever since.

Meteorologists tell us that what we call weather is caused by the uneven heating of the Earth's surface, and that the great clashes of warm and cold fronts and the swirling of high and low pressure systems is merely Mother Earth's effort to achieve balance. That's true, but that effort to achieve balance is what produces hurricanes, tornadoes, blizzards, and floods. I believe that human conflict comes from something similar. It comes from the uneven social development of mankind and the inevitable clash that takes place when those differing societies collide. Islamic extremism and Islamic Terror grows from the difficulty or the inability of Islam to find itself and its place in the modern world.

During the many centuries that the Muslim regions were isolated from the rest of the world, Islam served its societies quite well. It provided man a sense of his place in the great cosmic scheme, as well as religious certainty. It provided order to a certain degree. It provided a sense of unity and a codified law. It dictated how society should be organized and each individual's duties and rights within society.

It worked pretty well for a civilization stuck in time. But that time couldn't last forever. And as the rest of the world developed and changed, the Islamic world stood fast—until modern communication and transportation overwhelmed them. And that is the source of the problem.

If you hate something, ask yourself this question: What is it that I fear of this thing? Because hatred grows directly out of fear, and man fears nothing so much as the unknown. The world of Islam fears the rest of the world, but most of all, it fears change. We must remember this: The modern world of the West has only been widely visible to the Middle East since about 1970. And that's a terribly short period of time to absorb changes that have taken place in the West over many centuries.

I think of it as akin to lying in bed asleep on a winter's morning, when suddenly the lights are thrown on and the covers are jerked back, exposing you naked, cold, and startled. Your first response is to scream an expletive, pull the covers back to your chin, and throw something at the bastard who's done this to you.

During the Great Awakening of Thought, and for the next several centuries, the Christian Church persecuted and murdered the change-bringers that it viewed as a threat to its God-given authority. Islamic fundamentalists are doing the same. The Islamic world yearns for the good old days of simplicity and certainty, when thought and reason weren't a requirement, and dogma was sufficient. And now, in the face of overwhelming and sudden change, it has turned inward and reacted violently.

The bin Ladens of the world have no concern whatsoever of bringing down our government, or of destroying the American way of life, or of converting the West to Islam. Their objectives are simple: They want things they way they were, according to the myths of the good old days. Their view and desire is of a Pan-Islamic government encompassing the entire Muslim world—and oh, by the way, they, the Pure Ones, will lead that world.

The terrorists' tactic is to inflict pain and suffering upon us, as they believe they suffer from our existence and at our hands. They believe that if we suffer sufficiently, we will withdraw from contact and leave them once again to their own devices. The only problem is that the world is just too small these days for that to happen, and also, the good old days never were—neither in the Middle East nor the West. Which brings us now to the War on Terror and our invasion and occupation of Iraq.

Islamic Terror has morphed over the last thirty years. Once upon a time, it was the province of the Palestinian cause, but since the mid 1980s, the Palestinian factions have renounced the use of terror against America and the West. As the Palestinians were dropping that method of conflict with the United States, the Islamic Revolutionary government of Iran adopted it wholesale, and for the next decade or so, they and their surrogates were the ones perpetrating attacks against American targets and interests. Then along came the Iraqi invasion of Kuwait, the American-led war to push Saddam's forces back inside the Iraqi border (principally to protect the Saudis) and the outcome was: A boiling, rolling hatred within Saudi Arabia for the United States.

The original manifesto of bin Laden and Al Qaeda centered on the presence of the infidel on the sacred soil of Saudi Arabia. To say this idea appealed to the populace of that land is a wonderfully superb understatement. The Saudis have a fear and a loathing of foreigners that is astounding to anyone who has ever been witness to it, and not just for Westerners. Here is an example. It is a joke told by my Saudi friends and is simply hilarious to them at each telling:

A police corporal on duty at a traffic circle in Jiddah radios his sergeant with the report, "I am at the scene of a two-car accident. What should I do?"

The immediate reply from the sergeant is, "Arrest the foreigner."

After a short pause, the corporal responds, "They are both foreigners. What should I do?"

The sergeant instantly replies, "Arrest the Egyptian."

In Saudi Arabia, the Egyptians, no matter what position they hold in the Saudi workforce are viewed as nothing more than "wetback" labor, and they are the recipients of much ridicule and disrespect. Their only perceived redeeming quality is that at least they are Muslim. And that goes for almost everyone else in the Islamic world.

Saudi Arabia is the site of the two holiest mosques, at Mecca and Medina. In fact, the principal platform in the Saudi king's God-given right to rule is that he bears the title: "Keeper of the two Holy Mosques." The Saudis are the pure ones. The form of religion they practice is the only pure form, and almost no one else measures up. They are obsessive in their practice of religion, and they have worked diligently to spread their particular view and version throughout the Muslim world. The fundamentalist madrassas, the religious schools that preach such intolerance and hatred that have been established around the Muslim world, are funded and supported principally by the Saudis.

Please know this if you know nothing else: Islamic terrorism in its current form is a creation of the Saudis. It has its ideological source in Saudi Arabia. It has been funded by Saudi Arabians. It has been exported by Saudi Arabians. Fifteen of the nineteen hijackers of 9/11 were from Saudi Arabia. Al Qaeda was conceived and developed by a Saudi. Most of the members of Al Qaeda are Saudi, as are the bulk of the Al Qaeda prisoners held at Guantánamo Bay.

The Saudi monarchy expelled bin Laden because his first pronouncement was to replace the monarchy with his own movement. And that message has found traction with the people of Saudi Arabia because the royal family is so notoriously and publicly corrupt. But the Saudi government, at all levels, has been complicitous with Al Qaeda and other forms of extremism both before and since 9/11. So why the attack against Iraq and not a full court press against the Saudis and a demand that they change their ways? Good question. Let's take a look.

The Saudi monarchy, the vast house of Al Saud, the ruling family, wants one thing above all others: maintenance of their own power. This is an extended family that in essence owns a country, and a mighty rich one at that. It was not ever so. Saudi Arabia was created in 1932, when the patriarch of the family had, by ward and treaty, unified the tribes of the current state and announced the creation of Saudi Arabia, which means Arabia of the Saud family.

Vast oil deposits were found almost immediately, and the U.S. government, in order to forestall the British, moved in and cuddled up to the king. The result was "Aramco," the Arabian/American Oil Company, a consortium of the big American petroleum outfits that carved up the "pie" for the benefit of all. The pie stayed principally in American hands, with the Saudi ruling house receiving their royalties, until the early 1970s, when the host government took over the operation. The Americans at that point became clients and dependents. Since that time, the Saudis have wielded their incalculable wealth and vast oil reserves as an invisible yet terribly powerful weapon.

The political upper class of the United States, and that includes members of both political parties, down to third-level appointees, have kowtowed to the House of Al Saud for many years, and they have been well paid for their obeisance. The *Boston Globe*, the *New York Times*, and other respected periodicals have presented well-documented examples of the pipeline of Saudi money into American politics. Which brings us to our current situation.

The ruling regent of Saudi Arabia, Prince Abdullah, and the rest of the ruling faction of that nation, sit very precariously on the throne. I can tell you from firsthand experience, as one who has lived in the kingdom and worked in the House of Al Saud, that the common people hate the members of the monarchy with a quiet passion, and the monarchy knows this for a fact.

The CIA, in a quietly leaked report less than two years ago, predicted that the monarchy probably would not survive another five years. So, again, if all this is true, why attack Iraq? Because the only thing that can possibly replace the Saudi monarchy is an Islamic extremist government the likes of which the world has never seen. In fact, that government is waiting in the wings.

The Ulema, the Court of Senior Islamic Scholars, is the group that interprets Muslim law and advises the Crown on how the law should be enacted. Saudi Arabia is the only nation in the world where the Sharia, Muslim law, is the law of the land, and the Ulema is the entity that wields the power of that law. Its other function is to tell the people that the House of Al Saud rules by divine right and at the will of Allah. The Ulema is a group of religious extremists and fundamentalists who would put the rest of the world to the sword if they could and if that world would not follow their edicts. They can do so within their own country, and they are the ones who have exported their extreme views to the poorest and most desperate areas of the Muslim world. And the Ulema is only the tip of the clerical iceberg within Saudi Arabia.

The attack into Iraq, the overthrow of the regime of Saddam Hussein, and the imposition of a friendly or at least a compliant government in that country was conducted as a means of corralling and containing Saudi Arabia when the monarchy is deposed and a radical evangelical Muslim government takes over. Iraqi oil would be a counterbalance to the Saudi oil reserves. It would provide a base of operations from which to seize the Saudi oil fields, because there is no way an American government could allow that massive wealth to be used by the worst possible form of an extremist government.

Even with limited wealth, a radical Saudi regime would be a dangerous thing. The excesses of the Revolutionary Islamic government of Iran would be seen as child's play by comparison. The first place to experience its influence would be Egypt, a nation with a huge population of desperately poor people. It is only in the last ten years that Egypt has beaten down the extremists within its borders. Most of the survivors of that purge found refuge with Al Qaeda. But the worst of all possibilities, the nightmare scenario, is to be found farther east.

What would be your response to the idea of a radical Islamic nation that possessed not only nuclear weapons but also the ballistic missiles necessary to deliver them. Terribly frightening thought, isn't it? Well the world is only one coup away from such a nation. And that is Pakistan.

Consider the following: Pakistan is a Muslim nation. It was the largest recipient of Saudi money used to fund the madrassas. Pakistan's government was one of the few to recognize the Taliban regime of Afghanistan. Pakistan changes government by coup. The current Pakistani president, General Musharaf, seized power in a military coup. Large segments of the Pakistani government, especially within the army and the secret intelligence services were very sympathetic to Al Qaeda and the Taliban. Musharaf has been the target of at least three close assassination attempts since January 2005. And Pakistan has nuclear weapons and missiles.

Were an Islamic extremist government, one sympathetic to the aims of Al Qaeda to seize power in Pakistan, I believe India would have no choice but to attack with nuclear weapons. The reasons are simple. There is a long history of deadly violence between the Hindus of India and the Muslims of both India and Pakistan. At the partition of India, Muslims and Hindus fought viciously, and continue to do so to this day. But more than that, to the Muslim view, Hindus are the genuine infidels.

Under the teachings of Islam, Christians and Jews are known as "People of the Book," fellow monotheists who worship the same God as the Muslims worship. According to the Quran, Christians and Jews are to be well treated and even protected by Muslims (under some pretty bad circumstances, I have been afforded protection by my Muslim hosts). But Hindus, as polytheists, receive no such consideration and are to be considered enemies of God.

As recently as the summer of 2003, India and Pakistan rattled their nuclear sabers at one another, and otherwise intelligent people on each side of the border were clamoring for the final showdown. In Nevil Shute's classic novel, *On the Beach*, the war that destroys mankind starts as a nuclear exchange between India and Pakistan.

If even half of what I've said is true, how does any administration explain this to the American public, a public that usually gets its information through slogans and sound bites. Couple that with an administration that doesn't appear to genuinely trust the great unwashed mass of the electorate and what do we get: a smoke screen about weapons of mass destruction in Iraq, and transplanting democracy to the Middle East by force. A war by deception and wishful thinking. The use of brute force when subtlety and cunning were required. The war in Iraq has not yet succeeded in fixing any of the problems the world faces. So far it has only exacerbated them. It has shown the extremists that they can face the United States in a guerilla war and have a good chance of prevailing.

We didn't know the enemy, and I don't think we knew ourselves. I fear the cancer has metastasized. I fear we are in the opening phase of what may become the Third World War. I pray that I am wrong.

CHAPTER 2

From Shock and Awe to Aw Shucks

WILLIAM TERDOSLAVICH

It was the perfect war.

The United States and Britain brought four divisions to Kuwait. In two days, the British were at the threshold of Basra, doing what the Iranians could not do in eight years of war. In three weeks, American tanks rolled through Baghdad, seemingly without effort.

Losses were few.

Enemy casualties were many.

It was a one-sided blowout, a splendid little war that did not take long to win, just the way Americans like to fight them.

Two years later, over 1,300 American soldiers were killed in action in Iraq. Over 10,000 were wounded. Close to 150,000 were occupying a country where they were clearly being treated as unwanted guests, not liberators.

What happened?

The United States fought the war it wanted to fight. It was the war it had been training to fight since the Vietnam War ended. Training and technology were brought to bear on set-piece battle between two armies. Such a war would be fought at high tempo. At every level, from platoon to corps, unit leaders planned and attacked faster than their enemies, forcing them to react to every American move, ultimately reaching a point where the enemy was reacting to the last move as the next blow was delivered. Do this fast enough and the enemy will collapse, blind and confused, with all falling to ruin around them.

The United States fights this kind of war better than anyone else. It has developed a dizzying array of sensors to cut through the fog of war, collect and collate information on the enemy and forward it to the right commanders. (At least, that's how the system should work.) AWACs will find and identify anything that flies. JSTARs will do the same for anything that crawls on the ground. Rivet Joint will pick up any radio message anywhere on the spectrum and identify its source and frequency. Global Hawk will deliver a live TV picture of any spot on the battlefield. Predator will do that, too, only at a lower altitude. And the army would like to take all these data streams and put them into a computerized system called Blue Force Tracker that will show all enemy and friendly units, and put it all on a screen near you.

All of this stuff can't detect three Iraqi insurgents in a closed room, strapping a detonator to a pair of artillery shells and attaching a cell phone to act as the remote-controlled trigger. That homemade bomb will be used to blow up a passing American HUMV on patrol. No sensor can spot this bomb ahead of time.

And therein lies the problem.

While America eagerly trained for the war it wanted to fight, its enemies chose not to. Rather than try to match America's strength, it was easier to exploit America's weakness: the reluctance to suffer casualties in a long, drawn-out guerilla war.

Any army goes into battle with a doctrine—a codified method for fighting that becomes second nature through training. A commander does not have to write a detailed list of orders telling his soldiers what to do and when. They already know how to fight, so the commander only has to tell them what to do, not how to do it.

The U.S. Army already has a well-established doctrine for main force battle. Every battalion trains hard for this mission, culminating in exercises against the "opposition force" battalion at Fort Irwin, California. That is where every battalion commander gets to learn from his mistakes, winning one mock battle out of every five fought.

The doctrine and the training paid off handsomely in the second war against Iraq, much more so than the first. Now the sensor and communications network is far deeper. Accurate weapons are more plentiful. A brigade today punches far above its weight, every bit equal to a division of the previous generation. So it was no surprise that the United States only needed a few weeks to take Baghdad and oust dictator Saddam Hussein.

But there was no doctrine or training regimen for nation building and peacekeeping. After waging war, those same battalions of armor and mechanized infantry had to wage peace—rebuilding neighborhoods, then shooting at terrorists and insurgents. Fortunately, many sergeants and colonels could rely on their experience handling peacekeeping and nation building in Bosnia and Kosovo. This folk wisdom, plus common sense, enabled the Army to find its way in Iraq, albeit imperfectly.

Folk wisdom and common sense are not substitutes for training and doctrine. Playing a desperate game of catch-up, the Army is now training to fight the wars it didn't want to fight before. At Fort Polk, Louisiana, soldiers readying for Iraq deployment get some practice patrolling a small town inhabited by role-playing civilians who form crowds, stage riots, or just plain get in the way during sniper fire, just to give troops a real-life taste of enforcing order in ambiguous situations.

The United States dislikes counterinsurgency, nation building and peacekeeping. These are the downsides of the Vietnam War that still haunt—and hurt—to this day. It is the war without a front, where enemies and civilians are indistinguishable. There are no stand-up, set-piece firefights. There is no decisive battle to mark the turning point toward victory. Such wars mock advanced weapons and technology. Supersonic jet fighters, stealth bombers, carrier battle groups, armored divisions, and computer-linked sensors can't do much against a group of men armed with AK-47s, RPGs, and a willingness to fight and die for a cause, no matter how dubious.

In such wars, the enemy will lose ten times as many men as our side.

They will replace them.

And they will try to fight as long as it takes for us to give up and go away, frustrated with the cost in blood, money, and time.

That is how we lose.

Reaching for the Weapon

How the United States chose to fight Iraq is a long and complex story that cannot be analyzed or understood by shouting slogans or reciting clichés about Vietnam. Political passion clouds judgment. Seeing what goes right is not an implicit endorsement of Bush Administration policy. Showing what went wrong is not an explicit criticism of administration incompetence, either.

As Clausewitz once stated pithily, war is politics by other means. When a nation goes to war, it is for a political purpose. Force will be used to resolve a dispute that diplomacy or sanctions could not. A national leader, reaching for the weapon that is his nation's army, does so without fully knowing its sharpness and reach. How to fight the war is the challenge delegated to the generals. They have to win the fight in order to obtain the desired political goal.

Indeed, that was the case with Iraq. When George W. Bush took his oath of office in January 2001, he inherited a decade-old alliance cobbled together by his father, then-president George H. W. Bush. The original purpose was to eject Iraqi forces from Kuwait, which was invaded in August 1990. By the end of February 1991, the mission was accomplished.

Alliances are easy to build when nations face a common threat, but hard to maintain after the enemy is vanquished. The question of Iraq's possession of chemical, biological, and nuclear weapons (weapons of mass destruction—WMD) was still unanswered at war's end, so the alliance had to be maintained. The United Nations engineered an inspection program to make sure Iraq had no WMD stockpiles. To enforce the inspections regime, economic sanctions would be applied and maintained by the United Nations. In 1998, Iraq kicked out the U.N. inspectors before it could be fully determined that Iraq had no WMD. The United States responded with a brief air campaign against Iraq, meanwhile maintaining the sanctions and enforcing "no fly" zones that excluded the Iraqi air force over northern and southern Iraq.

Following these events, it became clear that the anti-Iraq alliance was going to be harder to maintain. France and Russia were becoming increasingly reluctant to continue pressing sanctions on Iraq. Saudi Arabia was inching toward rapprochement. The Arab "man in the street" viewed the sanctions with increasing disfavor, as ordinary Iraqis endured the hardships of poverty, lack of medicine, and food shortages. Al Jazeera showed the TV images of that suffering in living color. Even the United Nation's oil for food program was compromised, as Saddam Hussein paid multimillion-dollar bribes to key officials, who then allowed the sanctions to be evaded so weapons and proscribed goods could be imported. Hussein, in control of food rationing, increased his political grip. The presidential palaces were rebuilt as the people starved and suffered.

The downside facing the United States in 2002 was the possible collapse of sanctions against Iraq. Once freed from international constraint, Saddam Hussein would rearm and threaten the region again. The exact size and nature of Hussein's WMD arsenal was still unknown. And of course, the bloody repression of the Iraqi people would still continue at the rate of 30,000 killed per year, as it had for an entire decade.

None of this would have happened if the United States pressed on for Baghdad in 1991. But that is too easy to say with hindsight.

While then-president George H. W. Bush complained about the incompleteness of victory, it was politically impossible for the United States to finish what it started. Many allies signed on to the alliance to liberate Kuwait and cut Iraq down to size, not to overthrow Saddam Hussein and free Iraq. Saudi Arabia might turn off its fuel taps and close its ports if the United States decided to go it alone. The United States did not have the $60 billion to pay for the Gulf War, owing to high budget deficits and a weighty national debt. Liberating and rebuilding Iraq would be a far greater expense, tying down the army in occupation duty for an unknown number of years.

Caution proved to be the better part of valor for George H. W. Bush, so the war was limited to liberating Kuwait.

That was easily done.

Mission accomplished?

It would be all too corny to claim that the sins of the father are visited upon the son. George W. Bush did inherit an unfinished problem in Iraq from his predecessor, Bill Clinton, who got it from Bush's father, the president. Iraq was certainly in the strategic crosshairs of the current Bush administration since day one. By the spring of 2003, despite successfully obtaining a renewal of the U.N. inspection regime, Bush was maintaining his aim to remove Saddam Hussein. Along with Iran and North Korea, Iraq was part of the "axis of evil," a nice way to package several long-running foreign policy problems so that their sum demanded greater action. As U.N. weapons inspectors found no WMD, the United States failed to get U.N. Security Council approval to invade Iraq as punishment for Iraq's failure to comply with previous U.N. resolutions.

In the end, the United States would go to war without most of the world's approval.

Bush stated three war aims, though never at one time or in one place. This made the sale of the war to the American people a bit confusing. First, Saddam Hussein must be removed from power and the Baath regime overthrown. Second, Saddam Hussein's WMD arsenal must be found and destroyed. Third, Iraq must be returned to a liberated Iraqi people so they can form a democratically elected government. The first two aims the United States could accomplish. The third aim was up to the Iraqi people. These were the political goals that were worth fighting for. George Bush persuaded the American people this was so. With the appropriate Congressional resolutions giving the war a green light, Bush now turned to the military to use force to achieve these goals.

The War We Wanted to Fight

The previous Gulf War in 1990–91 saw the six-month buildup of a three-corps multinational army that would strike north into and around Kuwait to oust Saddam Hussein's massive mechanized army. The U.S. contribution alone amounted to over a half-dozen divisions, numbering over 500,000 troops.

For the Iraq War, Secretary of Defense Donald Rumsfeld wanted a lighter deployment. First figures called for a 250,000-man deployment to face a much depleted Iraqi Army that would be fighting to defend its homeland. But even that force was too large for Rumsfeld, who locked horns with Central Command chief Gen. Tommy Franks over the scope of the plan. When it finally took shape, the number was cut to around 130,000 men. The plan called for a British armored division to advance north from Kuwait to take Basra, while an American corps of two divisions moved north into Iraq from western Kuwait.

The U.S. war plan called for the Third Infantry Division's attack to be the primary effort. It would advance through open terrain northward on an axis west of the Euphrates River. To the Third Infantry Division's right, the First Marine Expeditionary Force would cross the Euphrates at Nasariyah and proceed north between the Euphrates and Tigris rivers as the secondary effort. The 101st Airborne, now an airmobile division, would be ready to support the Third Infantry Division. One brigade of the 82nd Airborne would also be held as a strategic reserve. Adding firepower to the primary effort would be the 11th Attack Helicopter Regiment, with its strike force of AH-64 Apache helicopter gunships. Plans also called for the Fourth Infantry Division to advance on Baghdad southward from Turkey. This required the political approval of the Turkish parliament, which as it turned out never came. The goal here was to pin down any Iraqi units deployed in the north to keep them from reinforcing the defense against the Third Infantry Division and the First Marine Expeditionary Force.

Some rules would be broken with the lighter approach. The plan called for the offensive to go forward before the U.S. buildup was completed. Such a penny-pinching approach to reinforcement ran the risk of the U.S. offensive being defeated in detail, but this could only happen if the enemy was competent. The Iraqi Army was not a sharp fighting force in the previous Gulf War, and had since degraded in the decade leading up to the Iraq War. Against an enemy so weak and questionably commanded, the United States could bend or break a few rules and get away with it. This theme would run throughout the campaign.

The Iraqi Army had fifteen divisions, clustered in five corps deployed in an arc from the south, facing Kuwait; to the east, facing Iran; then to the north, facing the Kurds. But the task of protecting Baghdad was entrusted to the six-division Republican Guard. Two divisions faced north toward Kurdish country while the remainder guarded the southern approaches to Baghdad. Add to this one division of Special Republican Guard to defend the capital. Also add the irregular Saddam Fedayeen—basically regime enthusiasts with guns but no training, deployed in every city. Toss in assorted Baath Party loyalists responsible for repressing the local population. Stir thoroughly upon invasion.

That's the recipe.

But the ingredients left something to be desired.

The Iraqi Army theoretically had the training and equipment to put up a fight. But desertion rates were high, maintenance was poor, and its job repressing the locals did not prepare it to fight a war of maneuver against the United States. Republican Guard divisions numbered about 8,000–10,000 each, but again equipment was old and not thoroughly maintained. The Saddam Fedayeen, foreign fighters, and Special Republican Guard had no more than small arms and mortars, and little training.

Aside from the collapse of several divisions in the south of Iraq, the Iraqi Army pretty much sat this one out. Massive desertions left abandoned equipment to mark its positions. The cities were packed with the irregulars—Saddam Fedayeen, Baath Party, and foreign fighters. Arms caches were plentiful and widespread. Knowing U.S. rules of engagement, the "bad guys" were not shy about using schools, hospitals, and mosques as bases of operations. (If the United States struck any of these militarized targets, the Iraqis could claim the United States was waging war as criminals and barbarians.) Only the Republican Guard was going to put up a conventional defense: Disperse the defenders to avoid giving the Americans any target, but concentrate forces for attack when the opportunities presented themselves.

While the Iraqis depended on a mix of guerilla and conventional defense, the United States was going to fight the war it practiced for. Between airborne and ground sensors (counter-battery radar and thermal sights on tanks and Bradley IFVs), any enemy would be spotted in night or day, in any kind of weather, and killed at great distance before he could engage.

The Iraqi strategy had a simple aim: kill lots of Americans. It sounds like something out of a bad movie or comic book, but there was some basis for this in recent history. In all of its post–Cold War interventions, the United States has avoided casualties, sometimes ending an intervention if too many servicemen were lost. In 1983, the suicide truck bomb that killed 241 Marines in Beirut was enough to convince President Ronald Reagan that the intervention was not worth the effort. In 1993, the U.S. deployment in Somalia ended at the cost of eighteen dead and over seventy-five wounded when American Rangers and Delta Force became operationally complacent during a routine raid. This was enough to persuade then-president Clinton to call it quits in Somalia. In both cases, the forces that "won" were little more than armed locals who had little to no military training and a desire to fight and die for their "cause." This perception was reinforced by the Kosovo War, which the United States fought entirely from the air, suffering no battle casualties. The Serbian military negated many American technical advantages by dispersing forces and setting up dummy tanks that would draw American air strikes from 15,000 feet. The Iraqi leadership studied these wars, as well as the recent American invasion of Afghanistan, trying to find the right tactics that would offset America's high-tech advantages. However, they did not understand how the United States learned from the mistakes made in these campaigns as well.

For the Americans, the one underlying idea that came out of that review was the concept of "shock and awe." Most Americans first heard this term at the beginning of the Iraq War. It became a buzzword for high expectations—an opening air strike so massive that the Iraqi command authority would collapse from fear. (The opening-night air strikes proved to be smaller than in the previous Gulf War, so "shock and awe" became a derogatory term used to mock the Bush administration.)

"Shock and Awe" was a term coined by Harlan K. Ullman and James P. Wade in their 1996 paper "Shock and Awe: Achieving Rapid Dominance." As the authors put it, the goal is to impose a "regime of shock and awe" on the enemy in order to achieve military objectives. That is done by Rapid Dominance, which requires the United States to go into battle with "total knowledge and understanding of self, adversary, and environment; rapidity and timeliness in application; operational brilliance in execution; and (near) total control and signature management of the entire operational environment."[1]

One military example given by the authors (and cited by many other analysts) was the Nazi German conquest of France in 1940. By marrying communications (two-way radio), concentrated armor (the panzer division), close air support, and decisive command near the point of action, Germany was able to fight its battle at a faster tempo than the French army. France's military was still operating as it did in

World War I, with centralized command managing a set-piece battle. Information flowed to the top of the command pyramid, where a decision was made and orders then sent back down the echelons of command to the front, then implemented by frontline units. Information flowed no faster than repeated phone calls cascading up the chain of command, or paper reports carried by couriers on motorcycles. With the Germans advancing so quickly, however, the French high command found itself issuing orders for situations that did not exist anymore. At a certain point, the command system broke down, unable to do anything.

"Shock and Awe" finds its roots in the work of the autodidactic Col. John Boyd, an Air Force fighter pilot who first codified what was known implicitly: He who can impose change the fastest, wins. From this, he derived the OODA Loop—Observation, Orientation, Decision, Action. A pilot in a dogfight will win if he can do this faster than the enemy, in effect getting inside the bad guy's decision cycle. As it is for fighter pilots, so it is for generals leading armies. A general who can gather information, make the right decision, and execute a plan faster than his enemy will dictate the course of the battle. Eventually, the enemy finds itself reacting to yesterday's information while blind to today's attack. The defense then becomes uncoordinated and is easily defeated in detail by the attacker.

Shock and Awe in Action

The conventional portion of the Iraq War can be divided into four distinct phases. First is the initial breakthrough and advance up to Najaf. Second was the pause forced by the *shamal*, or dust storm. Third was the resumption of the offensive, as the Army broke through at Karbala

Gap while the Marines crossed the Tigris near Kut. Fourth was the endgame, as U.S. units fought their way into Baghdad.

Running throughout all four phases was the air component, as enemy ground units were found and fixed for destruction by accurate air strikes regardless of time or weather. Making this possible was the extensive use of precision guided munitions (PGMs) including laser-guided bombs (LGBs) or Joint Direct Attack Munitions (JDAMs), which are basically dumb bombs guided to target by the Global Positioning System (GPS). All of this was augmented by a rich array of airborne sensors also able to find and fix targets.

March 19, 2003, became the war's start date, almost by surprise. When U.S. intelligence got word of an Iraqi government meeting where Saddam Hussein may have been present, orders were given immediately to bomb the building. An impromptu raid was flown by F-117 Stealth fighters, backed by cruise missiles, to hit the target. It was to be the first example of "Shock and Awe" in the war. A dictatorship is centralized command personified. Taking off the head disrupts command, as it is not always certain who is in charge when that happens, thus causing some confusion when action is needed. This tactic was repeated three weeks later when the United States thought it had knowledge of Saddam Hussein holding another meeting at a restaurant in Baghdad's Mansour district. A B-1 bomber on station dropped four bombs on the target, obliterating it. Again, it was not certain for a while whether Saddam Hussein was dead or alive.

March 20 saw the start of the ground war, as the Third Infantry Division crossed the Kuwaiti border, advancing through the open desert to points west of Nasariyah. The First Marine Expeditionary Force followed, aiming to take the bridges across the Euphrates at Nasariyah to begin a parallel advance northward, between the Euphrates and the Tigris rivers. British forces, with a regiment of U.S. Marines, captured

Iraq's lone port, Umm Qasr. Then the British First Armored picked up the pace, bound north for Basra.

The British could advance just as quickly as the Americans. But when it came to confronting the defenses of Basra, the First Armored Division slowed down the tempo of its operations. Sniper teams and special forces infiltrated the city to disrupt resistance, using meaningful information provided by the network of agents run by British intelligence. Iraqi Army attempts to break out of the city were futile, at best, as the tanks of the British Seventh Armored Brigade had no trouble picking off obsolete Iraqi T-55s at several miles' distance. Several battles were infantry-only affairs, done without air strikes or artillery to keep collateral damage and civilian casualties down. One fight for the Basra College of Literature pitted British infantry against three hundred foreign fedayeen who were eager to fight but lacked training. Relying on basic infantry skills, the British cleared the complex in four hours.[2] By April 7, Basra was taken. Here Britain's experience in Northern Ireland paid off, as the armored vehicles were pulled out of town and replaced with foot patrols by soldiers wearing hats, not helmets, to restore order and calm civilians. "Smile, shoot, smile" was the practice, not "shock and awe." It was a transition from war-fighting to peacekeeping that the Americans would have a harder time pulling off.

The tools of "Shock and Awe" were plentiful on the ground. Each brigade or regiment of the Third Mechanized Infantry Division and First Marine Expeditionary Force punched above its weight class, perhaps each equal to a division. Again, sensors, computers, and long-range weaponry combined to find, fix, and kill targets before they could get in range to attack U.S. units. For example, U.S. counterbattery radars would identify the trajectories of enemy shells as soon as they left their gun tubes, forwarding the target information to friendly artillery units, which would fire back instantly.[3]

"Speed kills" was another concept put into practice. If American forces advanced quickly enough, then velocity could compensate for lack of mass.[4] Iraqi commanders would find themselves being overtaken by events, never being able to react to American moves quickly enough to stop them. American subordinate officers were encouraged to bypass resistance and maintain the speed of the advance, leaving protection of the rear areas to follow-up forces. Iraqi forces would have to concentrate their units to attack supply lines, but as soon as they did that, they became vulnerable to air strikes. The downside is that ambushes for American units became more frequent, and the rear was never quite secure.

This was clearly seen in the battles of Nasariyah, Samawah, and Najaf. The Iraqis concentrated their irregular forces in the cities along the American's path of advance in the hope of forcing city fights that would produce a lot of dead Americans. (After all, it worked in Mogadishu.) The rapid advance of the Third Infantry made these bypassed cities problematic for follow-up units. The 507th Maintenance Company, a support unit for Third Infantry, found out the hard way that there was no such thing as "the rear" when it got lost at Nasariyah and blundered into an ambush. Between the bullets and the vehicle collisions, eleven Americans were killed. A number of soldiers were captured, including Private Jessica Lynch. (Unfortunately, her story would later overshadow that of her comrades in the 507th and other events in the Iraq War, thanks to massive media coverage.)

The First Marine Expeditionary Force had to fight its way through Nasariyah, using a task force to secure the town to permit the division to pass through. Likewise, Third Infantry had to peel off a brigade to cover Samawah and another to cover Najaf, keeping Iraqi reinforcements contained and away from the U.S. supply lines. That did not leave enough striking power left to plow through Karbala Gap, a bottleneck of open land between Lake Razzazah to the west and the city of Karbala to the east. The Republican Guard's Medina Division was holding this ground.

To crack the Medina Division, the commanders on the scene resorted to a long-range helicopter strike with the 11th Attack Helicopter Regiment. Deep strike was done before in the Gulf War. On opening night, AH-64s went deep into the desert to wipe out Iraqi early warning radars and SAM sites, complementing the air strikes. During the Battle of 73 Easting, VII Corp's Aviation Brigade launched two Apache strikes as a follow-up to 2nd Armored Cavalry Regiment's (ACR) battle with the Republican Guard's Tawakalna Division.[5]

But this time, the deep strike would be thwarted by a low-tech Iraqi defense. It did not help that a series of small, cascading mishaps hampered 11th Attack Helicopter Regiment's mission planning, a good example of what Clausewitz called "friction" in warfare. The Iraqi Army did get wind of the impending attack from several sources and had sufficient time to guess where the attack would be coming from, and line the approach with plenty of troops. As the thirty-two AH-64 Apaches banked toward their target, the streetlights below were turned off for two seconds—a signal for troops below to open fire with RPGs and small arms.[6] One Apache was downed, and all thirty-two machines took between ten and twenty hits in the three-hour attack.[7]

The United States was blindsided by the low-tech counterstroke.

"Shock and Awe" was now a shoe on the wrong foot.

The problem was generally foreseen, though not in such exact terms.

In the summer preceding the war, Marine Corps Lt. Gen. Paul van Riper dealt an embarrassing blow to the Navy during the free-play phase of the Millennium Challenge 2002 war game. As the "Red Force" leader of a simulated but unnamed Iran, van Riper used the muzzein's call to morning prayer as the signal to launch a simulated simultaneous attack by small boats, planes, and cruise missiles against a U.S. carrier battle group in the Persian Gulf. The game attack sank sixteen ships, including one aircraft carrier and two amphibious assault ships. The weapons were different, but the tactic was low-tech, bypassed electronic communications (always monitored by the United States), and achieved results through surprise.[8]

The loss of the 507th Maintenance Company, and the debacle of the 11th Attack Helicopter Regiment's attack were small setbacks that did not materially impede America's one-sided victory. But these small setbacks crudely foreshadowed the human problems that would challenge an army built on high technology to achieve "Shock and Awe."

Bad Weather and Good Hunting

On March 24, 2003, the U.S. advance was brought to a grinding halt. Not by Iraqi resistance, but by the *shamal*—or sandstorm. Visibility plunged to ten yards or less. U.S. forces were now halfway to Baghdad in less than a week, but strung out along the route of advance. If the United States lacked its high-tech advantage, its forces would have been very vulnerable to defeat in detail. An army strung out is vulnerable to attack on its flanks, a scenario for defeat originally confirmed by the Roman Army's defeat at the hands of barbarians at Teutoburger Wald in 9 A.D.

The Iraqis did indeed use the blinding sandstorm to move and concentrate units, hoping to cut the American supply routes and defeat the Third Infantry Division's battalions in detail. Yet no such thing happened. M-1 tanks and M-2 Bradleys, thanks to their thermal sights, still could fire on any gathering of Iraqi irregulars. Up above, JSTARs could still pick out the movement of ground units with its computer-aided radar systems. Targeting information could still be forwarded to orbiting U.S. aircraft, armed with GPS-guided JDAMs to destroy any Iraqi unit.

A change in air tactics also helped. As the Iraqi Air Force stayed on the ground and Iraqi air defense was totally neutralized, U.S. air commander Lt. Gen. T. Michael Mosely moved his tankers and JSTARs aircraft deep into Iraqi air space. Constant sensor presence and refueling of U.S. strike aircraft helped maintain the ability to destroy Iraqi ground targets. U.S. bombers and fighters were equipped with infrared sensors that could pick out targets on the sandstorm-clouded ground that the Mark I Eyeball could not.

The Air Force had a term for this: Find, Fix, Track, Target, Engage, Assess (F2T2EA), better known as "the kill chain."[9] Ideally, the kill chain must be as short as possible. For example, when Saddam Hussein's whereabouts became known later in the war, it took forty-five minutes from receipt of information to "bombs away" for an orbiting B-1 bomber to attack. Ideally, the Air Force would like to see this shrunk down to one minute or less.[10] Nonetheless, overwhelming American sensor superiority and massive air strikes reduced the Medina Division by 75 percent.[11] That changed Third Infantry's advance through Karbala Gap from a frontal assault into a cakewalk.

During the pause, V Corps Commander Lt. Gen. William Wallace got into some hot water when he commented on the unexpected attacks by a large number of Iraqi irregulars. The enemy he was fighting now was "a bit different than the one we war-gamed against, because of the paramilitary forces."[12] The fights were always one-sided wins for U.S. troops, who easily outgunned the attackers. But the guerilla attacks continued nonetheless, oftentimes frequent and intense.

Helmuth von Moltke the Elder once observed that no plan ever survives first contact with the enemy.

Why would Iraq be any different?

Critics pointed to the guerilla attacks as proof that the war's proponents got it wrong. The Americans were not being greeted as liberators, but as invaders. Many were quick to call the situation a "quagmire," with the presumed advantage going to the guerillas. Yet Nasairyah fell to the Marines by the third day of the war. Samawah was secured by the 82nd Airborne, while the 101st Airborne and elements of Third Infantry spent the first several days of April securing Najaf. Meanwhile, the British secured Basra by the first week in April. Guerillas lost every stand-up fight against American and British forces. But that didn't mean winning was easy.

Shock It Ain't

Concurrent with the main drive up from Kuwait was a secondary effort that nearly came to naught. The Fourth Infantry Division was supposed to land in Turkey and drive south through the Kurdish region on to Tikrit (Saddam Hussein's hometown), thence on to Baghdad.

But Turkey's parliament could not pass the measure allowing a foreign force to transit its territory to invade a neighboring state. The measure failed by a close margin. The half-plan went forward anyway. The 173rd Airborne Brigade was supposed to make a paradrop to spearhead the Fourth's advance. Now the brigade would go in, augmented by Army Special Forces' 10th Group, a tank company from the 1st Infantry Division, and the 26th Marine Expeditionary Unit (battalion-sized). This may seem a ridiculously small deployment to make in the face of 10–15 Iraqi divisions facing the north. But the United States had already negotiated a de facto alliance with the Kurds, who could back up the American task force with 50,000 *peshmerga* guerillas.

This portion of the Iraq War had a greater resemblance to the Afghanistan War than it did to the southern advance on Baghdad. Air strikes had to be delivered from carriers in the eastern Mediterranean, guided to target by Special Forces. After clearing out an Ansar-al-Islam terrorist enclave near the Iranian border, 10th Group shifted its attention southward, launching encirclement attacks that captured Mosul and Kirkuk. The Iraqi Army and Republican Guard defense left something to be desired. But the strategic goal was accomplished—no Iraqi units redeployed south to reinforce the defense of Baghdad.[13]

Shock and Awe in Motion

Once Najaf was secured in early April 2003, Third Infantry reconcentrated and blew through Karbala Gap with ease, but met resistance forcing the river crossing at Yasin al-Khudayr (Objective Peach) on the Euphrates. First Marine Expeditionary Force took Ad Diwaniyah and feinted toward Al Hillah. This drew a number of Iraqi units southward from Baghdad as they expected a frontal assault by the Marines. But that was not the American plan, as the Marines made a lateral move toward An Numaniyah to the east, crossing the Tigris, and resuming the advance on Baghdad from the southeast. Violent attacks, rapid breakthroughs, and quick advances brought American forces to the outskirts of Baghdad, reaching Saddam Hussein International Airport by April 3.

As theater commander General Tommy Franks was fond of saying, "speed kills."[14] More important, with speed came surprise, as American units would pop up closer to Baghdad than the Iraqi defenders had expected.

With the approach to Baghdad, the brigade and battalion commanders of Third Infantry were going to rewrite the rules again. Traditionally, any armor force entering a city without supporting infantry was doomed. The "Thunder Run" made by Task Force 1-64 of Third Infantry's second brigade had a simple task. The mixed force of M-1 Abrams tanks and Bradley IFVs drove down Highway 8 into downtown Baghdad, moving and shooting all the way, then looped out again to the airport, then back to Objective Saints (intersection of Highways 1 and 8, south of Baghdad). Even though every American vehicle was hit, only one tank was lost. The Abrams was impervious to RPG fire, as was the Bradley. The losses inflicted on the Iraqis made the Thunder Run another one-sided battle, with as many as 100 vehicles destroyed and 1,000–3,000 Iraqi troops killed. Unknown was the number of Iraqis who fled, as evidenced by discarded uniforms and abandoned tanks.

On the second "Thunder Run" into Baghdad, the United States had to secure three cloverleaf interchanges on Highway 8, leading north from Objective Saints. Nicknamed "Moe," "Larry," and "Curly," they secured Third Infantry's supply line to support the armored assault. The three interchanges were also the local high ground in the neighborhood—ideal for defense. The fight for Curly—the most lightly defended of the three—lasted twelve hours, as Iraqi irregulars and regime remnants pressed home repeated attacks, mounting anything they could find—pickup trucks, taxis, and motorcycles—and charging with guns blazing. The trouble was that none of these attacks were coordinated to strike simultaneously and overwhelm the company-sized task force holding Curly. Instead, U.S. troops defeated the attacks in detail, but were still hard pressed. Once Curly was reinforced, trucks could get through to resupply the two-battalion tank attack on downtown Baghdad.

Perhaps the last proof of "Shock and Awe" was the live TV appearance by Iraqi information minister Muhammed Said al-Shahhaf, who claimed there were no American tanks in Baghdad when they were merely a block away. The American presence in downtown Baghdad was proof that Saddam Hussein was no longer in charge of his own country. As Marine Corps Major General James Mattis put it, the Marines were in charge when they were drinking the other man's liquor.[15]

By April 9, the United States was in possession of the capital. And so were the looters. At Firdos Square, a U.S. tank recovery vehicle pulled down a statue of Saddam Hussein, live on TV. Soon after that, TV news crews had no trouble covering the widespread looting that followed, as angry Iraqis (and more than a few crooks) carted away anything that wasn't nailed down from a variety of Iraqi government buildings, military sites, and Baath party facilities. This quickly soured any "honeymoon" that the U.S. forces may have enjoyed with the locals, who expected law and order to be restored after the fall of a despised despot. (Even though 30,000 Iraqis a year "disappeared" in Saddam's Iraq during the embargo period, the streets were still safe enough to walk at night.)

The war was over.

Or was it?

We Told You So

Iraq quickly descended into a persistent and bloody guerilla war against U.S. troops and any Iraqis aiding the "occupation." The problems of counterinsurgency took many Americans by surprise, primarily because of the Bush Administration's expectations that U.S. troops would be greeted as liberators.

That was the political selling point.

It did not come true.

And the problems *were* foreseen.

The U.S. Army War College's Strategic Studies Institute undertook a study that ran from October 2002 to February 2003, looking at all possible problems that could crop up if Iraq proved to be a difficult case in nation building and peacekeeping. The study's authors, Conrad C. Crane and W. Andrew Terrill, were not far off the mark.

First, the authors assumed that Arab attitudes toward occupation would shift from gratitude for Saddam's overthrow to suspicion that the United States intervened for its own reasons. Resistance to a U.S. presence could also be fueled by religion, as Muslims have no duty to submit to rule by non-Muslims. Other problems identified include Sunni discontent following the loss of power and privilege; Turkish fear of an independent Kurdish state in the north; the possibility of a Shiite theocratic ascendancy; possible Iranian influence in Iraqi internal affairs; mishandled tribal politics that could produce retaliation against U.S. forces; the unwelcome return of Iraqi exiles that could upset local politics; the loss of the Iraqi Army as a unifying institution (U.S. proconsul L. Paul Bremer disbanded it by decree); insufficient occupying forces; the possibility that terrorists would base in Iraq to fight U.S. forces; the need to pay for the occupation and rebuilding (the $100 billion estimate was not far off the mark); and the very real possibility that a popular uprising could occur against the U.S. presence (and it very nearly happened!).[16]

Making the Iraq invasion yet more unpromising was a quick examination of past U.S. efforts that mismanaged the transition from conflict to nation building, which at best were improvised, challenging, and problematic. Back in 1989, when the United States ousted Panamanian dictator Manuel Noriega, the effort was followed up by a very rough year as U.S. troops tried to restore law and order with insufficient numbers of military police. The 1994 invasion of Haiti to restore elected president Jean Bertrand Aristide was followed by a more detailed effort to rebuild the nation on the quick. But any chance of success vanished with the pullout of U.S. troops in 1996. Going into Bosnia in 1995 and Kosovo in 1999 saw the United States undertake more long-range planning to maintain a peacekeeping presence there for years. Nevertheless, these efforts faced challenges because the force mix lacked sufficient engineering, liaison, civil affairs personnel, linguists, and intelligence assets.[17]

What was not seen in the Iraq War was anything like the major planning effort the United States undertook for Germany, Italy, and Japan during World War II. Civil affairs planning began in 1942—three years before the war actually ended in Europe—and the mechanics of regime change and nation rebuilding were mapped out. Soon after the first U.S. units crossed into Germany, a civil affairs unit had a local occupation government up and running within four days in Roetgen, the first occupied town. In short, Crane and Terrill pointed out many shortcomings in the past practice of nation building, hard-learned lessons that U.S. military policy makers and planners willfully ignored when it came to Iraq.

The State Department had detailed plans on how to run the country during occupation. But the Pentagon kept the effort out of the Army's planning until February 2003—a month before the war began. This left too little time to study the blueprint and plan for implementation. Some expected problems did not happen, like environmental damage from burning oil fields or massive numbers of refugees that would need food and shelter. But the unexpected did happen: stiff resistance from Saddam Fedayeen, Baath Party remnants, mercenaries recruited from Syria and other Arab countries, and even Al Qaeda operatives. By Summer 2003, any plans to reduce the size of the U.S. occupying force were shelved. The United States also did not count on many Iraqi government workers, police, and civil servants to stop coming to work after "liberation," literally shutting down the administrative apparatus that kept Iraq going on a day-to-day basis.[18]

Movie Versus Real Life

The United States won the war it wanted to fight.

Now it was the Iraqis' turn.

By staging an insurgency, former regime loyalists and other disaffected Sunni factions were aiming for victory through stalemate. Again, the goal is to kill a lot of Americans, only not right away. By maintaining a bloody and violent resistance to American occupation over time, the insurgents make the claim through action that the United States (and the later sovereign Iraqi government) is not in control.

Democracies are politically vulnerable to long wars without result. The political support needed to fight a war is eroded by mounting casualties and expenses suffered over time. At a certain point, the goodwill of the voters is expended, and the ruling government must bring the war to an end or be ousted in the next election. Knowing this, any nation that can fight such a war can defeat the United States.

The untrained hordes of light infantry were totally useless making frontal assaults on U.S. armored columns. It was as if everybody had seen *Black Hawk Down* and were copying the tactics that worked in the movie. But once the conventional war was over, the United States shifted to a greater reliance on HUMVs—basically the light truck that replaced the WWII-style jeep—and away from tracked armor. Now the soft-skinned HUMVs and trucks were much better targets for the gun-toting militias, just as they were in Mogadishu. Shifting tactics from uncoordinated frontal assault to ambush/hit-and-run, the Iraqis seized the initiative. As guerillas, they could choose the time and place of attack and break contact when the battle began moving against them. Even the Americans noticed over time an increasing sophistication in small-unit attacks up to platoon level, supported by mortars and RPG fire.

Roadside bombs, called "improvised explosive devices" proved deadly. Oftentimes these were nothing more than a couple of artillery shells lashed together, with a cell phone, garage opener, or radio toy car controller to provide the switch needed to complete the electrical circuit to the detonator. The blasts shredded HUMVs and trucks with ease.

By the summer of 2003, the insurgency was already averaging about twenty attacks a day. U.S. plans to begin unit pullouts were put on hold, and a rotation of troops had to be planned.

Shock and awe was out.

"Aw shucks" became the norm.

One-sided victory gave way to bloody stalemate. The insurgency was not strong enough to oust the United States in the short run. Nor was the United States able to crush the insurgency.

The U.S. Army did enjoy some intelligence successes during the first year of occupation. Saddam's two sons Uday and Qusay were cornered and killed in a shoot-out with a company of the 101st Airborne in July 2003. With their deaths ended any political possibility of succession for the regime of Saddam Hussein. That following December, Saddam's turn came when he was captured by Delta Force commandos operating with the Fourth Infantry Division near his hometown of Tikrit. He now faces trial for crimes committed against the Iraqi people, as befitting a fallen dictator.

The United States worked with anti-Saddam Iraqis to set up a replacement government. But this proved to be slow work. The task was given to the State Department's L. Paul Bremer, ensconced in Baghdad as proconsul. By mid-July 2003, a twenty-five-member interim "Governing Council" was installed as a temporary government until sovereignty could be restored in about a year. Nation building had to be done against the growing head wind of the insurgency, starting first as a disturbing breeze that would later grow into a nasty and persistent storm.

Punctuating the dreary procession of daily low-level ambushes were several high-profile strikes. By mid-August, terrorists successfully bombed the Jordanian embassy in Baghdad. The United Nations left Baghdad shortly afterward, when its headquarters was also bombed. The attack killed twenty-two, including U.N. envoy Sergio Vieira de Mello, who recently arrived after successfully overseeing the nation-building effort in East Timor. In late August, a car bomb in Najaf killed 100 at the Imam Ali Mosque. Among the dead was Ayatollah Muhamad Bakar al-Hakim, head of SCIRI (one of two major Shiite parties).

By February 2004, it finally became apparent that no WMDs were to be found. The Bush Administration lost one of its major reasons for justifying the war.

On March 2, 2004, 180 Shiites were killed in car bombings in Karbala and Baghdad. Al Qaeda, Sunni militants, foreign jihadists are all reasonable suspects.

Despite all this, ground forces commander Lt. General Richard Sanchez had expected to draw down the U.S. troop level from 135,000 to 110,000 in the spring of 2004. About one-third of the troops present were from the Reserves or the National Guard.[19] Events would dictate otherwise.

April is the Cruelest Month

Four battles would sharply punctuate the bloody routine of occupation: The First Battle of Fallujah (April 2004), First Battle of Najaf

(April–May 2004), Second Najaf (August 2004), and Second Fallujah (November 2004). The sum total of these four battles taught some very harsh lessons to insurgents and Americans on city fighting and the use of force in the struggle for control of Iraq's political destiny.

Of the four, only Second Fallujah had a deliberate start. The other three were the outgrowth of accidental events, much like huge forest fires that erupted from carelessly setting sparks to dry tinder.

In Fallujah, tensions were already pretty high when the 82nd Airborne handed over responsibility for policing the town (and Anbar province) to the First Marine Expeditionary Force, which also had fought in the Iraq War a year before. Many press accounts leading up to the handoff had quoted unnamed Marine officers criticizing the 82nd's laid-back, low-presence policing of the town. Tactically, the Marines believed in maintaining an aggressive presence that did not back down from confrontation. In public statements, officers from both services tried to avoid an open feud over the tactics and objectives of occupation and counterinsurgency.

The feud touched on two approaches to counterinsurgency—"go in" or "hang back." Each approach has its advantages and disadvantages, militarily and politically. Hanging back may reduce political tensions, but it makes the occupier look weak and bullied, perhaps emboldening the insurgents. Going in is a race against time—can the attackers wipe out the insurgents before the fighting (and increased civilian casualties) triggers a backlash among the populace?[20] There are no easy answers to these questions, but practice gained in the four major occupation battles sheds some light on the issue.

Fallujah boiled over in late March 2004 when four American security contractors were surrounded, killed, and mutilated. TV images were reminiscent of the debacle in Mogadishu a decade earlier, when

Somali insurgents dragged the body of an American serviceman through the streets.

On April 5, the Marines went into Fallujah with the battalion on hand. Typically, Marines would advance to draw out enemy fire, responding with air strikes and artillery to destroy the strong point. The only problem is that in this case, it would happen in a city full of people, so collateral damage and civilian casualties were tragically inevitable. As the Marines advanced, they were attacked by groups of Sunni insurgents, numbering 10–60 fighters, mostly armed with AK-47s and RPGs. The attacks marked a break from the "shoot and scoot" tactics of months past, when rebels contented themselves with exploding large bombs while U.S. patrols passed by, or shooting at them and running away. The Marines were cautious at first, not calling in artillery or air support, but with casualties mounting and progress lagging, they gave in and brought on the firepower. In one instance, Marines took fire from a mosque. An air strike from an AC-130 gunship leveled the minaret, killing forty insurgents. After two days of fighting, Marines controlled one-quarter of Fallujah.[21]

But the Iraqis claimed six hundred civilians killed, mostly elderly, women, and children. Marines claim most of the wounded are fighters. And therein lies the problem. Iraqi Arabs getting their Al Jazeera TV coverage live via satellite dish believed the hospital officials.[22] The last thing the Americans wanted was an Iraqi general uprising, which would make the occupation bloody and untenable. That was the risk the United States was running in its attack on Fallujah.

Events in Najaf would add fuel to the fire.

Najaf is the spiritual capital of Shia Islam. Many Shia Muslims make pilgrimages to the Imam Ali Mosque located there, especially for holy days on the Shia calendar. A huge five-square mile cemetery—twice the size of New York's Central Park—is nearby, a place where many Shia faithful hope to be buried. Grand Ayatollah Ali Sistani, who is the faith's acknowledged head, is also based here.

But he has competition.

Young Shia cleric Moqtadeh al Sadr wants to take over. Not in thirty years, after he has proven his scholarship to assume the rank of grand ayatollah. Now would be preferable.

The young al Sadr was already wanted for conspiracy to commit murder, as his associates killed rival pro-Western Ayatollah Abdul Majid al Khoei upon his return to Najaf, shortly after Saddam Hussein's overthrow. The Americans want to arrest al Sadr. U.S. troops in late March shut down al Sadr's newspaper in the Baghdad slum of Sadr City (al Sadr's political base), and arrested a key aide. Al Sadr's response is to take over the Imam Ali Mosque in Najaf. His Mahdi Army numbered about 3,000 fighters.

Now the United States has a replay of its Mogadishu problem, when it sought the arrest of local Somali warlord Mohammed Farah Aideed. To arrest al Sadr, U.S. troops will have to fight their way into Najaf. But if their attack endangers the Imam Ali Mosque, then Shiites will have a good reason to rebel, and that would risk losing the war in Iraq a year after it was "won."

Now the choice must be faced.

Hang back or go in?

The Army hangs back.

To add to the occupier's woes, al Sadr widened his rebellion. Mahdi Army detachments raised hell in Amarah, Nasariyah, Karbala, and Kut. After these flare-ups, however, al Sadr decided to concentrate his efforts in three locations: Karbala (where two holy Shia shrines are located), Kufa (al Sadr's home, across the river from Najaf), and Najaf proper.

By mid-April, the war in Iraq was not well in hand. U.S. policy makers feared that the two separate rebellions would fuse into one and spread nationwide.

That fear was not unfounded.

Limited low-level cooperation did arise between the Mahdi Army in Najaf and the Sunni rebellion in Fallujah. But the sectarian and political differences between the two blocs were too great to be overcome by the common purpose of ousting the Americans. The Sunni—former Baath party officials, civil servants, Republican Guard, Mukhabarat (intelligence service), and Iraqi Army veterans—were fighting for the restoration of the pre-war privileges they enjoyed under Saddam Hussein. Under the dictator, oppression of the Shia and their limitation to second-class citizenship was the norm. Young al Sadr also wanted power, and to get it, he was going to fight the unpopular American occupation to prove he was more worthy than Sistani to lead Iraq's Shia. Many in Sadr City were willing to follow, but control of the slum was not the center of gravity in Shia. Ownership of Najaf was, and the locals were not willing to follow al Sadr. (It seems that open warfare was bad for the pilgrimage business.)

Beyond hatred of the Americans, there was nothing to really bind the two rebellions into one, and the Americans were smart enough to exploit these differences.

Do Things One At a Time

Go in or hang back?

Lt. Gen. Ricardo Sanchez decided to do a little of each.

The Marines in Fallujah would be going in, reinforced by a second battalion. They would mount aggressive raids to find, fix, and kill insurgents. The Iraqi Civil Defense Corp's 36th battalion would also join the fight (it was one of the few dependable Iraqi units available at the time). But there eventually was some reluctance to press the blade home. Iraqis were becoming increasingly disaffected by news of heavy civilian casualties. After renewed fighting, following one broken cease-fire, the lead Marine commander, Lt. Gen. James T. Conway, struck the deal that ended the battle, allowing the Fallujah Brigade to be formed by local Iraqis for self-policing (which eventually proved unsuccessful).

A few weeks after the truce was signed, joint patrols between Marines and the Fallujah Brigade ceased. The insurgents increased their grip on the city, eventually manning the checkpoints with the Fallujah Brigade "volunteers." The fight was shut down in time for the June 30 restoration of Iraqi sovereignty under the hand of appointed prime minister Ayad Allawi, a secular Shia and former CIA informant. But in the interim, the city became a haven for terrorists and rebels, prime among them Abu Musab al Zarqawi, head of the Al Qaeda franchise in Iraq. Hostages would soon be losing their heads to Zarqawi's hands, as his faction—Ansar al Islam—used Fallujah as a place to keep their captives until their videotaped deaths could be broadcast on Al Jazeera. (It was just "payback" for the prison abuse going on at the Abu Ghraib under the Americans.)

For Najaf, the decision was made to hang back.

A multibattalion U.S. task force cordoned off the city to prevent reinforcements and supplies from reaching the Mahdi Army. But getting troops from Baghdad to Najaf proved problematic. Mahdi Army irregulars successfully blew up one bridge and damaged two more to impede the movement of U.S. troops.[23]

In the first battles between the U.S. Army and the Mahdi Army, the insurgents proved their mettle—or their incompetence. One five-hour firefight pitted a platoon-strength group of rebels against a company of the 25th Infantry Division's first battalion, 14th regiment. It took place in a palm grove on the Najaf-side of the Euphrates, across from Kufa. The company surrounded the enemy and hit their position with 150 rounds of mortar fire, but they did not surrender or break. Mahdi Army reinforcements began crossing the bridge from Kufa, or crossing the river by small boat. U.S. Army snipers killed three. But the Americans were ordered to withdraw to avoid getting sucked into an unplanned city fight.[24]

The flip side was seen in Kufa, when a six-vehicle U.S. Army convoy sped through to cross the bridge to Najaf. Two lines of Mahdi Army irregulars lined the sidewalks on either side of the convoy and raked it with automatic gunfire. Not a single soldier was hit, though some insurgents managed to shoot each other across the street and hit some bystanders, too.[25]

Toward the end of April 2004, the United States turned to Najaf officials and Shia representatives to figure out how much support al Sadr and the Mahdi Army had, as well as what the boundaries of operations would be if the United States had to go in to defeat and capture the wanted cleric. It was determined that al Sadr had no local support. The people of Najaf wanted him out, and they would reluctantly countenance a battle in their own backyards if the Imam Ali Mosque was not damaged or taken.

The fight to retake Najaf, Kufa, and Karbala began in earnest on May 6. It was going to be a series of stand-up firefights between the mixed armor and infantry forces of the First Armored Division, supported by airpower and artillery, and the Mahdi Army irregulars, who could only bring AK-47s, RPGs, and mortars to bear.[26]

Concurrently, the First Cavalry Division had to defeat about 200–300 Mahdi Army insurgents in the Sadr City slum of Baghdad. Insurgents used concealed attacks to hit U.S. armored columns in the rear, combined with small arms and RPG fire from several sides. This did not stop U.S. troops from destroying both of al Sadr's offices, and this was not the decisive battle, as al Sadr's bid for power depended on holding Najaf.

In Karbala, several armor and infantry raids were launched by the First Brigade of the First Armored Division. The goal was to kill al Sadr's insurgents wherever they put up a fight. The Mukkhaiyam Mosque, near the two shrines, was taken in an eleven-hour firefight from a force of about 50–75 Mahdi Army irregulars. Special Forces led the attack on the mosque, followed by Iraqi commandos, to lessen religious sensitivities over "infidels" entering the holy place. The remaining Mahdi Army forces regrouped 600 feet away in the shrines of Abbas and Hussein. Air strikes, delivered by AC-130, killed one group of irregulars just 160 feet away from the shrines. By May 23, al Sadr conceded control of Karbala to the Americans.[27]

Kufa did not get much attention until late May, when U.S. and Iraqi commandos took the Salah Mosque, depriving the Mahdi Army of a base and an arms cache. (Again, the presence of Moslem Iraqi commandos provided the political cover the Americans needed to take the mosque.) Two other positions, a technical college and a building called "Saddam's Palace," were also taken. About thirty-six insurgents were killed in the trio of assaults.[28]

Najaf was a more delicate job, given the presence of the Imam Ali Mosque. The governor's office was retaken and a new governor was installed. That undercut any political claim that al Sadr controlled the town. One attempt was made to broker a truce. The offer included dropping charges against al Sadr, disarming his militia, and converting it into a political party.

Al Sadr balked.

So it was no surprise two days later when U.S. tanks entered Najaf's five-square-mile cemetery. The United States did not press home the attack, letting al Sadr sit in the Imam Ali Mosque while maintaining a cordon around Najaf that prevented rebel reinforcements from entering. A truce brokered by local Shiite and town officials got the United States to remove its forces from the town. Mahdi Army irregulars from other cities also had to leave Najaf. The arrest warrant for al Sadr was voided. The United States was allowed to maintain outposts in the city.[29]

The first battles of Fallujah and Najaf ended on unsatisfactory notes for the Americans. Al Sadr, while successfully isolated, was not eliminated as a threat to the interim Iraqi government, which took power as scheduled on June 30, 2004. Likewise, Fallujah was pacified, but later devolved into a rebel-held sanctuary that clearly belied any claim that the interim government was in charge.

The Americans suffered over 120 killed and almost four times that number wounded in April, making it one of the worst months in the occupation. Fortunately, American political and military leaders sized up the situation quickly and managed to keep the separate rebellions from combining, which could have led to defeat well before Iraqi sovereignty was restored.

But avoiding defeat was not victory.

Promises Are Made to be Broken

Like the Sunnis in Fallujah, Moqtadeh al Sadr never kept his promise to disarm. The truce imploded in early August, when Iraqi police surrounded al Sadr's home. (He was not in.) The Mahdi Army retaliated by attacking a police station, failing twice to take it. During the third attack, the Iraqi police called for reinforcements and got the 11th Marine Expeditionary Unit, which repelled the attacking insurgents.

The Marines, who were new to the area, would not back down from a firefight, much like their newly arrived counterparts in Fallujah a few months before. It was a replay of the hang-back/go-in dilemma, with go-in as the default setting for the Marines. They attacked Mahdi Army positions in the cemetery, gambling that a quick offensive would take the battalion to the walls of Najaf's old city. It only took a day, but the 11th Marine Expeditionary Unit was in need of reinforcements.

The cavalry did not arrive in the nick of time.

First Cavalry Division had its hands full putting down yet another blowup in Baghdad's Sadr City section. First Battalion of the Fifth Cavalry regiment was dispatched, but took forty-eight hours to make the drive down to Najaf, having to fight its way through insurgent-held areas south of Baghdad.

As the cavalry battalion was unable to fight upon arrival, the exhausted Marines pulled out of Najaf's cemetery. When the attack resumed the next day, First Battalion of the Fifth Cavalry advanced into the cemetery under strict orders not to fire in the direction of the Imam Ali Mosque without explicit permission from higher-ups. Unlike the Marines, the army never reached the southern edge of the cemetery.[30]

A cease-fire was arranged. The United States brought in another Marine unit—First Battalion, Fourth Marine regiment. The Marines and soldiers put up a cordon for a one-mile radius around the Imam Ali Mosque, making sure no supplies or reinforcements reached al Sadr. Prime Minister Ayad Allawi of the Iraqi interim government delivered an ultimatum to al Sadr—disarm and leave the Imam Ali Mosque, or else.[31]

The battle resumed. In Bagdhad, the First Cavalry pushed two miles into Sadr City. Concurrently in Najaf, dozens of tanks and Bradley IFVs hit Mahdi Army positions to the south and west of the Imam Ali Mosque while taking great care not to shoot at the holy building.

Al Sadr began the battle with as many as 1,000–2,000 fighters, and his losses at the hands of the United States were pretty heavy—well over 300 after two weeks of battle. Due to desertions, al Sadr was probably down to no more than 200–300 fighters inside the Imam Ali Mosque. U.S. forces slowly constricted the cordon line, killing more insurgents with every move.

It took over three weeks for the United States to push its cordon to the walls of the old city, reaching the line that the Marines occupied on day one of the battle. U.S. forces ended up only 400 yards away from the Imam Ali Mosque. The ubiquitous 36th battalion of the Iraqi Civil Defense Corps cleared the neighborhood south of the mosque, ready to go into the mosque alongside the Americans to provide political cover, should that need arise.

By the end of the month, Grand Ayatollah Ali Sistani successfully brokered another truce. By this time, Americans were within seventy-five yards of the Imam Ali Mosque. Sistani regained possession of the mosque, and under the agreement, both sides had to pull their forces out of Najaf.[32]

Lessons were learned the hard way—again. It became clear that armor was now key to fighting and winning city battles. The numbers were telling. Seven Marines were killed and twenty wounded retaking Najaf. Army losses were two killed and a handful wounded. When the Marines started the battle, they had only four tanks that were part of the 11th Marine Expeditionary Unit and had to borrow seven more M2 Bradleys. With Marine airpower handy, the 11th MEU could count on air strikes to make up for its lack of armor and artillery. This was the so-called "light" profile that many advocates of army transformation were arguing for. Light units with sensor dominance and airpower should be able to win battles. But bombing city blocks is clumsy, causing a lot of collateral damage and civilian casualties. The armor, on the other hand, could fight more easily in the city without destroying it. (Battle still makes a mess, though.) The M1 Abrams tanks and M2 Bradley IFVs were impervious to RPG fire. Even the Marines admitted privately that more armor would have helped going in again.[33]

The lessons of these three city battles were taken to heart when the final assault to retake Fallujah was planned for November. It was important that Iraqi sovereignty be upheld before the January 30 elections chose a government that would draft the Iraqi constitution.

Unfinished Business

Since May 2004, Fallujah had become a sore point for the United States. The truce had allowed the town to morph into a terrorist and rebel sanctuary. Fallujah could not be allowed to exist outside of the control of the Iraqi Interim Government, especially by the election planned for January 30, 2005.

Fallujah was still within the 1st Marine Expeditionary Force's area of operations in Anbar province. However, the assault was going to be massively supplemented by U.S. Army units packing far more armor punch than the Marines.

The attack was long-expected. About 80 percent of Fallujah's 300,000 residents fled in the weeks leading up to the battle. Urban fighting would still produce a lot of collateral damage, but the possibility of heavy civilian casualties was now reduced.[34] The downside was that many insurgents and foreign fighters also left, free to seek action on more promising fronts. It came as a surprise later during the battle when rebels mounted a major attack on Mosul, shattering the city's 5,000-member police force.

During the pre-battle phase, the United States launched numerous probing attacks and feints along Fallujah's southern edge. This caused the insurgents to orient their defense toward the south, and many fighters would be in the wrong place when the battle started.

The United States also focused on winning the propaganda battle as well. Unconfirmed reports of high civilian casualties made U.S. commanders reluctant to press the attack home back in April 2004, settling for an ineffective cease-fire that only shut down the problem in the short run. When the second Battle of Fallujah began in early November, U.S. Special Forces and Iraqi commandos (the Iraqi 36th CDC battalion, again) took over the hospital. It was the source of civilian casualty claims in the last battle, and would play no role for the enemy in the next one.[35]

About six American battalions hit Fallujah along its northern edge and spent the next week fighting their way to the town's southern line. Following were several Iraqi battalions doing mop-up operations to make sure no insurgent stay-behinds plagued the rear. A strong five-battalion cordon would keep out enemy reinforcements and supplies. About 1,000–3,000 insurgents were estimated to be holding Fallujah.

Route 10, a major east-west road cutting through Fallujah's center, marked the halfway point. It was reached in three days by Army battalions posted on the left and right flanks. But going down the middle was a bit tougher for the 1st Battalion, 8th Marine regiment. At one point, its advance was stalled for a few hours by a single sniper. The apartment building in which the sniper hid was pounded by bombs, artillery, and AC-130 gunfire. He survived and continued to take pot-shots at the Marines. The same battalion took the Muhammadia Mosque after a sixteen-hour firefight. One platoon had to cross the street to take the building—and was hammered by crossfire from two machine guns. Five Marines were wounded, one mortally.

Throughout the battle, the United States maintained a robust line of communications to its line of advance, quickly evacuating wounded soldiers to nearby aid stations. There would be no lack of food and ammo for the frontline units. And the attack would be sustained without pause to keep the enemy on the defensive at all times. Units would be rotated out of the line to be rested while the relieving units maintained the offensive.

Time-fused bombs were used to level buildings—exploding a few seconds after hitting their targets. This cut down on a lot of expected collateral damage, especially to nearby mosques. Separate gun sights for commanders and gunners on M1 tanks and Bradley IFVs allowed crews to keep all in view while staying buttoned up. This allowed armor to operate in the city without the need for vehicle commanders to stand in the open, hatches up, to see what was going on to issue orders (and get shot).[36]

The defense was low-tech and stubborn. Individual fighters hid themselves in holes and trenches to pop up and snipe at American platoons after they had passed. If artillery and air support could not kill the stay-behinds, then armored bulldozers buried them alive. Also, the defenders would mark their line of contact with the Americans by flying black flags from rooftops that could be easily seen from other parts of town, and insurgents would send reinforcements there. It was another example of low-tech operating despite high tech's presence.

It took roughly one week for U.S. forces to take Fallujah. About 1,200–1,600 insurgents were killed, which amounted to about half of the estimated garrison. U.S. losses were fifty-one killed, 425 wounded. Even so, many resistant pockets of 5–30 fighters were still being encountered, and numerous arms caches were found. One standard insurgent tactic was firing on advancing U.S. units and then retreating into the next line of buildings. Eventually, the rebels ran out of town to retreat through, hitting the anvil of the U.S. cordon while receiving blows from the six-battalion hammer advancing from the north.

While all the hard-learned lessons of city fighting were well applied to retaking Fallujah, it was harder to discern what affect this had on the overall war. The United States claimed a decisive victory over the Sunni insurgency. But that did not stop the insurgents from starting a new front in Mosul. Throughout the occupation, enemy losses were always made up and the insurgency still increased in tempo.

The Violent Background

The four major occupation battles stand out in stark relief against the daily, bloody grind that U.S. troops had to endure. Not a day went by without dozens of attacks on U.S. forces, ranging from bombings to shoot-outs. Many of the insurgents were disaffected Sunnis taking their best shots for a variety of reasons—revenge against mistreatment of family members or tribal peers by American troops; restoration of Saddam-era Sunni privilege; loss of Army posts or civil service jobs due to the Coalition Provisional Authority's abolition of the Army and de-Baathification policy; the chance to make a buck (criminals were often involved); and the chance to kill Americans for a cause (jihadists, terrorists, foreign fighters).

By the end of April 2004, the Abu Ghraib prison scandal broke. American prison guards had beaten and abused Iraqi inmates, even taking photographs of Arab prisoners being sexually humiliated. The United States was already unloved and unbelieved by the Arab Street. The scandal did not help matters any, and provided a political rallying point for Sunni rebels, as well as Al Jazeera's pro-insurgent coverage of events in Iraq. Indeed, Al Qaeda was no less shy, posting its own video footage on the Internet of American hostage Nicholas Berg being beheaded. Abu Mussab al Zarqawi, who headed Al Qaeda's operations in Iraq, could claim that the killing of a hostage was justified retaliation for the abuse of Arab prisoners at Abu Ghraib.

Taking a look at the occupation after one year, defense analyst Anthony Cordesman saw an imperfect picture of American policy in action. Cordesman still credited the Coalition Provisional Authority (CPA) with improvising solutions where plans were lacking. But he also noted the growing anti-American attitudes of the Sunni minority that was picked up by political polling—in effect the tinder needed to start the insurgency. There were 203 attacks in the last week of March 2004, compared to only 179 weekly attacks as an average for the previous eight weeks. U.S. casualties were 514 dead and 3,419 wounded after nearly a year of occupation, compared to 138 killed for the three-week war itself.[37]

Further adding to occupation woes was the lag in development aid needed to rebuild the Iraqi economy. Out of $18 billion in budgeted aid, less than $4 billion had been spent after a year because of cumbersome contracting rules and the lengthy assessment process for projects.[38]

By the end of 2004, the insurgency had clearly worsened. Cordesman criticized the Administration for failing to notice the problem, terming it "denial as a method of counterinsurgency." While the Bush Administration claimed only 5,000 insurgents, estimates by the CPA put it more at 12,000–16,000. Attacks against American troops, Iraqi civilians and infrastructure also got a lot of detailed press coverage. This became a useful channel between various insurgent groups that effectively measured and communicated the results of their attacks.

Here, Cordesman does not provide any detailed Order of Battle for the insurgency, but don't hold that against him. No one has. About thirty-five Sunni groups, by his count, have claimed some credit for a number of attacks. Baathists, criminal gangs, religious insurgents, foreign fighters, Al Qaeda operatives, and various Sunni tribes all contributed to the insurgency.[39] Many insurgents were killed and captured when the United States finally seized Fallujah. But this did nothing to stop the insurgents shifting forces to other cities, principally Mosul, where they attacked with ease.

Ballot Box vs. Cartridge Box

With the January 30 elections now weeks away, the Sunni insurgency refocused its efforts on killing Iraqi police, Civil Defense Corps troops, civilians, and anyone connected with conducting the election. Attacks were reaching up to 100 per day. Iraqi casualties were running at 10–20 per day, punctuated by the occasional spectacular bombing that killed many more. Despite all this, the numbers worked against the insurgency. Election day saw 8 million Iraqis go to the polls, despite the low turnout in Sunni areas. Election-day attacks could not hit all the polling places and kill all the voters. The event changed the complexion of the war in ways the U.S. occupation could not. The insurgency became anti-Iraqi, anti-government. The voters became less anti-American and more pro-Iraq.[40]

To really press the insurgency, the United States had to find a way of shifting its combat burden to a rebuilt Iraqi Army. Throughout the occupation, the United States persisted in training a new Iraqi police force, civil defense corps, and army. The results were less than successful. As of early February 2005, less than one-third of the 136,000 members of all Iraqi security forces could be used to tackle all missions. Of the total number, 79,000 made up the Iraqi police, while 57,000 belonged to the army and other bodies. The semantics of service became easier when in late February, the 38,000-strong Iraqi Civil

Defense Corps was officially incorporated into the army, which by this time only had 12,000 soldiers. The merger created a 50,000-man force that would be raised to 100,000 by July 2005, then up to 150,000 by the end of 2005. Casualties among the pro-government Iraqis have also been far heavier than U.S. forces. They suffered 1,342 killed in action between June 2004 and February 2005.

To achieve the changeover, the United States has to devote more troops and resources to training and less to policing and maintaining security in a contested Iraq. That will mean assigning 8,000–10,000 American officers and NCOs to the job.[41] The goal is to cut desertion rates and train capable Iraqi officers to lead from the front. It is hoped that American trainers will stiffen the resolve of Iraqi units in the field by working alongside Iraqi commanders. The goal is to make sure Iraqi units are more likely to stand their ground against the insurgents.

Lt. General Daniel Petraeus, who commanded the 101st Airborne during the Iraq War, was placed in charge of the U.S. effort to train the new Iraqi Army. He has his work cut out for him trying to find enough capable Iraqi officers, for the leader sets the tone for his unit. Leadership in the old Iraqi Army was autocratic and did not encourage initiative at the lower echelons. The badly led troops were prone to desertion in the face of battle. While competent junior leaders can be found to command the platoons and companies, field-grade officers with leadership abilities are much harder to find. In the old Iraqi Army, rank had its privileges, contrasted with the U.S. Army, where rank has its responsibilities. The American Army's "corporate culture" stresses local initiative, leadership from the front, candor, and accuracy in reporting to the upper echelons, and a dedication to training to achieve high levels of battlefield competence. The Iraqi perception of officer privilege can be undermined by such American practices as having a strong NCO corps, relying on competent subordinates who can exercise initiative, and the honest reporting of "bad news." Bad leadership accounts for much of Iraq's lackluster successes and stunning defeats on the battlefield.[42] Training a new Iraqi Army in the Western mold is not going to be easy. Only Great Britain ever trained an Arab army to be as good as its own, and that was Jordan's Arab Legion, the most competent force on either side during Irasel's 1948 War of Independence.[43]

Another problem that could not be resolved was the infiltration of Iraqi police and military units by insurgents who pass the vetting process, then forward intelligence back to their allies. Ethnic and tribal loyalties also complicate the training picture, as not every member of a unit may be serving Iraq first.

Irregular brigades also cloud the training picture. Nicknamed "pop-ups" by the Americans, these disconnected units are basically militias that are formed by some Iraqi factions or follow the command of a charismatic leader who can pick and choose his troops. Among them are the Special Police Commandos under Gen. Adnan Thavit (currently at about battalion strength), Muthana Brigade (serving the former prime minister, Ayyad Allawi), Defenders of Baghdad (Baghdad Shiites), the Second Defenders of Baghdad Brigade, the Amarah Brigade (Baghdad vicinity), another five Shiite units scattered throughout southern Iraq, and the Defenders of Khadamiya (a security force for a Shiite shrine in northern Iraq).[44] Some of these homegrown units are every bit as capable as the trained Iraqi Army units now being sent out by U.S. trainers. Not known at the time of this chapter's writing is what military or political role they will play in Iraq's future.

All these factors do not spell out a sure victory over the Iraqi insurgency.

By the end of January 2005, the United States had killed or captured 32,000 insurgents. Another 8,000 Iraqi rebels were then being detained on suspicion of insurgency. This surpasses older American estimates that placed the insurgency's strength at 5,000–12,000. Iraqi intelligence estimates there are 40,000 hard-core rebels, supported by 160,000 sympathizers. (U.S. force level in Iraq that January was 150,000, plus 25,000 provided by coalition allies.)[45]

One thing is clear. The rebellion has replaced its losses and grown, despite American claims regarding its size. To date, no one has produced an order of battle for the Sunni insurgents. Generally, the group is fractured into many factions, with no clear leader. If there is a principal faction, it might be the former regime elements presumably guided by senior Baathists hiding out in Syria.[46] The Sunni factions agree the United States must go. Beyond that, they have no unifying political agenda.

As of April 2005, the number of daily attacks has edged up to about sixty a day, half of which prove unsuccessful. This looks like a big improvement from the 150 attacks logged the day before the January 30 elections, but it is up from the forty daily attacks logged shortly after the polling. While U.S. losses are down, Iraqi casualties are up as insurgents try to discredit the present Iraqi government. But Iraqis are also more willing to provide intelligence on insurgents to Iraqi security forces, which have also been increasing in number as new units come on-line following U.S. training.[47]

The Impact on the U.S. Military

The counterinsurgency effort in Iraq has forced two basic changes on the U.S. military. First, the Pentagon rearranged its priorities away from purchasing high-tech weapons for the Air Force and Navy, placing more resources with the Army to pay for interventions abroad and counterterrorism operations. The shift will amount to a $55 billion cut over the next six years, impacting the F-22 fighter and the C-130J transport. One carrier will be cut, fewer of the new DDX destroyers and Virginia-class submarines will be purchased. The Army will get $25 billion more for its restructuring from large divisions to smaller, more deployable brigades, as well as more military police, civil affairs units, psychological warfare specialists, and assets needed for "post-conflict stabilization and reconstruction operations."[48]

The other challenge is to relearn counterinsurgency. Lt. Gen. William Wallace, who commanded V Corps in the Iraq War, pushed to renew counterinsurgency doctrine as head of the Combined Arms Center at Fort Leavenworth, Kansas. A draft of the manual was written in five months, which is blindingly fast compared to the thirty-six months it normally takes to turn doctrine into the printed word. Prior to this, the Army could only turn to two Special Forces manuals describing the techniques of counterinsurgency—in the early 1960s. The only other source was the Small Wars Manual, a 1940-vintage distillation of the Marine Corps' experience fighting rebels in various banana republics in the teens and twenties. (It has many useful tips on the loading and handling of mules.) As Wallace explained in a newspaper interview (for which he did not get into trouble this time), to do counterinsurgency, the United States has to strike the right balance between military operations, economic development, and the defense or construction of political institutions.[49] Indeed, the lessons of Iraq are filtering into the Army's training centers at Fort Irwin (where mechanized maneuver warfare is practiced) and Fort Polk (devoted to counterinsurgency and urban warfare).

Déjà Vu All Over Again

After failing to win a counterinsurgency war in Vietnam, the U.S. Army swore there would be "no more Vietnams." It worked hard to master modern warfare, envisioning the sensor array and armament needed to have perfect information on the battlefield—and the perfect aim to kill the enemy. Fighting the Iraqi military twice in one decade, the United States showed it could win such wars with ease, but only if our enemies oblige us by fighting on our terms.

Conventional wars did not form the bulk of America's post–Cold War deployments. Rather, these were brushfire wars that were characterized by brief, sharp fights followed by some form of occupation, peacekeeping, and nation building. The list is a depressing confirmation of the obvious: Panama (1989), Somalia (1992–93), Haiti (1994), Bosnia (1995), Kosovo (1999), Afghanistan (2001–present), and now Iraq (2003–present).

Rogue state dictators and terrorists are not obliging enough to fight on our terms. They have noticed America's failures in Lebanon and Somalia. All it takes for them to win is time. Prolong the war, kill lots of U.S. servicemen, and the American people and their leaders will figure out that it pays to quit. For the United States, long, bloody, low-level wars are not worth fighting due to their great expense and heavy casualties relative to a paltry gain.

The Iraq occupation has turned out this way. But declaring victory and going home is the worst thing that the United States can do. The nation will have to see the effort through to the end, at great expense in dollars and lives. That will demand patience—a virtue Americans don't have in abundance. Victory in Iraq will depend on Iraqis successfully establishing a viable government and how well it can keep Iraqis safe from insurgents and criminals. Success cannot be measured by charting the rise and fall in the daily number of attacks, and a successful counterinsurgency will take years to achieve.[50]

If the past is prologue, the United States will probably have to fight this kind of war again some time in the next decade. It cannot be done by purely military means, but will require a fusion of political and economic means. Civil agencies will have to coordinate their work with the military. The United States will have to place greater reliance on the Army's military police, engineers, civil affairs, light infantry, and intelligence assets rather than tanks, jet fighters, and carrier battle groups. Human factors will count for more than technological expertise.

The Army is now applying hard-won wisdom to making these needed changes. It already possesses a doctrine for war-fighting. Now it must develop a doctrine for peacekeeping, and train its units to achieve equal competence in this field. The goal is to have units capable of shifting from war-fighting to peacekeeping seamlessly when hostilities cease, and to support the changeover with a different mix of supporting units.

If the United States succeeds in this endeavor, present and future enemies will be deprived of the means to defeat American forces by unconventional means.

Because the next time, there will be no shock and awe.

ENDNOTES

1. Harlan K. Ullman and James P. Wade, *Shock and Awe: Achieving Rapid Dominance* (Washington, D.C.: NDU Press Book, 1996) http://ndupress.ndu.edu

2. John Keegan, *The Iraq War* (New York: Alfred A. Knopf, 2004), 181.

3. Williamson Murray and Robert H. Scales, *The Iraq War* (Cambridge, MA: Harvard University Press, Belknap Press, 2003), 103.

4. Ibid., 245

5. Michael R. Gordon and General Bernard E. Trainor, *The Generals' War* (Boston and New York: Little, Brown and Co., 1995), 392.

6. Murray and Scales, op. cit., 105–9.

7. Todd S. Purdum and the Staff of the *New York Times*, *A Time of Our Choosing* (New York: Times Books, 2003), 129.

8. Sean D. Naylor, "Wargames Rigged? General Says Millennium Challenge '02 Was Entirely Scripted," *Army Times*, 16 August 2002.

9. Col. Walter J. Boyne, *Operation Iraqi Freedom* (New York: Forge, 2003), 96.

10. Boyne, op. cit., 149.

11. Purdum, op. cit., 182.

12. Purdum, op. cit., 161.

13. Linda Robinson, "Masters of Chaos: The Secret History of Special Forces" *Public Affairs*, (New York: 2004), 296–341.

14. Purdum, op. cit., 194.

15. Bing West and Maj. Gen. Ray L. Smith, *The March Up* (New York: Bantam, 2003), 235.

16. Conrad C. Crane and W. Andrew Terrill, "Reconstructing Iraq: Insights, Challenges, and Missions for Military Forces in a Post-Conflict Scenario," Strategic Studies Institute of the U.S. Army War College, February 2003, 18–42.

17. Ibid., 3–18.

18. Purdum, op cit., 232–6.

19. Carla Anne Robbins, Christopher Cooper, and Neil King, Jr., "Decision Time: As Insurgency In Iraq Rages, Bush Faces Unappealing Options," *Wall Street Journal*, 9 April 2004.

20. Ibid.

21. Carla Anne Robbins, Greg Jaffe, and Michael M. Phillips in Washington and Farmaz Fassihi in Doha, Qatar, "Iraqi Insurgents Mount Attacks on many Fronts," *Wall Street Journal*, 7 April 2004.

22. Farnaz Fassihi, "Iraqis Increasingly Sympathize With Rebels," *Wall Street Journal*, 12 April 2004.

23. Thomas E. Ricks, "Insurgents Display New Sophistication," *Washington Post*, 14 April 2004.

24. Edmund Sanders, "U.S., Cleric's Forces Clash for Hours in Iraqi South," *Los Angeles Times*, 17 April 2004.

25. Edmund Sanders, "Cleric's Forces Have Surprised American Forces," *Los Angeles Times*, 18 April 2004.

26. Edward Wong, "G.I.'s Kill Scores of Militia Forces in Three Cities," *New York Times*, 8 May 2004.

27. Edward Wong, "U.S. Strikes Mosque Held by Iraqi Cleric's Militia," *New York Times*, 12 May 2004; "U.S. Forces, Under Attack, Strike Rebel Cleric's Fighters Near Shrine," *New York Times*, 18 May 2004; "U.S. Military Says Shiite Rebels Seem to Have Conceded Karbala," *New York Times*, 23 May 2004.

28. Edward Wong, "G.I.'s Report Killing 36 Insurgents Around Kufa Mosque That Held Arms," *New York Times*, 24 May 2004.

29. Dexter Filkins, Edward Wong contributing, "Agreement by U.S. and Rebels Ends Fighting in Najaf" *New York Times*, 28 May 2004.

30. Alex Berenson and John F. Burns, "8-Day Battle for Najaf: From Attack to Stalemate" *New York Times*, 18 August 2004.

31. John F. Burns and Sabrina Tavernise, "Iraq Chief Gives Final Warning to Rebel Cleric" *New York Times*, 20 August 2004.

32. Alex Berenson and Sabrina Tavernise, "Overwhelming Militiamen, Troops Push Closer to Shrine," *New York Times*, 24 August 2004; and Alex Berenson and Dexter Filkins, with Erik Eckholm and Sabrina Tavernise contributing, "Rebel Iraqi Cleric is Told to Give Up or Face Attack," *New York Times*, 25 August 2004.

33. Alex Berenson, "Fighting the Old-Fashioned Way in Najaf" *New York Times*, 29 August 2004.

34. Dexter Filkins and James Glanz, "All Sides Prepare for American Attack on Fallujah" *New York Times*, 6 November 2004.

35. Richard A. Oppel Jr. and Robert F. Worth, "G.I.s Open Attack to Take Fallujah from Iraqi Rebels," *New York Times*, 8 November 2004.

36. Thom Shanker and Eric Schmitt, Dexter Filkins contributing, "Past Battles Won and Lost Helped in Falluja Assault," *New York Times*, 22 November 2004.

37. Anthony Cordesman, "One Year On: Nation Building in Iraq—A Status Report," Center for Strategic and International Studies, Working Paper revised 16 April 2004, 2–8.

38. Ibid., 20.

39. Anthony Cordesman, "The Developing Iraqi Insurgency: Status at End—2004," Center for Strategic and International Studies, Working Draft updated 22 December 2004, 12–13.

40. Doug Struck, "Iraqis Cite Shift in Attitude Since Vote," *Washington Post*, 7 February 2005.

41. Eric Schmitt, "General Seeks Faster Training of Iraq Soldiers," *New York Times*, 23 January 2005.

42. Mark Bowden, "When Officers Aren't Gentlemen," *Wall Street Journal*, 8 February 2005; and Greg Jaffe, "A Marine Captain Trains Iraqi Colonel to Take Over the Fight," *Wall Street Journal*, 24 February 2005.

43. Kenneth M. Pollack, *Arabs at War* (Lincoln, NE: University of Nebraska Press, 2002), 355–7.

44. Greg Jaffe, "New Factor in Iraq: Irregular Brigades Fill the Security Void," *Wall Street Journal*, 16 February 2005.

45. "Hopeful Turning Point or Descent Into Chaos?" *The Economist*, 29 January 2005.

46. Thomas E. Ricks, "General: Iraqi Insurgents Directed From Syria," *Washington Post*, 17 December 2004.

47. Bradley Graham, "Pentagon Plays Down New Rise in Iraq Violence," *Washington Post*, 27 April 2005.

48. Bradley Graham, "Pentagon Prepares to Rethink Focus on Conventional Warfare," *Washington Post*, 26 January 2005.

49. Douglas Jehl and Thom Shanker, "For the First Time Since Vietnam, Army Prints Guide to Fighting Insurgents," *New York Times*, 13 November 2004.

50. Thomas X. Hammes, "War Isn't Fought in the Headlines," *New York Times*, 21 April 2005.

CHAPTER 3

French Algeria and British Northern Ireland: Legitimacy and the Rule of Law in Low-Intensity Conflict

LIEUTENANT COLONEL JAMES D. CAMPBELL

The post–Cold War world, with its small wars of ethnic nationalism, tribal and religious conflict, and localized and global terrorism, is not so different from Europe during the era of decolonization in the late 1950s and 1960s. The ethnic and religious roots of many of the world's current conflicts derive from the period when Europe shed its empires and much of the developing world gained independence. One critical lesson of the European wars of decolonization is the need to maintain legitimacy while conducting low-intensity conflict (LIC) operations. Without legitimacy, a democratic nation cannot hope to prosecute operations to a successful conclusion.

Counterterrorism and counterinsurgency operations in Algiers from 1957 to 1958 and in Northern Ireland from 1970 to 1999 reveal significant truths about legitimacy and the rule of law. Insurgent warfare based on ethnic nationalism is inherently political. If, during the course of such a war, a government and military abandon the principles that put them above the level of the terrorists they are fighting, they lose the legitimacy of their cause and face political and military defeat.

In 1958, after several years of war in the then-French province of

Algeria, which resulted in thousands of military and civilian casualties, the French Fourth Republic collapsed and was replaced by a new republican government hostile to the war. In 1962, the French Army left in defeat and Algeria became independent. Ironically, by all accounts, the French Army had decisively defeated the Algerian Front de la Libération Nationale (FLN) rebels and retained control of the country militarily at the time Algeria gained independence.[1]

The government of the Fourth Republic lost credibility and most of its popular support because of a perceived loss of control of the military waging the war and its toleration, if not encouragement, of the army's widespread use of torture, assassination, and violent intimidation. The French Army's ruthless counterterrorism campaign in Algiers from 1957 to 1958 was a classic Pyrrhic victory. The French Army crushed the FLN in the city, but the methods it used caused an international outcry that led to the Fourth Republic's downfall and, with it, the loss of any real hope for an "Algérie Française."[2]

By contrast, since 1969, in an attempt to force the separation of Northern Ireland from Great Britain, Irish nationalists have waged a war of terrorism against the British presence. Hundreds of combatants and innocents have been killed, yet Northern Ireland remains solidly British. In fact, the cease-fire, Good Friday peace accords, and subsequent political developments suggest the Irish Republican Army (IRA) has virtually given up hope of achieving its aims through violence.

The British Army's counterterrorist and peacekeeping campaigns against the many paramilitary groups in Ulster have seen their share of mistakes, crises, and political failures but, on the whole, compare favorably with the French effort in Algeria. The British Government has insisted on maintaining civilian and police control over military operations, using the minimum possible level of violence in attacking terrorists, and has held fast to the rule of law in conducting military operations.[3] Despite some well-publicized exceptions, the British military has remained under the firm control of civilian authorities, and transgressions of law have been publicly investigated and prosecuted. This adherence to the rule of law has allowed the British Government to retain its legitimacy in the paramount view of domestic public opinion.[4]

Although these two wars differ in their causes, historical context, and geography, they are similar enough to help draw some important conclusions about LIC operations and government policies. In both wars, terrorists and insurgents fought on behalf of an ethnically distinct population residing in an area geographically separated from but still rhetorically and politically an integral part of the home country. Both provinces had or have a significant resident population vociferously loyal to the home country that generated its own paramilitary and terrorist organizations, adding another violent, unstable element to the conflict. And, in both wars, political considerations overshadowed military ones and became the most important factors in determining the success or failure of government attempts to end the wars.

Algeria

Following unwritten but perfectly clear rules . . . on the orders of the socialist government . . . intelligence officers used two methods of questioning[:] electric shock and water.

—Jean-Claude Goudeau[5]

The causes and dynamics of the French war in Algeria are complex and, in many ways, prototypical of late-twentieth-century wars of "national liberation." The war contained all the now-familiar patterns of idealistic nationalism, cynical power politics, international posturing, and brutal, senseless violence, the victims of which were more often than not guilty of nothing more than being unlucky. The war in Algeria was different from many, however, in that the insurgents were defeated militarily and yet still achieved their aims, not through force of arms, but largely through the French Government's loss of public support and consequent loss of will to continue the fight.[6] The methods the French Army used in its antiterrorism campaign in Algiers from 1957 to 1958 became widely accepted military and government policy, a policy that led directly to failure and defeat.

By early 1956, the FLN had the Algerian provincial government on the defensive. The French military had just been extracted from the debacle at Suez, hard on the heels of defeat in Indochina, and was not yet reestablished in Algeria. Many units that had fought in Indochina were still being reconstituted after their destruction at Dien Bien Phu and the internment of their leaders in Viet Minh prisons.

In Summer 1956, the FLN began a stepped-up campaign of urban terror in Algiers with bombings, assassinations, and strikes, all calculated to bring the government to its knees.[7] By August, the terror campaign had brought chaos to Algiers. To be a government official or employee was to invite death. The Arab quarter of the Casbah, a warren of ancient buildings, alleyways, and tunnels, was under FLN control and off-limits to police, white Europeans, and Algerians loyal to France. Terrorism and vigilante attacks by loyalist settlers (*pieds-noir*) brought the violence to a crescendo that paralyzed the city.[8]

In January 1957, Algeria's socialist governor-general, Robert Lacoste, under strong pressure from the government in Paris, decided to fight fire with fire. He ordered the French Army's 10th Airborne Division, a crack unit led by a hard core of Indochina veterans recently returned from Suez, into Algiers with orders to end the terrorist attacks at all costs.[9] The 10th Division's commander, General Jacques Massu, had full authority to maintain order in Algiers with no civilian influence or interference in the military's operations. The army had a free hand to do whatever was necessary to restore order. This carte-blanche authority would not be rescinded for five years. The transfer of absolute authority in Algiers to Massu proved to be "the death warrant of the Fourth Republic."[10]

Although 10th Division soldiers called the assignment a "cop's job," they worked with zeal, determined to erase the ignominious memories of Suez and Dien Bien Phu.[11] Ruthlessly efficient, they made scores of illegal arrests and quickly and violently ended a general strike by breaking open stores and forcing people to work at gunpoint. Through the uninhibited use of torture, "disappearances," public beatings, and other forms of intimidation, the army quickly broke the FLN terrorist network.

By March 1957, the terrorist problem in Algiers was effectively ended.[12] But at what price? Although torture and murder occurred throughout the war, following the operations in Algiers, such actions became systematic and even institutionalized. From then on, with the tacit approval of the government, the French Army consistently relied on these methods in all its dealings with the FLN.[13] Clearly, such methods were effective. Coupled with a successful campaign in the countryside (with free-fire zones, forced resettlement, and other tactics familiar to students of the American war in Vietnam), the tactics used by the French Army rendered the FLN incapable of mounting any large-scale resistance by the end of the decade.[14]

The widespread, ruthless recourse to barbarity by forces that stood for "civilization" destroyed what legitimacy the French had among ethnic Algerians, and this had major political repercussions in France. By late 1957, clear evidence of torture and other government-sponsored or condoned forms of brutality and illegal behavior by the army fed a popular outcry that grew until Charles De Gaulle was elected to the presidency in 1958, ending the Fourth Republic.[15] As De Gaulle was later to claim, he had every intention from the beginning of his presidency to end the war in Algeria by granting it independence.[16]

The groundswell of antigovernment feeling in France that destroyed the Fourth Republic can in large part be directly attributed to the unrestrained, government-condoned, illegal acts of the French Army in conducting its highly successful campaign against the FLN.

Northern Ireland

You are to operate as directed by the Gilbraltar Police Commissioner . . . Act at all times in accordance with the lawful instructions of the senior police officer . . . Do not use more force than is necessary . . . Only open fire if he/she is . . . committing an action likely to endanger lives.   —British Ministry of Defence[17]

The British experience in Northern Ireland is even more complex than that of the French in Algeria. The roots of political repression, terrorism, military force, and violence in Northern Ireland are centuries old and firmly embedded in the culture.[18] The British Army has been fully involved in the government's attempts to restore order in Ulster since 1969 when the "troubles" began, primarily in a peacekeeping and counterterrorist role.

However, a major difference exists between the British Army's status in Ulster and that of the French Army in Algeria after 1957. Since its initial involvement in Northern Ireland, the British Army has been tasked to reinforce the Royal Ulster Constabulary (RUC) and has remained under at least nominal police and civilian control throughout.

After attempts at an internment policy during the early 1970s, the government realized the danger of involving the British military in running prisons and conducting interrogations. Allegations of torture still dog the army today. As a consequence, the army turns over anyone it arrests to the civilian police and does not conduct independent interrogations or operate prisons.[19]

Perhaps because violence in Ireland has long been a part of British life, there may exist a certain tolerance for it among the public. Even so, the British government consistently conducts investigations and even judicial proceedings each time a soldier is involved in violence, whether fatal or not.[20] Even in cases of clear self-defense, or when a known terrorist or group of terrorists is caught in the act of committing violence, due process of law has been generally followed. Inquests, investigations, and trials have been conducted publicly and on the record.

A dramatic illustration of this process comes from an incident in Loughall, Northern Ireland. On May 8, 1987, acting on information provided by the RUC, British soldiers of the Special Air Service (SAS) ambushed and killed eight members of the provisional Irish Republican Army while they were attempting to detonate a bomb near the Loughall post office.

The SAS ambush came in broad daylight in the midst of a suburban area and caused two accidental civilian casualties. The outcry in the press was significant, and the resultant investigation into the incident was extensive. Detailed information, including the specific numbers of rounds fired by each soldier, their precise points of impact, and an exhaustive search into the decisions leading up to this action, were compiled and revealed at a public inquest. After due process, the soldiers involved were cleared of any wrongdoing. This action was treated with the same scrutiny one might expect each time a police officer resorts to deadly force in the execution of his duties.[21]

Clearly, even a cursory examination of the British record in Northern Ireland since 1969 reveals instances of illegality, brutality, and cover-up, but the salient point in comparison with the French example in Algeria is that, in Ulster, the British government and military have scrupulously adhered to the forms and functions of civilian control and maintained the rule of law and military restraint.

Military restraint, the constant effort to hold to the rule of law in the prosecution of a protracted, complex military campaign, has been the major factor in the British government's ability to retain legitimacy in British popular opinion, which has allowed successive administrations to continue prosecuting the war. Government forces, civilian and military, demonstrated to the public the differences separating them from terrorists. Unlike the French Army in Algiers, they did not sink to the terrorists' level of inhumanity and brutality.

Lessons Learned

The critical importance of civilian control of the military, rigid adherence to the rule of law, and accountability of soldiers for their actions are just a few of the lessons we can draw from a comparison of these two wars. Perhaps the most important of these lessons is that in a low-intensity conflict, a key—if not *the* key—operational center of gravity and balance is domestic public opinion and the retention of legitimacy. Because of the nature of war itself, particularly in a LIC environment, soldiers and governments must remain true to legal principles and not descend into brutality. In Algiers in 1957, the French Army descended to that level, playing into the terrorists' hands and costing the government its popular mandate and, eventually, the war. The responsibility for those actions rests squarely with the Fourth Republic's civilian leaders.

In contrast, by consistently attempting to hold to a legal and fully accountable prosecution of warfare, the British government and military in Northern Ireland have retained the public's mandate to prosecute the war and might yet see it to a successful conclusion. While such a strict adherence to the principles of law and legitimacy might considerably lengthen a campaign, the lessons of the long British experience in Northern Ireland suggest that a longer campaign might be the only way to ensure success.

ENDNOTES

1. Edgar O'Ballance, *The Algerian Insurrection 1954–62* (Hamden, CT: Archon Books, 1967), 143.

2. John Talbot, *The War Without a Name: France in Algeria, 1954–62* (New York: Alfred A. Knopf, 1980), 247–8.

3. J. Bowyer Bell, *The Irish Troubles, A Generation of Violence 1967–1992* (New York: St. Martin's Press, 1993), 230.

4. Ibid.

5. Jean-Claude Goudeau, Director-General, "Minute," on French military operations in Algiers in 1957, quoted in Tony Geraghty, *March or Die: A New History of the French Foreign Legion* (New York: Facts on File Publications, 1986), 284.

6. Paul Johnson, *Modern Times: The World from the Twenties to the Eighties* (New York: Harper & Row, 1983), 495–505.

7. Geraghty, *March or Die*, 252.

8. Alistair Horne, *A Savage War of Peace, Algeria 1954–1962* (New York: The Viking Press, 1977), 183–7.

9. Geraghty, *March or Die*, chap. 14.

10. Horne, op cit., 188.

11. Talbot, op. cit., 85.

12. Horne, op. cit., 207.

13. Ibid., 197–8.

14. O'Ballance, op. cit., 143.

15. Horne, op. cit., 206–7.

16. Johnson, op. cit., 503–4.

17. Excerpt from "Rules of Engagement for the Military Commander of Operation Flavius," British Ministry of Defence, 1988. Operation Flavius was a British Special Air Service counterterrorism operation in which three Irish Republican Army terrorists were shot to death. See Tony Geraghty, *Who Dares Wins: The Story of the SAS 1950–1992* (London: Warner Books, 1993), 284.

18. Alfred McClung Lee, *Terrorism in Northern Ireland* (Bayside, NY: General Hall, Inc., 1983), chap. 2.

19. Bell, op. cit., 230.

20. Ibid.

21. Geraghty, *Who Dares Wins*, 274–8.

CHAPTER 4

The Ascent of Knowledge-Based Warfare

PAUL A. THOMSEN

Since the rise of the first nation-states in antiquity, two premises have guided every leader, every army, and every battle plan. First, in order to defeat an enemy one must know an adversary's location, military capabilities, and exploitable weaknesses. Second, with the proper amount of force applied to the appropriate weak point, in theory, a targeted enemy will dissemble and disintegrate time and again. In other words, a diminutive shepherd boy could bring down a giant, a silencer-toting busboy could eliminate a rising leader of a threatening state, a ragtag rebel army could drive a superior force to despair, and, in theory, an entire war could be fought and won against overwhelming odds by a few well-informed and capable soldiers. Little used, but often successful in limited tactical engagements and operations throughout history, these are the main tenets of knowledge-based warfare, a terribly effective tool in the twilight of the twenty-first century and a central tenet of future strategic war-fighting.

Previously considered the exclusive purview of nation-state intelligence organs and special forces units, throughout the 1990s Al Qaeda cells repeatedly demonstrated the key elements for bringing the long-theorized form of warfare from small-scale tactical origins to grand-scale practical application: excellent intelligence-gathering skills, frugal financial management, and an ardent resolve to take the fight to their enemies through inventive and unconventional means.[1] Where nation-states once tasked the skills of small elite forces (such as Nazi Germany's *Jagdkommandos*, the British Special Air Services (SAS), the Russian *Spetznaz*, and the United States Seal Team Six and 1st Special Forces Operational Detachment-Delta [more commonly known as Delta Force]) to provide a rapid response to international crises from sabotage operations and assassinations to snatch-and-grab and tide-turning battlefield operations, on the morning of September 11, 2001, four groups of largely inexperienced clandestine operatives proved beyond any doubt that a small, determined force could paralyze an entire country with some reconnaissance, nearly two dozen box cutters, the threat of violence, and a few pilot lessons. Policy makers and journalists alike have called this "a new kind of war,"[2] but the nineteen box cutter–wielding 9/11 hijackers were practicing a very old form of war in a very new way with great intrepidity.

Since antiquity, military leaders have sought to gain an edge over numerically superior adversaries through the adoption of new technologies, the implementation of improved training regiments, and exhaustive strategic planning. In order to augment their war-making capabilities, nation-states have frequently employed spies to gather data on their adversaries, saboteurs to slow an enemy's progress, and dissident elements to stir fear and disharmony into targeted civilian populations. Sometimes, the gathered information has offered weaker powers sudden opportunities to ambush or neutralize their foes. At other times, clandestine operatives have tied down entire regiments with a few well-placed shots. At still other times, information glimpsed on a few scraps of paper and clandestinely delivered have turned the tides of battle. Yet, the constraints of time, command-level clearance, and limits of period technology have habitually relegated the utility of crippling surgical strikes to the periphery of battlefield application. As a result, hesitant battlefield commanders and their political leaders have repeatedly chosen to exercise overwhelming force instead of the perceived less-certain advantages of surgical operations, decapitation strikes, and covert infrastructure degradation. In essence, rather than invest in a sharpened scalpel, history's leaders have consistently opted to perform delicate policy surgery with a tablespoon.

Throughout history military commanders have relied on the motions, methods, and intimidating effects large armies enjoyed to enforce the political will of their state. Restricted solely by their ability to furnish weapons and secure supplies, warfare between principalities have frequently devolved into either two or more forces clashing on contested terrain, or one group laying siege to another less-ready opponent. As greater resources were acquired, the average size of armies grew from a few hundred or a few thousand men in the ancient world to standing forces numbering in the tens and hundreds of thousands in the modern era. Until the advent of the atomic bomb, both the proportional size of military forces on land, sea, and air and the resource capabilities of their nation-state oftentimes mattered more in deterring potential aggressors and winning wars than nearly any other warfighting factor. As a result, those nation-states less populous than their competitor normally either resorted to deferential treaties, or sought technological solutions that might offset their disadvantage, or heroically stood their ground and died for their convictions.

Still, the unilateral submission of a conquered populace to the designs of occupying armies was seldom a certainty. Rather oppositely, most communities habitually bred small enclaves of politically, philosophically, or socially discontented individuals, which frequently needed to be weeded out by effective rulers and security services. With the removal of the established authority, however, those groups not enfranchised by the new leadership often sought measured revolutionary action to undermine their new leaders. Around 166 B.C.E., for example, disenfranchised Jewish rebels of the Hasmonean Dynasty (more commonly known as the Maccabees) exploited their occupiers need for geographic stability to overthrow Seleucid rule and successfully brokered a nonaggression pact with their former overlords. At other times, growing dissident movements turned to unbridled violence to intimidate their new overlords and security measures to promote a more "enlightened" form of governance (usually their's), exact revenge for past wrongs, or failing both, appropriate a modicum of the region's new wealth and bide their time for a more opportune moment to make their moves. Best exemplified by another contingent of rival militant Jewish dissident groups (most notably the curved-dagger wielding *Sicarii*),[3] in the years preceding the 70 C.E. destruction of the Second Temple of Solomon, radicals galvanized crowds to overthrow Roman rule through acts of terror in the streets of Jerusalem and throughout the countryside, but lacking political skill and a listening adversary, fell before the sandals and *gladi* of rival Roman cohorts. A few, such as legendary Grand Master Hasan-i-Sabbah's *Assassins* who raided Middle Eastern highways and trade routes between Christian-occupied settlements,[4] were motivated by revenge and the accumulation of wealth, and offered measured responses to new leadership to obtain short-term goals without jeopardizing their own property. Finally, still other dissident groups, such as the Irish Republican Army (IRA) in Ireland (most effectively led by commander Michael Collins),[5] the colonists in North America, and a multitude of factions in opposition to the Raj in India (primarily the Indian Nationalist Army of Sarat and Subhas Chandra Bose),[6] fought with small guerrilla raids and acts of terror and reprisal over the course of decades and sometimes centuries, as disaffected members of the British Empire benefited from the force-multiplying effects of communication and weapons technology to bleed their occupier dry.

With a solid group of supporters willing to hide, supply, and reliably inform the dissident elements about opposition movements, occupying leaders were frequently frustrated by insufficient leads, never-ending chases, deadly ambushes, and routes. In annoyance, rulers were frequently at a loss as to how they might neutralize the disruptive acts of such rebel groups without inviting further dissent. Overwhelming force rarely worked. Clandestine activities expertly carried out occasionally neutralized opposition forces with little fear of resurgence, but effective spymasters who never desired to rise above their station, such as British Queen Elizabeth's advisor Sir Francis Walsingham, were often the rarest of feudal commodities. Most often, however, appeasement, partial enfranchisement, and the granting of limited fiduciary concessions cooled rebellious tempers. Still, no matter how agreeable either side behaved with their settlements, the fear of what a few future reactionaries might yet do continued to haunt most ruling sovereigns until their dying hour.

The American Revolutionaries of the 1770s, facing a numerically superior, veteran-trained, and well-supplied force for control of continental sovereignty, were the first to successfully prosecute a war with modern guerilla warfare tactics and gathered actionable intelligence. They were small in number, inexperienced war-fighters, and held only their personal frontier gear, but they also had allies and the means of coordinating intracolonial and international actions. Learning beforehand of the massing of a veteran force of British Light Infantry and Grenadiers in Massachusetts, on April 15, 1775, enabled a mixed group of colonial militia and minutemen to assemble, break into small units, and fire on the enemy behind walls, rocks, and trees at the Battle of

Lexington and Concord (reportedly killing approximately seventy-three and wounding 174 of the king's men).[7] On June 17, 1775, the colonials again resorted to small-unit tactics, inflicting heavy casualties on the advancing ranks of enemy soldiers before relinquishing the field at Breed's Hill (according to Harold Selesky, the British incurred over 1,000 casualties in taking the abandoned Patriot battery).[8] Unaccustomed to fighting such an unconventional enemy and unable to gain a tactical intelligence advantage, the British grew more frustrated with each engagement and were eventually bled dry of their will to fight.

Later in the war, the Patriots realized that stand-off guerilla fighting tactics did not guarantee victory. General George Washington and his adjutants, after the disastrous 1776 fall of New York to the British, shifted the Patriot's overall direct war-fighting strategy toward a more dynamic combat intelligence doctrine, relying heavily on a semi-autonomous command structure, intelligence gathering efforts, hit-and-fade attacks, and, as Thomas Fleming has posited in the case of Nathan Hale, incendiary sabotage.[9] In 1778, General Washington, as spymaster, cultivated fledgling intelligence assets through Major Benjamin Tallmadge (who operated under several cover identities, including John Bolton and Sir James Jay), yielding reams of valuable and exploitable information on enemy force sizes,[10] including the plans of British General Sir Henry Clinton, the defection of Major General Benedict Arnold, and an impending British attack on colonial forces at Newport, Rhode Island.[11] Similar semi-autonomous intelligence efforts by other Patriots, likewise, enabled Ethan Allen and guerrilla fighters to launch successful operations against British outposts in the north. After the fall of Charleston in 1780, Francis Marion, Charles Sumter, Andrew Pickens, and theater commander General Nathaniel Greene, likewise, led their region's special forces in surgical attacks against enemy movements through a series of posted sentries and like-minded civilians who regularly reported on enemy troop movements. Knowing the enemy's size, strength, and location, they were able to lead a brigade of Patriot guerrilla fighters on daring raids against British convoys, stifle the punitive actions of local Tory bands, come to the aid of fellow colonial forces, outdistance the enemy's attempts to pursue them, and effectively force British General Lord Charles Earl Cornwallis to either invest heavily in securing the outback of South Carolina or flee and lose not only the colony, but also the war.

After the American Revolution, knowledge-based warfare fell into disuse as the nation moved to build large armies, erect fortifications, and maintain fleets with which they might deter a potential aggressor. During the Civil War, brief personal fears and fleeting moments of inspiration forced Union General George B. McClellan to enlist the assistance of the Pinkerton Detective Agency to spy on Confederate troop movements (the effort was dismally inaccurate, led to numerous overcalculations of enemy troop strength, and likely needlessly extended the duration of the conflict),[12] and Confederates in the western states to suffer dozens of Union partisan raids as well as enemy sabotage operations preceding the arrival of conventional forces (the chaos caused by the burning of bridges and firing of Confederate posts little aided the Union either in taking entrenched enemy positions or in capturing the fleeing units).[13] Similar knowledge-based warfare operations undertaken during World War I met with inconclusive results. For example, in July 1916 and January 1917, a group of German Army soldiers and civilian recruits detonated explosives on Black Tom Island in Brooklyn Harbor, at a Kingsland munitions plant in New Jersey, and aboard several transatlantic cargo vessels. They had hoped to deter the United States from entering the war. Contrarily, neither the country nor the White House linked the operation to the war raging in Europe. Noticeably unaffected, the U.S. entered the war in 1917.

Although repeated failures in communication, resource allocation, intelligence-gathering, and rapid response led to thousands of deaths in the German Blitzkreig, Operation Barbarossa, the Japanese attack on Pear Harbor, the slow start of Operation Torch, as in the American Revolution, during the Second World War fears of superior enemy capabilities fostered a renewed tactical acceptance of knowledge-based warfare. Through the 1942 efforts of Lieutenant Commander Joseph J. Rochefort's United States Pacific Fleet cryptanalysts and Vice Admiral William Halsey's Task Force 16 (TF-16), bombers from carriers *Enterprise* (CV-6), USS *Yorktown* (CV-5), and *Hornet* (CV-8) were able to trap Vice Admiral Chuichi Nagumo's fleet, sinking three Japanese carriers at the battle of Midway Island.[14] Later, code-breaking efforts and the capture of a German Enigma machine resulted in the turning of the tide in the Battle of the Atlantic and a few inconsistent tactical victories during the invasion of Europe.

Still, in the early 1940s, some progress was made toward integrating intelligence into strategic war-fighting by both Axis and Allied elements. On the frontlines, Allied combat interrogators extricated details on enemy troop strength, disposition, armaments, and battle plans from captured prisoners of war.[15] In operational planning, General George S. Patton relied heavily on Third Army Intelligence Colonel Oscar Koch to furnish pertinent G-2 analysis, aerial reconnaissance photography, and battlefield assessments of enemy capabilities, aiding in the Breakout, the penetration of the Siegfried Line, and the turning back of the Nazi Ardennes counteroffensive.[16] On the opposite side of the conflict, Europe's "most dangerous man,"[17] SS-Sturmbannführer Otto Skorzeny, and his *Jagdkommandos* cultivated their own indigenous assets and organized their own behind-enemy-line operations, successfully exfiltrating Fascist Italian dictator Benito Mussolini imprisoned atop an Allied-guarded mountain chalet and nearly succeeded in penetrating enemy lines to assassinate members of the Allied High Command. Likewise, as new alliances were forged, both sides attempted to gain comprehensive assessments of the other's military, scientific, social, and industrial advancements in the form of defections, aerial/orbital photography, wiretaps, and moles. American, British, and Russian intelligence officers were instrumental in tracking down and "disappearing." At the war's end, German weapons program staff, material, and scientists were used to further each country's own aviation, nuclear, and ballistic missile technologies. Still, neither the Allied nor the Axis advances either fundamentally shifted the nature of the war or decisively shifted the tide of rolling campaigns.

Over the following decades, both American and Soviet leaders drove their respective intelligence communities to produce greater and greater quantities of intelligence in the pursuit of policy victories and led both nations further away from more cost-effective precision warfighting strategies. Advances in weapons and industrial technologies bred competition, and increased competition fueled each nation's hunger for greater access to resources. By the end of the Reagan-Gorbachev Era, it seemed Cold War brinkmanship and runaway military-industrial complexes had derailed the development of knowledge-based warfare with multimillion dollar submarines, smart bombs, surveillance satellites, laser designators, fast-attack helicopters, and nuclear-powered warships, but three post–World War II occurrences returned the focus of military doctrine to intelligence and the strategic application of military force: the 1979 Soviet invasion of Afghanistan; the 1983 truck-bombing of a United States military compound in Beirut, Lebanon; and Al Qaeda's increasingly successful intelligence-heavy war against the United States.

Where the eighteenth-century American Revolutionaries had fought off the might of the British Empire, near the end of the twentieth century, a cadre of ill-equipped and factionalized Afghanistani rebels faced a similar seemingly never-ending tide of veteran military units and the best hardware the Soviet Union could muster. Like the Continental Army, the Afghanistani repeatedly frustrated their opponents with hit-and-fade attacks, ambushes, and firing retreats, consistently inflicting heavy enemy losses before conceding ground. But for years they could not staunch the flow of Russian troops flowing into the region. Luckily, like the American Revolutionaries, the Afghanistani had allies in the Soviet Union's enemies. As a response to Moscow's deployment of Spetsnaz Special Forces, Airborne assault units, and flights of heavily armored Hind-D gunships (designed to be nearly impervious to small arms fire), in the early 1980s, Saudi Arabia and the United States funneled a steady stream of experienced dissident leaders, criminals, and religious extremists (many of which had previously been incarcerated for crimes against the Saudi royal family), who had been trained by American advisors in Pakistan and equipped with American-built weapons systems (most notably infrared-seeking Stinger anti-aircraft missiles and the wire-guided British Javelins) into the region. With the assistance of the new foreign fighters, called *Mujahideen* (meaning "Holy Warriors"), the Afghanistani had done what was believed impossible. They effectively turned back the Soviet offensive[18] and, by 1988, had forced Moscow to withdraw their military assets from the region. Knowledge-based warfare, employed tactically and used judiciously, had for the first time, changed the course of a war.

During the late 1970s and 1980s, another multinational crisis was developing in parallel with the fighting in Afghanistan. With the 1979 toppling of the Shah of Iran, new radical interpretations of Muslim orthodoxy had spawned numerous state- and privately sponsored militant groups throughout the Middle East, including Hamas, the Palestinian Liberation Organization (PLO), the Mujahideen, and Hezbollah.

While larger dissident groups waged a scorched-earth policy against Israel and its allies, dozens of lesser coordinated and less well-financed
extremist groups, heartened by Ayatollah Rouhallah Khomeini's effective humiliation of the United States with the seizure of fifty-three
United States diplomats for 444 days and the disastrous aborted Delta
Force mission to rescue the hostages, fell back on the traditional violent
tools of the disenfranchised and attempted to bring world attention to
their respective causes through the application of terror. In 1985, Trans
World Airlines (TWA) Flight 847 was skyjacked by members of Abu
Nidal, leaving two Americans dead.[19] In 1988, agents of Libyan dictator
Colonel Moammar Gadhafi detonated an explosive device aboard Pan
American (Pan Am) Flight 103.[20] In 1983, splinter cells of the PLO engi-
neered the bombings of the United States embassy in Beirut and the
Marine barracks at the Beirut airport, killing over sixty people and 241
U.S. military personnel, respectively.[21] Finally, in 1996, an explosive de-
vise concealed inside a water truck parked outside Building 131 at the
Dharhan Khobar Towers in Saudi Arabia was allegedly detonated by
members of Hezbollah, killing nineteen American servicemen quar-
tered in the facility.[22]

Although independently planned and privately undertaken, these
terrorist actions were predicated on operational considerations, real-
time intelligence analysis, and near-immediate tactical application in
the pursuit of perceived achievable short-term goals, including policy
education and public relations through homicidal/suicidal acts. Indeed, the entire Soviet-Afghanistani war had played out in a series of
lessons in the application of precisely administered doses of pain and
punishment to wear down superior forces. Similarly, the 1980 failure of
Delta Force in the Iranian desert (Operation Eagle Claw) had embold-
ened the Iranians, offering rhyme, reason, and support approval for the
facilitation of Qods Force activities (a branch of the Iranian Revolution-

ary Guard responsible for expanding the reach of Hezbollah-sponsored cellular activities throughout the region). Knowledge-based warfare was moving from the hands of isolated radicals and intrepid battlefield commanders toward more expanded usage.

The events subsequent to the 1983 Beirut bombings are even more telling. Rather than expand U.S. military operations in response to the attacks (as the Romans had in Palestine, the British had in Ireland, Scotland, and India, and the Russians continued to follow into twenty-first-century Chechnya), military leadership ordered the swift removal of American troops and authorized the shelling of Beirut by the battleship *New Jersey* (BB-62) prior to their departure from the theater.[23] America's enemies did not miss the lesson that, with sufficient knowledge, dedication, and pressure even small uncoordinated groups could move/remove superpowers.

Ironically, both the Afghanistani-Soviet War and the 1980s Mid-East dissident activities, which culminated in the 1983 Beirut bombings, provided appreciable impetus for the U.S. military to reevaluate its long-standing military doctrine of overwhelming force. Born of geopolitical necessity by the Carter Administration, Army Colonel Charles Beckwith's Delta Force learned the lessons of history's small-action groups, modern police units, and special forces units from around the world to become the preeminent hostage-rescue rapid response unit. As time passed, however, Delta operators came to be increasingly relied upon to neutralize/resolve tactical threats to the global interests of the United States, including deployment as snipers in Beirut, strike teams in Grenada,[24] rescuers in Panama,[25] and abductors in Somalia.[26] Likewise, their Naval counterpart, Naval Special Warfare Development Group (designated NSWDG, but more commonly known as the Navy SEALs) were similarly deployed in crisis situations, but, as the years passed, they were more frequently retasked to support broader, more hazardous, intelligence gathering efforts off foreign shores. By the end of the twentieth century, both groups had countered a number of U.S. national security threats, applying integrated civilian and military intelligence into tactical usages and projecting American military power into every corner of the globe with surgical precision and, when sanctioned, deadly results.

Still, the special forces remained only one minor component of America's new late-twentieth-century war-fighting machine. After World War II, with the American public adverse to the notion of retaining a large standing military presence, and facing a retinue of potential aggressors (including the USSR, China, North Korea, and Vietnam), some with numerically superior populations, the United States married advanced weapons and intelligence technologies to the projection of military power. The atomic bomb marginalized concerns of mass armies of invasion. Satellites, high-altitude surveillance planes, and wiretaps minimized the chances of undetected advances made by competitors and prepared, but unnoticed, enemy first strikes on American infrastructure. Advanced guidance systems utilizing laser designators, GPS systems, and computer-enhanced topographic imaging technology provided less potential for collateral damage than a battleship's cannons, and greater accuracy. Consequently, stand-off missile attacks grew more common. In response to the 1988 bombing of Pan Am 103, a flight of Navy fighters and bombers were able to deliver precision-guided munitions to the doorsteps of Colonel Moammar Gadhafi's residence and his intelligence agency.[27] Laser-guided ordinance was able to eliminate Slobodan Milosevic's ability to make war in Kosovo,[28] and Tomahawk cruise missiles were able to neutralize Iraqi troop installations during the First and Second Gulf Wars.[29]

By the mid 1990s, Saudi national Osama bin Laden and his Egyptian-born Al Qaeda second-in-command, Ayman Zawahiri, were also learning from past dissident movements as well as America's now traditional heavy-handed military approach, to revise the direction of terrorism as a weapon of war and learn from their adversaries. Unlike most past terrorist groups, Al Qaeda functioned as a long-term-oriented, privately backed, multinational, military force. Nominally, they wanted the United States removed from Middle East affairs. Secondarily, they sought to remove Western influences from Middle Eastern regional governance. And, thirdly, they desired the creation of a new pan-Islamic state.[30]

With private funds, an aggressive Western-style marketing campaign (replete with Internet websites, publicly aired product advertisements, and songs), modern office equipment, a handful of training camps, and regional franchise rights granted to the most promising candidates, Al Qaeda was able to launch and sustain a nearly undetectable intelligence-heavy campaign against the United States for several years (starting with the October 1993 training of Somalis with rocket propelled grenades [RPGs],[31] continuing with the February 1993 bombing of the World Trade Center,[32] and rising to broad awareness with the 1998 simultaneous suicide attacks on America's embassies in Kenya and Tanzania).[33] Even after achieving international notoriety and the dubious distinction of playing fox to Central Intelligence Agency's hunter-killer team GE/SENIOR's hounds,[34] bin Laden's network was able to succeed in two out of three subsequent attacks against the United States, including the 2000 attack on the USS *Cole* and the September 11, 2001 attack (as of date of publication, released government reports indicate that the Millennium Plot to raze Los Angeles International Airport remains the solitary victory of the United States federal government in successfully intercepting an Al Qaeda–launched operation).[35] By the end of the twentieth century, knowledge-based warfare had become Al Qaeda's strategic doctrine for the creation of the amassing of personal profit and the creation of a pan-Islamic state.

Until September 2001, few outside special forces and America's Intelligence Community (IC) had considered the benefits of blending real-time intelligence gathering efforts with elite military expertise to produce devastating real-time theaterwide paralysis. While many nations had suffered the shock and awe of carefully planned preemptive strikes on military assets (most notably, the March 1904 attack on Russia's Port Arthur, the June 1941 Nazi commencement of Operation Barbarossa, and the December 1941 attack on America's Pearl Harbor naval facility), few however, could compare to either Al Qaeda's systematic, multipronged, knowledge-based attacks or their staggering mortal results.

Minutes after both hijacked planes hit the World Trade Center complex, the federal government was locked down. Simultaneously, cabinet members and their adjutants were whisked into vaults and shelters in compliance with continuity of governance protocols. Next, the nation's financial center fell silent. Within an hour, the nerve center of America's defensive capabilities was bleeding black smoke into the blue Virginian sky. Shortly thereafter, over 2,500 civilians lay dead beneath glass, mortar, plaster, asbestos, and steel in lower Manhattan.[36] Thirty-seven more, the passengers of United Airlines Flight 93 who had attempted to interdict Al Qaeda's plans, lay dead in a Pennsylvania field amidst aviation parts, unspent fuel, and the bodies of their attackers.[37] One hundred and eighty-nine military personnel were being pulled from the gouged earth and smoldering infrastructure of the Pentagon.[38] Within a handful of hours, the Air Force had erected a defensive screen over Washington, D.C., the nuclear-powered aircraft carrier *George Washington* (CV-73) was sortieing fighter wings over Brooklyn Harbor and New York coastal waters. By late afternoon, every plane inside the airspace of the Continental United States had been grounded.

In the weeks, months, and years following Al Qaeda's largest and most complex attack, the United States has begun to learn from its enemies and incrementally alter its war-fighting doctrine. The Intelligence Community (IC), depleted by years of congressional underfinancing and previously stymied in its attempts to eliminate emerging national security threats by risk-adverse policy makers and military coordinators (including several pre-9/11 attempts to capture/kill bin Laden),[39] found new friends on Capitol Hill, at the White House, and in sections of the Department of Defense. America's special forces, now brimming with eager new talent and equipped with the requisite tools, were being deployed on operations geared for knowledge-based warfare. On September 9, 2001, CIA Counter Terrorism Center leader Coffer Black authorized his new Northern Afghanistan Liaison Team (NALT), code-named Jawbreaker, to ". . . Go find Al Qaeda and kill them . . . Get bin Laden . . . I want his head in a box."[40] In October 2001, U.S. Special Forces Team-555 was dropped into Afghanistan to provide eyes-on and laser targeting of Taliban and Al Qaeda positions for Allied fighters and bombers.[41, 42] By November 3, 2001, four CIA paramilitary and three Special Forces teams inside Afghanistan and several more waiting to be flown in-country were ordered to degrade enemy troop concentrations in advance of the ragtag army of the Northern Alliance.[43] On November 11, 2001, Team-555 reportedly inflicted a loss of twenty-nine tanks, six command posts, and 2,200 enemy casualties surrounding Bagram Air Base via twenty-five air strikes.[44] By December 7, 2001, approximately 110 CIA officers and 316 members of America's Special Forces had forced the Taliban to surrender 85 percent of the country to the American-backed Northern Alliance.[45]

Later, in the Second Gulf War and the occupation of Iraq that followed, the application of knowledge-based warfare saw wide dissemination beyond IC paramilitary and American special forces teams. In the opening hours of the war, approximately three hundred members of the American Special Operations Forces (SOF), clandestinely helicoptered and air-dropped into the theater, began securing missile sites, capturing airports (specifically H-1 and H-2), and designating targets for the first wave of attacking Allied aircraft.[46] While units such as Task Force 121[47] hunted first Iraqi President Saddam Hussein,[48] and, later, Al Qaeda theater commander Abu Musab al Zarqawi,[49] new tactics and weapons systems were allowing real-time intelligence to more directly alter the outcome of enemy encounters and weaken the Iraqi Army's ability to fight. In the early morning hours of March 19, 2003, numerous laser- and satellite-guided bombs shut down several Iraqi power facilities, communication nets, and command and control facilities.[50] Later, GPS units were employed to track Allied troop movements, mark key enemy weapons sites, and target enemy positions in preparation for air strikes.[51] As combat moved into urban centers, snipers were deployed to "target command and control elements and other high-value targets."[52] During the January 2005 siege of Fallujah, Unmanned Aerial Vehicle's (UAV) acquired, identified, and tracked potential targets for Marine Corps units, limiting the possibility of civilian casualties, minimizing friendly casualties, and maximizing the effectiveness of Allied firepower.[53] Finally, and most extraordinarily, the Fourth Infantry Division (nicknamed "the Digital Division"), equipped with digital radio networked personal computers (including a monitor, sealed keyboard, six-to-ten Gigabyte hard drive, and upwards of a 333MHz processor) in their vehicles carrying the Force 21 Base and Command Brigade and Below system (FBCB2), were able to communicate with Central Command via an instant messenger program, plot the locations of enemy units with icons on constantly updating digital maps shared with system users, read and interpolate combat intelligence in real-time, issue commands, and coordinate division activities.[54]

Since September 11, 2001, the U.S. Army has begun to change its doctrinal concept of war-fighting toward an increasingly dominant knowledge-based warfare approach. Rather than a single amorphous mass of troops expected to rotate into frontline action as needed, long-tested sports strategies (such as the American football concept of defined offensive and defensive teams—one for rapid attack, and one to hold the line while the primary team continues to advance the army's sphere of control) have led the military to economize and prioritize the distribution of cached armor, intelligence, provisions, equipment, and ammunition to where they are most needed. Fading also are the days of front- and rear-echelon fighting. Instead, the new axiom of ground war has become, in the words of one general, "deep, close, and rear,"[55] allowing mass army fighters greater flexibility of movement and the ability to strike at the vitals of an enemy mass. In both instances, the desire for actionable battlefield intelligence and the time needed for a reallocation of combat assets toward either taking advantage of an unaware adversary or interdicting an enemy response has become a paramount concern. As a former chairman of the Joint Chiefs of Staff described, ". . . you can develop military operations until hell freezes over, but they are worthless without intelligence."[56]

Since the failure to detect the Japanese fleet at Pearl Harbor and the National Security Act of 1947, the United States IC has traditionally followed the five steps of intelligence gathering called the Intelligence Cycle: Planning/Direction (identifying Administration data collection needs), Collection (the amassing of information via human operatives, signal intelligence, image intelligence . . .), Processing (pooling usable all-source intelligence into readable packages), Analysis (evaluating the collected data and the drawing of conclusions), and Dissemination (providing finished intelligence products to pertinent political and military consumers).[57] In a given amount of time, tens of thousands of pages of information are produced by workers within the fourteen agencies that make up the IC, but, due to time constraints, only a handful of distilled paragraphs reach the eyes and ears of the president. As has been revealed through various congressional inquiries, much of the information available to analysts or field agents of one agency has in several cases failed to reach the hands of another agent within that agency (for example, the notorious FBI 9/11 Phoenix Memo) or other intelligence producers working on parallel projects from different orientations within the IC.[58] Furthermore, in recent history, valuable time has been wasted in the pursuit of limited information to the exclusion of other equally mission-pertinent information. As follow-up queries are made, critical opportunities can rapidly vanish.

Some have theorized the use of artificial intelligence to accelerate the information cycle and expand the IC's ability to cull all-source intelligence into manageable analytical products.[59] Others have moved to streamline the intelligence process into a noncollection/nonanalytical position, the National Intelligence Director. Others still have clamored for greater congressional oversight, claiming they might best be able to direct intelligence collection more accurately if they had a greater hand. And others have even pressed for supplementing intelligence analysis with private vendors. As exemplified by the failure of Soviet leader Joseph Stalin to receive, comprehend, and order his Red Army to counter Nazi Germany's invasion of Russia, despite valid intelligence demonstrating clear signs of an imminent attack in the weeks, days, and hours in advance of Operation Barbarossa's commencement, slow intelligence analysis, lengthy command protocols, and resistant/risk adverse policy makers have meant the difference between mortal combat and massacre.

In order to combat these deficiencies, an effort has been made to centralize intelligence on the policy end, but, in recent years, few have addressed the concerns of the intelligence operators. Useful information is often missed. With the exception of Delta Force members, discussions of mission parameters are frequently held above the level of tactical planners. Isolated from the worlds of headquarters and capital politics, agents in the field frequently have few resources that they might apply to new situations in a timely manner outside the items that they either brought with them or managed to obtain in the time since their arrival in-country. While centralization of intelligence is sound with respect to physical security (if classified information is available at only a handful of locations, less availability means a decreased likelihood of information theft/defections), it does remove the information from the field operatives and parallel-working analysts.

With the ever-expanding pool of intelligence data that modern technology can troll from the electronic ether (e.g., images, web conversations, net postings, e-mails, cell phone conversations) and the increased number of special forces/CIA paramilitary missions being launched, there will be a great necessity for the adoption of new intelligence handling and retention guidelines. Whereas new technologies are positive avenues that governments should explore, nothing can surpass placing knowledgeable people in touch with the source material. With security of information at a premium, every government has compartmentalized intelligence data by subject and/or geographic area. But the IC need not sacrifice productivity for security. In the millennia prior to the advent of electronic communication, the Roman Catholic Church and numerous feudal lords used trusted servants to convey pieces of information to needed parties. When the Church found information of value, they were laboriously hand-copied and shelved away in monasteries, abbeys, and private libraries for posterity. In the world of limited physical space made infinite by PC hard, jump, floppy, and writable CD drives, there is little reason not to follow the old Church's lead. While domestic intelligence headquarters should retain originals and backups, like the mass mailing feature in most e-mail programs, analysts across the entire stateside IC could theoretically send sorted information by subject to a collection drive, where each subject is encrypted, broken into parts, copied separately onto transportable media at the end of every week or month and conveyed by carefully screened individuals to designated points around the world under the control of the intelligence producer's government for use by cleared individuals.

In this model, the information would remain as secure as if it went to a policy maker. It would be available for practical application as real-time events dictated, without compromising peripheral data use. As at headquarters, only a limited number of individuals would be allowed access or dissemination rights for the information. And, above all, those with a need to know would be pooling their resources to better understand ongoing events and, in time of war, get inside the enemy's learning/action curve. What might have happened had the December 1941, Department of Defense MAGIC crypt analyst's deductions reached Pearl Harbor prior to the Japanese attack or, more recently, what might have been gained by FBI, CIA, and NSA headquarters' sharing of even part of their 2001 intelligence on Al Qaeda operations with the FBI Phoenix field office, holding Zacarias Moussaoui, or had knowledge that two of the individuals who perpetrated the 9/11 attack been identified as terrorists by the CIA, and subsequently watch-listed by the FBI prior to entering the United States in the months before the attack?

Next, the opportunities for the mining of additional present and future intelligence data are immense. Every year, satellite imaging technology gains in accuracy, resolution, compass, and depth. Since the end of the First Gulf War, a portion of the imagery obtained by the U.S. military's web of orbital satellites has, indeed, been processed by civilian companies.[60] Not knowing what might be considered sensitive material until the images are developed and handed over to governmental officials, the situation is ripe for industrial espionage and sabotage. Similarly, the lines between the protection of one's privacy rights as a U.S. citizen are also becoming blurred by an increasing number of private companies.

Still, American law does not preclude the use of such collected information against noncitizen. In the late 1990s, the FBI launched an Internet application, called Carnivore, capable of culling e-mail server information for evidence of illegal activities on the part of Internet Provider (IP) users. Although unpopular with the privacy conscious pre-9/11 American public, as the Internet grows, the venture, as well as other similar programs (such as key loggers, data sifters, and, offensively, logic bombs and other forms of denial-of-service-attacks), does have merit in monitoring, manipulating, and in certain cases, shutting down the new preferred ether of dissident conversations, terrorist planning, information warfare, and propagandist ventures. Similarly, the rise of PC usage in businesses and the pooling of consumer databases (such as aviation, banking, credit card companies, real estate, hospitalization, utilities, driver's licenses, visa applications, hotel reservations, etc.) has made "living off the grid" an increasingly difficult proposition for individuals desiring to avoid paper trails,[61] but desirous of interacting with society beyond an agent's deep cover. On a global level, it will be nearly impossible to hide evidence of increased weapons production, the logistical procedures necessary for readying a military contingent for battle, or tracking a force en route to a war zone (the noticeability of force allocation and troop buildup in Kuwait was one of Defense Secretary Donald Rumsfeld's major concerns prior to launching the Second Gulf War).[62]

Likewise, as the world becomes more dependent on electronic technology, new opportunities for tracking, espionage, and disruption of adversaries have also multiplied. While enemies of a given nation-state can use and trade in cell phones over limited periods of time in the hope of avoiding detection, rudimentary programs have been created to infect cell phones (one script kitty's attempt managed to spread an infection across several time zones over the course of a month, repeatedly depleting each infected user's battery).[63] Similar think-pieces have questioned the virus communicability/traceability of car electronics.[64] Conversely, teenagers or adults with limited prospects, could be given cell phones, an immediate monetary incentive, promise of relocation, and citizenship, in exchange for infrequent calls notifying intelligence collection points when certain neighborhood personalities or military units might be moving. On a smaller level, several institutions are rapidly developing the ultimate bugging devices, robotic cockroaches, flies, and nanobotic smart dust, which could easily be employed for disposable intelligence gathering purposes.[65] Finally, recent advances in optical/visual spectrum technology has enabled local and national security to follow the moves and motions of sources of Infrared Radiation (IR) (e.g., humans and pack animals) from increasing distances for monitoring, tracking, apprehension, and defensive capabilities.[66] If the abundance of surveillance cameras in urban centers and the number of companies developing software capable of distinguishing biometrics are any indication, over the next century, in more economically advanced/vulnerable states, few known dissidents or enemy units will be able to act more than once without being watched, recorded, tracked, and, likely, downed by notified security services or military units.

As evidenced by the downsizing and specializing trend of twentieth- and twenty-first-century conflicts and the entities that have fought them, placing traditional large armies on battlefields to face and annihilate other large armies, like the war chariot and the battleship before it, is fast falling into obsolescence. In Afghanistan, regular army units were brought into the theater only after special forces units and the Northern Alliance had diminished much of the Taliban's hold on the region. Why send 100,000 men to bring down a targeted nation-state or extranational dissident group, when a thousand elite trained and ably equipped ground-pounders could effect the same outcome with actionable intelligence, keen judgment, timing and, when needed, outside theater support (e.g., naval bombardment, UAV/satellite reconnaissance, and aerial transport)?

With the advent of real-time communications and miniaturized analytical technology, the small, isolated, and uncoordinated actions of prior special forces groups will eventually give way to the practical advantages of small, increasingly autonomous, and intelligence-rich battlefield units. While the multiplication of special forces units might not make them as "special" anymore, as in comparison between the early and later NASA astronaut corps members, there will be an increasing demand for soldiers with special skills in the sciences (e.g., primarily chemistry, biology, and rudimentary nuclear physics), dialects, urban cultures, and industries. Similarly, unlike many of their naval and aviation counterparts, special forces teams frequently have to expend time transiting to their launch point (usually submarines, carriers, and air bases), awaiting the "go" order, and being conveyed to the targets. With the creation of the Strategic Support Branch (SSB) of the Defense Intelligence Agency (DIA), crucial time need no longer be expended in trouble spots. On a more proactive level, special forces personnel, chosen for their ability to blend into the surroundings or a reasonable business cover, working clandestinely could be secreted into a civilian populace, potentially develop a relationship with the surrounding community, gather intelligence passively and remain in position for a handful of years before being rotated home or ordered to become operational. (In British imperial history, the similar planting of agents, most notably British Army Colonel Richard Meinertzhagen,[67] for lengthy tours of duty in rural corners of the empire often yielded vital information in times of crisis and action.) As one special forces officer reported during his 2005 tour of Afghanistan, "In order to defeat the enemy, you first have to love him and his culture."[68]

According to Richard Clarke, in 1998, reports surfaced of a Sudanese facility, funded by Osama bin Laden's Taba Investment Company, possibly manufacturing chemical weapons for the Al Qaeda leader, but before action could be taken to shut down the facility in the hostile country, soil samples needed to be surreptitiously obtained and analyzed.[69] In response, the CIA delegated an agent to travel to the site, gather the sample, and convey it to a laboratory outside the country for testing. The tests confirmed the presence of nerve-gas-agent byproducts. Shortly thereafter, the Clinton Administration launched several Tomahawk cruise missiles at the facility, but only baby powder was found.[70] Had a team with the proper training and equipment been in the region, a chemical specialist would have been able to analyze the sample on the spot, decreasing the time in which the facility could have been swapped via dual-usage procedures before the attack. The team could have tracked the chemicals from processing to storage, and/or the team could have directly sabotaged the plant without the ramifications of an international incident or the multimillion dollar price tag of the missile.

In taking a page from the employment of Al Qaeda, Soviet, Nazi, and Japanese clandestine actions of the twentieth century, sleeper cells are highly profitable methods of passively gathering intelligence, gauging popular reactions, launching sabotage operations, and inciting civil unrest amongst indigenous populations. If fifth columnists remain vigilant, they are seldom noticed until they are activated (with minimal conversance in English, nineteen of the 9/11 hijackers were able to enter and remain undetected by the American IC). They are adept at storing material necessary for fomenting revolution. (According to Christopher Andrew and Vasili Mitrokhin, the KGB were able to secure several weapons caches throughout the West for eventual deployment in the presumed worldwide Communist Revolution, which never came. They remained unknown by domestic intelligence until being informed on by a KGB defector in the 1990s.)[71] Most important, they are adept at creating timetables of military and paramilitary movements, charting the precise locations of key installations and weapons supplies, and providing cover for follow-up intelligence needs (best exemplified by Japanese imperial spy Takeo Yoshikawa, who under civilian cover, provided much of the intelligence that made the 1941 attack on Pearl Harbor possible). Finally, as in the Al Qaeda Madrid train bombing, imagine the damage that could be inflicted by a hundred individuals scattered across a nation-state, able to plant disposable, remote surveillance devices at will, leave time-delayed sabotage devices in key locations (e.g., rail lines, utility stations, communication hubs, marketplaces, the parameters of military depots), gather into groups, wait for the ordered time, and, while the bombs are going off and aerial support is flying overhead hitting their own targets, making for the target objective before the enemy can respond. With minimum friendly casualties, maximum yield, precise intelligence painstakingly planned, an entire country could be brought to its knees in a few hours and, if targets were selectively chosen, a new, more favorable government could be installed via a coup d' état. It would take the precision-guided weapons displayed nightly in the first Kosovo and both Gulf Wars to an entirely new level. It would be knowledge-based warfare at its finest.

Still, several administrative, legal, logistical, and oversight concerns need to be addressed before there can be any further evolution/integration/application of knowledge-based warfare into the present intelligence and military command structures. First, as in every modern military war, more individuals are needed behind the lines in support of operatives in-country. In facing the Soviet Union during the Cold War, the American IC cultivated experts to cover nearly every facet of Soviet life. After the fall of the Berlin Wall, elected officials in search of a "peace dividend" effectively stripped the CIA's Soviet divisions of its experts, did not reallocate assets to other divisions, and allowed the agency to fall behind in technology. (According to one source, it took years for the agency to acquire discretionary funds to outfit analyst desktops with basic Internet search capabilities.)[72]

Second, staff increases should be made to two sectors: multisubject experts and data organizers. The experts would be able to repopulate long-vacant positions, relieving overworked analysts and, like their knowledgeable special forces counterparts, augmenting the IC's ability to deal with more cases in greater detail, with greater recall. Data organizers would be able to prioritize, categorize, maintain, and disseminate gathered intelligence and analysis to the appropriate parties.

Third, a panel should be formed for every special forces unit placed in-country, consisting of military commanders and experts, a case-experienced intelligence expert, an Administration/State Department representative, a consultant with experience/knowledge of the target, and a member of the congressional legislature able to report on actions to the appropriate select committee. Borrowing in part from modern tactical operations, these individuals would act as an ad hoc command and control center via digital/voice link with the fielded teams, overseeing, briefing, and advising actions during active phases and ensuring compliance with intelligence requirements, legal constraints, and political wishes.

Fourth, a new policy for covert military intelligence operations would need to be formed. Whereas certain orders barring the assassinations of foreign leaders has been rescinded, several issues still remain unresolved, including the limits of Title X of the United States Code, covering Department of Defense activities with respect to Title L, which has governed civilian intelligence since the onset of the Cold War.[73] Similarly, respect needs to be paid to the findings of the 1976 Church Committee Report, which set forward the parameters and guidelines of proper conduct for the IC.[74] Although an 1837 precedent exists (affirming that the forces of one country may enter another in pursuit of a threat to national security), considerable thought must be given to the U.S. military's ability to conduct clandestine military operations on foreign soil without the nation's knowledge.[75]

The increasing rate of information acquisition has led to a revolution in intelligence gathering and the ascent of knowledge-based warfare. With the expanding ranks of IC and special forces recruits, the modern military units have expanded the concepts founded by their rebel, guerilla, and terrorist predecessors. Today, they are conducting vital and delicate missions, including the rescuing of hostages, snatching-and-grabbing political/military targets, assassinating opposition members, and conducting raids deep into enemy territory as parts of greater campaigns. In the future, knowledge-based warfare will play a dominant role for large nation states and minor dissident groups alike. Like the great wooden horse as night fell on the walled city of Troy, the concept still holds great hidden danger for targeted and unsuspecting enemies, blending intelligence and military force into decisive real-time actions writ on a theaterwide level.

ENDNOTES

1. Although Al Qaeda has been consistently identified by policy makers and analysts as a terrorist organization, if one looks at the group's methods, resources, goals, and actions, no comparison can be made with any previous terrorist group. Instead, they function more like a franchise/brand-driven corporation. The solicited global appeal through the generation of public relations material (including speeches, videos, and global recruiters). As far as declassified intelligence documentation revealed, they are funded entirely through private (non-state) ventures. Their goals are incremental, systematic, and specific in both the short and long term. And, above all, in the period between 1993 and 2004, they waged a clear and consistent knowledge-based war campaign against United States targets of both symbolic and tangible value.

2. "Target America," *Frontline*, Program #2001. Airdate: October 4, 2001 Reuters Newmedia Inc./Corbis. Transcript. http://www.pbs.org/wgbh/pages/frontline/shows/target/etc/script. html

3. Richard A. Horsley, "The Sicarii: Ancient Jewish 'Terrorists,' *Journal of Religion* 59, no. 4 (October 1979): 435–58.

4. Laurence Lockhart, "Hasan-i-Sabbah and the Assassins," *Bulletin of the School of Oriental Studies, University of London* 5, no. 4 (1930): 675–96.

5. Tom Bowden, "The Irish Underground and the War of Independence 1919–21, *Journal of Contemporary History* 8, no. 2 (April 1973): 3–23.

6. Leonard Gordon, *Brothers Against the Raj: A Biography of Indian Nationalists Sarat and Subhas Chandra Bose* (New York: Columbia University Press, 1990).

7. Ketchum, Richard, ed., *The American Heritage Book of The Revolution* (New York: American Heritage Publishing, 1958), 115.

8. John Chambers II, ed., *The Oxford Companion to American Military History*. (New York: Oxford University Press, 1999), 96.

9. Thomas Fleming, *Liberty: The American Revolution* (New York: Viking, 1997), 206.

10. George Washington, September–December, 1778, Revolutionary War Expense Account. George Washington's Accounts of Expenses While Commander-in-Chief of the Continental Army 1775–1783. With Annotations by John C. Fitzpatrick. http://memory.loc.gov/cgi_bin/ampage?collId=mgw5&fileName=gwpage022.db&recNum=26

11. Christopher Andrew, *For the President's Eyes Only: Secret Intelligence and the American Presidency from Washington to Bush* (New York: HarperCollins, 1995), 8.

12. Edwin C. Fishel, *The Secret War for the Union: The Untold Story of Military Intelligence in the Civil War* (New York: Houghton Mifflin Co., 1996).

13. Noel Fisher, *War at Every Door: Partisan Politics and Guerrilla Violence in East Tennessee, 1860–1869* (Chapel Hill: University of North Carolina Press, 2001); W. Todd Groce, *Mountain Rebels: East Tennessee Confederates and the Civil War, 1860–1870* (Knoxville: University of Tennessee Press, 2000).

14. Gordon Prange, *Miracle at Midway* (New York: Penguin Group, 1983).

15. Paul Thomsen and Joshua Spivak, "Through an Interrogator's Eyes," *Military History Magazine* (April 2002).

16. Carol D'Este, *Patton: A Genius For War* (New York: HarperCollins, 1995) 637; Nathan Prefer, *Patton's Ghost Corps: Cracking The Siegfried Line.* (Novato: Presidio Press, 1987), 10.

17. Charles Whiting, *Skorzeny: The Most Dangerous Man in Europe.* (Conshohocken: Combined Publishing, 1998).

18. According to the Bill Clinton and George W. Bush administrations' counterterrorism chief, Richard Clarke, upon receipt of their Allies' newfound services, the Mujahideen were rapidly able to bring down 270 Soviet aircraft. Richard Clarke, *Against All Enemies: Inside America's War on Terror* (New York: Free Press, 2004), 50.

19. Chambers II, ed. op. cit., 716.

20. Ibid.

21. Ibid., 387.

22. Counterterrorism Threat Assessment and Warning Unit National Security Division "Terrorism in the United States: 1997." United States Department of Justice, 1997. 7; Clarke. *Against All Enemies*. 113–14.

23. "Target America," *Frontline*, Program #2001. Airdate: October 4, 2001 Reuters Newmedia Inc./Corbis. Transcript. http://www.pbs.org/wgbh/pages/frontline/shows/target/etc/script.html

24. Eric Haney, *Inside Delta Force: The Story of America's Elite Counterterrorist Unit*,(New York: Delacorte Press, 2002), 253, 296.

25. "Air Power and Special Forces: A Symbiotic Relationship." Paper #14. Air Power Development Centre: Commonwealth of Australia, 2004. http://www.raaf.gov.au/airpower/publications/papers/apdc/APDC14_Air_Power_and_Special_Forces.pdf

26. Mark Bowden, *Black Hawk Down: A Story of Modern War*, (New York: Signet, 2001), 3–4.

27. "Suspects arrested in 1986 German disco bombing," *CNN.com* October 11, 1996. http://www.cnn.com/WORLD/9610/11/germany.arrests/index.html

28. "The Blast in Belgrade," *Airman* (September 1999) http://www.af.mil/news/airman/0999/misile2.htm

29. Air Force AGM-86B/C Missiles Fact Sheet. March 2001. http://www.af.mil/factsheets; "DoD News Briefing—Secretary Rumsfeld and Gen. Myers." Transcript. Presenters: Secretary of Defense Donald Rumsfeld and General Richard Myer. March 28, 2003 http://www.defenselink.mil/transcripts/2003

30. Peter Grier and Faye Bowers, "Inside the Mind of Al Qaeda," *Christian Science Monitor* 13 October 2004.

31. National Commission on Terrorist Attacks Upon the United States, *The 9/11 Commission Report: Final Report of the National Commission on Terrorist Attacks Upon the United States.* (New York: W. W. Norton & Co., 2004), 60.

32. Counterterrorism Threat Assessment and Warning Unit National Security Division, "Terrorism in the United States: 1997," *Against All Enemies*

33. Clarke. op. cit., 5.

34. Bob Woodward. *Bush at War.* 6–7.

35. National Commission on Terrorist Attacks Upon the United States. op. cit., 177–9.

36. Ibid., 311.

37. Ibid., 11.

38. Ibid., 314.

39. Woodward. *Bush at War.* 5–6.

40. Ibid., 141.

41. Ibid., 249.

42. Both NALT and Team-555 worked in tandem for approximately a month. Ibid., 264.

43. Ibid., 293.

44. Ibid., 309.

45. Ibid., 314, 312.

46. General Wesley K. Clark, *Winning Modern Wars: Iraq, Terrorism, and the American Empire* (New York: Public Affairs, 2003), 26, 33.

47. By 2004, Task Force 121, formerly known as Grey Fox, was comprised of Army Delta Force, Navy SEALs, Green Berets, British SAS, and British and Australian SAS-trained soldiers and was supported by the 160th Special Operations Aviation Regiment. Rowan Scarborough, "Agencies Unite to Find Bin Laden," *The*

Washington Times, 15 March 2004; Michael Smith, "Secret Teams were Constantly on the Trail of 'Number One," *The Daily Telegraph (London)*. December 15, 2003.

48. Niles Lathem, "GIS Pounce on Ultimate Tip, Taxi Clue Triggered Farm Raid, Saddam Resigned to His Fate," *New York Post*, 15 December 2003.

49. Ian Bruce and Michael Settle, "Special Forces Sent to Hunt Down Bigley's Killer Zarqawi; SAS and US Troops Switched from Afghanistan," *The Herald (Glasgow)*, 11 October 2004.

50. Bob Woodward, *Plan of Attack* (New York: Simon and Schuster, 2004), 385, 389, 398.

51. "Special Defense Department Briefing on Al-Qa'ida Munitions Facility in Iraq." Presenter: Principle Deputy Assistant Secretary of Defense for Public Affairs Lawrence Di Rita and Major Austin Pearson, 24th Ordnance Company, 24th Corps Support Group. Transcript. United States Department of Defense. October 29, 2004. http://www.defenselink.mil/transcripts/2004; "Briefing From Tallil Forward Air Base." Transcript. Presenter: Deputy Commanding General Jack Stoltz of the 377th Theater Support Command. United States Department of Defense. April 17, 2003 http://www.defenselink.mil/transcripts/2003

52. Eric Schmitt, "In Iraq's Murky Battle, Snipers Offer U.S. a Precision Weapon," *New York Times*, 2 January 2004.

53. Jim Garamone, "ScanEagle Proves Worth in Fallujah Fight," *American Forces Press Service*, 11 January 2005. http://www.defenselink.mil/newsJan2005/

54. Alphonso Van Marsh, "How the Army Used Latest Tech to Nab Saddam." CNN.com January 6, 2004. http://www.cnn.com/2004; Jim Garamone. "Digital World Meets Combat During Desert Exercise," *American Forces Information Service*, 18 April 2001. http://www.defenselink.mil/news/Apr2001, "Force XXI Battle Command, Brigade-and-Below (FBCB2). http://www.fas.org/man/dod-101/sys/land/fbcb2.htm

55. Clark. op. cit., 43.

56. Report of the Joint Inquiry into the Terrorist Attacks of September 11, 2001—By the House Permanent Select Committee on Intelligence and the Senate Select Committee on Intelligence. S.Rept. No. 107–351. 107th Congress, 2d Session. H. Rept. No. 107–792. December, 2002, 106.

57. *Factbook on Intelligence*. (Washington, D.C.: Central Intelligence Agency Office of Public Affairs, 2002). http://www.odci.gov/cia/publications/facttell

58. National Commission on Terrorist Attacks Upon the United States. op. cit., 272

59. Gina Murray Stevens, "Privacy: Total Information Awareness Programs and Related Information Access, Collection, and Protection Laws," Congressional Research Service, Library of Congress 21 March 2003.

60. Douglas B. Rider, "Establishing a Commercial Reserve Imagery Fleet: Obtaining Surge Imagery Capacity from Commercial Remote Sensing Satellite Systems during Crisis." Chairman of the Joint Chiefs of Staff Strategy Essay Competition, 2000. http://www.ndu.edu/inss/books

61. Robert O'Harrow Jr., "In Age of Security, Firm Mines Wealth of Personal Data," *Washington Post*. 20 January 2005.

62. Bob Woodward. *Plan of Attack*. 62–3, 137.

63. Spencer Swartz, "Mobile Phone Virus Found in United States," *Reuters* 18 February 2005.

64. Tom Zeller Jr. and Norman Mayersohn, "Can a Virus Hitch a Ride in Your Car?" *New York Times*, 13 March 2005.

65. Tim Weiner, "A New Model Army Soldier Rolls Closer to the Battlefield," *New York Times*, 16 February 2005; John Schwartz, "In Kingdom of Cockroaches, Leaders are Made, Not Born," *New York Times*, 7 December 2004.

66. "Students Notes and Comments: Does Heat Emanate Beyond The Threshold?: Home Infrared Emissions, Remote Sensing and the 4th Amendment Threshold," *Chicago-Kent Law Review*, 1994.

67. Colonel Richard Meinertzhagen, *Army Diary: 1899–1926* (Edinburgh: Oliver and Boyd, 1960).

68. Robert D. Kaplan, "'The Interrogators' and 'Torture:' Hard Questions," *New York Times*, 23 January 2005

69. Clarke. op. cit., 145–6.

70. "Sudan Demands U.S. Apology for Missile Attack," CNN.com 23 August 1998. http://www.cnn.com/WORLD/africa/9808/23/sudan.apology

71. Christopher Andrew and Vasili Mitrokhin, *The Sword and the Shield: The Mitrokhin Archives and the Secret History of the KGB* (New York: Basic Books, 1999), 365.

72. David Kaplan, "Mission Impossible," *U.S. News & World Report*, 2 August 2004.

73. U.S. Code Collection Title X Armed Forces. http://www.law.cornell.edu/uscode; U.S. Code Collection Title L, Chapter 15-National Security. http://www.law.cornell.edu/uscode

74. U.S. Congress. Senate. Select Committee to Study Governmental Operations with Respect to Intelligence Activities. Final Report. 94th Cong., 2d sess. S. Report No. 94-755, 6 Volumes. (Washington, D.C.: Government Printing Office, 1976).

75. Hunter Miller, ed. *Treaties and Other International Acts of the United States of America*, volume IV (Washington, D.C.: Government Printing Office, 1934.) Documents 80–121.

CHAPTER 5

Some Thoughts on Justice in America's Future Wars

JUDGE EUGENE R. SULLIVAN (RET.)*

"It is not merely of some importance but is of fundamental importance that justice should not only be done, but should manifestly and undoubtedly be seen to be done."[1]

When America wages its war against terror in the future, America should plan a fair system of justice for suspected terrorists captured in combat operations. The plan should take into consideration that the justice system for suspected terrorists must be constructed so that not only Americans, but most people all over the world should view the justice system provided to suspected terrorists as a just one. Please note that where the term "suspected terrorist" is used in this chapter, this term will refer to a noncitizen who is a suspected terrorist. It is assumed that any American citizen who is charged of terrorism-type criminal activity will be prosecuted in the U.S. civilian court system.

---

*Judge Sullivan is a retired federal judge and the CEO of the Gavel Consulting Group, a judicial consulting group. The views expressed herein are personal, not official views.

Generally speaking, America has two separate federal systems of justice for its civilian population and for its military. All over the world, these two American systems of justice have been generally cited and praised as fully complying with "Rule of Law" principles. The system of justice that America should construct for the suspected terrorists it captures as it wages its ongoing war against terrorism should attempt to resemble, if possible, the fair and open systems of justice that America has established for its own civilian population and for its military forces.

In order to analyze what justice system America should construct for this new war on terrorism, let's first look at a chart that gives a general comparison of the present systems of justice that are available in the U.S. federal government. The fifty state systems of justice that exist in America will not be examined here because these systems all closely resemble the U.S. federal civilian court system of justice. Keep in mind when viewing the following chart that the U.S. civilian court system and the U.S. military justice system have been enacted into federal law and are currently in force and being used daily, but the Military Commission system mandated and authorized by President Bush has been established into U.S. law by President Bush in an Executive Order and by regulations issued by the secretary of the U.S. Department of Defense, not by federal legislation.

Although it is remarkable how many similarities exist between these three federal systems of justice, there is a major difference among the three systems: The U.S. civilian courts and the U.S. military justice systems each have judicial oversight, both during trial and on appeal. However, the Military Commission system has neither a judge presiding at trial nor an appellate court process.

As will be shown later, this major difference of judicial involvement has been pointed out as a fatal flaw in the Military Commission system by many countries that hold to the cardinal "Rule of Law" principle that any valid system of justice must have an independent judiciary overseeing its operation.

Now let's take a look at the comparison of the three federal systems of justice—all of which could be used to give justice to a suspected terrorist caught by America in its war on terrorism.

U.S. Civilian Court System

A suspected terrorist could be tried in the U.S. court system. However there are difficulties in using the U.S. District Court system to try suspected terrorists, specifically delay and security.

The case of the suspected conspirator in the 9/11 attack upon America, Zacarias Moussaoui, is not completely illustrative of the point that delay is a problem in trying this type of case because Moussaoui pled guilty, and the district court where his case was brought is the U.S. District Court for the Eastern District of Virginia, a court known for such speed that the court is nicknamed "the court with the rocket docket." However, where a suspected terrorist is charged in a U.S. District Court with a normal backlog of cases, it could be argued that such a court is not a forum that can expedite a critical case of a suspected terrorist. Delay normally occurs in the regular course of litigation in most typical district courts.

Moreover, security for the courthouse, the judge, court personnel, the attorneys, the defendant, the jurors, and the public could be a massive and costly undertaking. In addition, the security of classified military and intelligence information is another problem that may be encountered in a typical district court not usually accustomed to handling of such sensitive information. Even though there is a federal law for the

STRUCTURAL COMPARISON OF AMERICAN CRIMINAL TRIALS IN FEDERAL CIVILIAN COURTS, MILITARY COURTS-MARTIAL, AND MILITARY COMMISSIONS

	U.S. Civilian Courts	Military Courts-martial	Military Commissions
Subject Matter Jurisdiction	Federal Crimes	Military Crimes	Law of war and other offenses to be tried by military commissions
Personal Jurisdiction	Any person in U.S. territory	All members of the U.S. Military	Suspected terrorists who are not U.S. citizens
Situs of trial	Federal District Courthouse in USA	Courtroom on a military base or a ship anywhere in the world	Place designated by appointing authority (probably outside USA)
Judge	Presidential appointee Civilian Judge	Military Judge appointed by Judge Advocates General	No Judge but Presiding Officer who is a Military Lawyer
Fact-finding Body	Civilian Jury or Judge	Military Jury or Judge	3–7 Military Officers-Members
Sentencing Body	Judge	Military Jury or Judge	Commission Members
Prosecutor	Civilian-U.S. Attorney	Military Lawyer	Military lawyer or special trial counsel (Justice Dept.)
Defense Counsel	Public Defender or retained civilian counsel	Detailed JAG or retained civilian counsel	Detailed Military lawyer or retained civilian counsel with security clearance
Rules of Evidence	Federal Rules of Evidence (FRE)	Military Rules of Evidence (very similar to FRE)	"All evidence having probative value to a reasonable man"
Rules of Procedure	Federal Rules of Criminal Procedure (FRCP)	Rules for Courts-martial (MCM) (similar to FRCP)	Military Commission Rules (similar to FRCP)

	U.S. Civilian Courts	Military Courts-martial	Military Commissions
Right to Witnesses	Yes	Yes	Yes
Right to Cross-examination	Yes	Yes	Yes
Trial Presumption	Presumption of innocence and burden of proof on Prosecution	Presumption of innocence and burden of proof on Prosecution	Presumption of innocence and burden of proof on Prosecution
Standard of Proof	Proof Beyond a Reasonable doubt	Proof Beyond a Reasonable doubt	Proof Beyond a Reasonable doubt
Hearsay Rule	Strict Hearsay Rule	Strict Hearsay Rule	No rule against hearsay
Professional Judiciary	Trained Judge (Civilian)	Trained Judge (Military)	No judicially trained officer but presiding officer must be a qualified military lawyer
Verdict	Must be unanimous	Less than unanimous, (2/3, 3/4)	2/3 of members
Courtroom Order	Summary contempt powers for Judge	Summary contempt over military Must refer civilians to U.S. Attorney	Power to maintain order over persons before it
Death Penalty	Yes	Yes	Yes
Death Penalty Procedure	Unanimous vote of 12 jurors	Unanimous vote of 12 members	Unanimous vote of 7 members
Appeals	U.S. Courts of Appeals (USCA) and Supreme Court	Military Courts of Criminal Appeals; USCA (AF) and Supreme Court	Approving authority, Board of Review, Secretary of Defense, President

protection of classified information used in federal trials, much discretion exists with the trial judge, and the government may feel the military forum option is more uniformly protective of classified information.

Accordingly, the Bush Administration believes that all of these potential problems with the trials of suspected terrorists are better managed in a legal forum (court-martial or commission) on a secure military base with military personnel who already usually have security clearances and experience in handling classified documents and information.

Although the Bush Administration has indicated that the trial of a suspected terrorist is more suitable in a military setting and not in a U.S. civilian court, there are respected critics of the present administration that will argue that the U.S. Court system is adequate to try all suspected terrorists.

U.S. Military Justice System

A suspected terrorist possibly could be tried in the U.S. military justice system. America's military does have a premier military justice system for American servicepersons, and its jurisdiction applies worldwide. The American court-martial system is based on the U.S. Constitution and guarantees American military personnel a fair trial. The military justice system is called the Uniformed Code of Military Justice, and in 1950 it was enacted into federal law (47 United States Code, Section 801 et seq.).

The military justice system has been generally accepted as a fair system. Some observers have stated that the military justice system has safeguards that equal or surpass those of trials in civilian trials in America. For example, the military justice system provided for Miranda-type warnings (self-incrimination warnings) to criminal suspects in the military for more than a decade before the U.S. Supreme Court provided for such rights in the Miranda case. Noted trial attorney F. Lee Bailey once stated, "If I had an innocent defendant, I would elect a trial in the military. If I had a guilty client, I would prefer to have the trial in U.S. district court." Moreover, the U.S. military justice system has been used as a model for other countries such as Taiwan and South Korea.

Hallmarks of the American military justice system include among other due process rights: the right to a free and qualified defense counsel, the presumption of innocence at trial, the prosecution has the burden to prove guilt, the right to call witnesses, the right to cross-examination, the standard of proof is beyond a reasonable doubt, the right to an impartial judge and military jury, and the right to appeal to an impartial appeals court.

Arguably, a suspected terrorist could possibly be tried under provisions of the U.S. military justice system if the suspect was classified as a "prisoner of war." There is a specific provision of this law that provides jurisdiction for prisoners of war: Article 2(a) ((9) of the Uniform Code of Military Justice (UCMJ). Although this provision exists, it is unlikely that a suspected terrorist who is not part of an opposition regular army would be treated as a prisoner of war under the UCMJ. That has been the position of the Bush Administration for suspected terrorists captured in Iraq and Afghanistan, and it is unlikely to change.

Although the Bush Administration doesn't seem inclined to use the UCMJ for suspected terrorists, another administration may well do so. If they did, then world opinion may support such an initiative. America would be in a more popular position of treating its enemies (suspected terrorists) with the same fair system it uses for its own servicepersons. That would probably make any sentence received by a suspected terrorist under the UCMJ more likely to be viewed by world opinion as a fair and just result.

The Military Commission Plan and
a Public Reaction to It

America's war on terrorism following the 9/11 terrorist attack in New York and the subsequent military offensive operations in Iraq and Afghanistan has spawned the birth of a new system of justice for noncitizens captured or detained in America's war on terrorism. This special system is called the Military Commission Plan.

Just following the 9/11 tragedy, President George W. Bush issued a presidential order establishing the Military Commission Plan to detain and conduct trials of noncitizens in the war against terrorism. (Military Order of November 13, 2001, published at 66 F.R.57833.) This order was implemented by the secretary of defense in 2002, in an order that established the rules and procedures to be used in these military commissions (Department of Defense Military Commission Order No. 1, March 21, 2002).

Immediately after the issuance of the Department of Defense implementing order, there was an unusual opportunity for a large convention of judges from all over the world to discuss and to debate the America's plan to use military commissions in its war on terrorism.

On May 22–24, 2002, at an international judicial conference, sitting at the Palais de l'Europe, the headquarters of the Council of Europe[2] in Strasbourg, France, two United States Federal judges presented their personal views of President Bush's Military Commission Plan for the trial of suspected terrorists. The plan provides for a tribunal of three to seven commissioned officers using rules, procedures, standards of proof, and the presumption of innocence that are similar to U.S. civilian criminal trials and U.S. military courts-martial.

Two notable exceptions to the similarity with U.S. military and civilian courts are: (1) that rules of evidence are relaxed; and (2) that there is no judicial appeal to any court.

Any appeal from a verdict of a Military Commission will be reviewed sequentially by an approving authority, then to a Board of Review (consisting of three military officers), then to the secretary of defense, and finally to the president.

At the Strasbourg conference, both U.S. judges who presented a favorable view of the Military Commission Plan were subjected to tough but enlightening questions and criticisms from many of the judicial delegates to the Conference. Attending the conference were over 140 chief justices and justices from sixty-six countries, including thirty-seven chief justices of supreme courts or their equivalents from countries such as India, the Russian Federation, Turkey, Ukraine, Philippines, Hungary, Austria, Czech Republic, Poland, and the European Court of Human Rights.

The majority of criticism of the Bush Plan focused on the following three areas:

1. Concerns about "judicial independence" since the commission members would be military officers with no judicial training.

2. Worry that the relaxing of the rules of evidence would lead to an unfair trial.

3. Shock that no court would review the verdict of the Military Commission.

Over the course of the two-day conference, the two U.S. judges attempted to convince the conference delegates that the Bush Plan was a sound one, and that it was needed in a time of national emergency to ensure swift and safe justice to a suspected terrorist. The U.S. judges argued that swift justice was needed to quickly resolve the guilt or innocence of a suspected terrorist. Giving a suspect a lengthy "OJ Simpson" type trial by a functioning U.S. court already burdened with an existing heavy backlog of criminal and civil cases is not the type of trial needed for this crisis situation. Concerns over the safety of the fact finders in a terrorist trial may have been one of the reasons a military tribunal was selected over the option of a civilian court with a judge and jury and a large number of court personnel. Protection of a military commission operating on a military base would be understandably easier. Also the necessity to protect sensitive, classified evidence made the option of a military tribunal undoubtedly more attractive.

Answering the criticism about the independence of the military commission was not as difficult as it may seem. Although this concern by many of the countries may have been rooted in past experience with military trials, America has a good record using military commissions in time of a special need for fair and independent justice. In fact, the first trial in America by an American tribunal was one using a military commission for Thomas Hickey, a member of General Washington's staff who was accused of a plot to poison General Washington. The trial was conducted in New York City the month before the Declaration of Independence. General Washington, then in command of the American Army, for obvious reasons, did not want to bring Hickey to a British court for justice. An American tribunal of thirteen officers was used at this critical time because only British courts were available in America.

There were two other times of crisis when America relied upon military commissions: (1) the military trial of the conspirators involved in the assassination of President Lincoln at the end of the Civil

War; and (2) the secret military commission that tried the Nazi sabo-teurs during World War II. It is interesting to note that the U.S. Supreme Court did review the death sentences given to the Nazi sabo-teurs. *Ex Parte Quirin*, 317 U.S. 1 (1942).

There were other uses of military commissions by America that are helpful to analyze. As to a prediction of the independence of the Amer-ican military officers sitting on a commission envisioned by President Bush's plan, one only needs to look at the conviction rates at the post–World War II military commissions that operated in occupied Japan and in occupied Germany immediately following the end of World War II. In Japan, there were 996 military commissions that were used to handle suspected military and civilian criminals on charges from mass murder and torture of Chinese civilians to rape and espi-onage. There were 800 convictions in these trials (a conviction rate of 80 percent). In occupied Germany, there were 1,692 trials by military commissions and 1,416 convictions (a conviction rate of 84 percent).

When you compare these conviction rates of military commissions that operated in Japan and Germany with the present conviction rate in U.S. military courts-martial of approximately 92 percent and with a conviction rate of over 95 percent in a typical civilian U.S. District Court trial, you get a sense that the American military officers serving these post-war military commissions were independent and that the verdicts were fair.

Moreover, there is a definite possibility that members of a military commission under the Bush Plan could be civilian judges who would be temporarily commissioned under 10 USC § 603. Using this fed-eral statute, the president could easily commission several federal or state judges and assign them to be on a commission. In fact, President Bush did exactly that for the Board of Review section of his military commission plan. He appointed some respected civilians as temporary military officers and appointed them to the Board of Review to give stature to this body, which has yet to be used. Whether this act would compensate for the lack of judicial oversight from a regularly constituted court is questionable.

As to the criticism about the relaxing of the rules of evidence for a military commission, one must realize that the evidence in any trial of a suspected terrorist from the Al Qaeda network may be evidence of an unusual nature (i.e., a videotape found in a cave in Afghanistan or recordings of a cell phone conversation pulled off the airways by a spy satellite). Traditional rules of evidence may not be able to easily cope with admissibility questions of such evidence.

The Bush Plan proposed rule of evidence, as set forth in the March, 2002 directive, is stated as: *"All evidence having probative value to a reasonable man" will be admissible by majority vote of the commission.* This simple, broad rule may well be what is necessary to handle the admissibility of unusual evidence in the present national crisis. As the old saying goes, unusual times require unusual measures.

One further important point on the evidence issue is that, in a military commission, the rules of admissibility will be relaxed for *both sides* (the prosecution and the defense). Accordingly, there will be a level playing field for both parties before the commission.

As to transparency, a military commission will operate for the most part open to the public, except where evidentiary matters of national security or safety require closed sessions. It is expected that almost all evidence will be presented during open sessions of a commission. This almost completely transparent process will allow the public to view the quality of evidence when judging the results of a commission. Therefore, it may be wise for world opinion in judging the fairness of this unusual rule of evidence to adopt a "wait and see" attitude.

As a final point, at the Strasbourg Conference, both U.S. judges told the delegates that they thought the Bush Plan was a structurally sound and fair one, considering that it would be used only in this time of a national emergency and in the face of an unusual threat. The Bush Plan can be viewed as a thoughtful, closed-loop, Executive Branch justice system for the noncitizen, suspected terrorist. One of the practical good points of the plan is that the plan can be used anywhere in the world on short notice and with commonsense security not only for its fact finders, but also for the sensitive evidence that may come before the tribunal. Some people have described it as a system based on the American-style judicial model, but modified to fit the special need of bringing swift justice to noncitizen suspects outside the United States.

Although American history has proved that an American military commission could be a fair and independent one, nevertheless the Strasbourg Conference and other samplings of world opinion have indicated that a military commission system without judicial oversight might always be viewed as an unfair system.

Modifying the Military Commission Plan

If America wants the verdicts of its military commissions to be viewed by world opinion as complying with "Rule of Law" principles, then prudence dictates that the Bush Plan should be modified. America has always set high standards for fairness in its judicial process, so it might be better to modify the Bush Military Commission Plan to provide for a judge to preside at the trial stage and to authorize a full court review of any verdict, all the way to the Supreme Court.

Adding a full court review to the plan almost certainly would require federal legislation in order to grant jurisdiction to federal courts for the review of sentences from commission decisions.

If the Bush Plan is modified to provide such judicial oversight, then America will have a better chance to have the sentences given by these commissions viewed as fair and just. In my view, the Military Commission Plan as modified with the inclusion of judicial oversight would not only be capable of doing justice, but showing the world the appearance of justice under normal views of the "Rule of Law" principles.

A Proposal for the Future of
U.S. Preventative Wars

When and if America decides to invade a country like Iraq in the future as a preventative measure in its war against terrorism, America should not take on any other role except that of a war fighter. The host country where the warfare is occurring should take on the roles related to the holding of prisoners and the administration of justice to those captured during the invasion by U.S. and allied troops.

Specifically, the function of detaining, interrogating, and conducting criminal trials to those suspected terrorists captured during the fighting should be performed by the host country if it has a functioning democratic government with an independent judiciary.

If the host country cannot perform those missions, then the roles pertaining to prisoners should be handled by an ally of the United States in support of the preventative war action. America would turn over the prisoners it takes in combat operations to this designated ally. America should then have no say in the processing of the prisoners after the turnover. If the ally in charge of administering justice wants to release a prisoner, America would and should have no control over the release decision. This could be a way that America can avoid any alleged abuses with prisoners or detainees, sometimes called "Victors' Justice," a traditional charge that not only alienates world opinion but becomes a major factor in any insurgency movement against America as an occupying force.

An Alliance Against Terrorism

Just as America helped build the North Atlantic Treaty Organization (NATO) as an organization to protect Europe against Communist aggression during the Cold War, America should begin to organize a standing coalition of nations to fight terrorism. In this new alliance of nations, certain countries could be assigned the duties of war-fighting, rebuilding infrastructure, developing economic plans, handling and interrogating detainees, administering justice to suspected terrorists, training police and army personnel in the occupied country, administering to the health and sanitation problems of an occupied country, and other duties expected in conducting preventative wars to obtain global peace against terrorism. America should take the lead role in war-fighting and leave the noncombat roles to other countries. One of the basic problems encountered in Iraq is that America has the lead role in all missions (combat and noncombat) in the occupation of Iraq.

One problem with this theoretical idea is the practical one of funding such an effort. What will be the sharing arrangement among the countries in the alliance for the duties and the cost of the war and the postwar reconstruction effort? Another problem is, who will have the discretion to award contracts in any reconstruction effort?

The Detainees at Guantánamo

Keeping suspected terrorists detained for interrogation purposes at the U.S. base at Guantánamo, Cuba, may have been a good idea initially. Extracting vital information from suspected terrorists by humane means in a safe and secure military base far from the combat operations was a proper decision. However, now the Guantánamo detainees are viewed generally by the world legal authorities as men kept in unjustified confinement by the U.S. government. America cannot keep these men prisoners for years without trials or hearings to determine whether or not they have committed crimes under the law of war or other defined criminal statute. A U.S. district court has recently recognized that due-process guarantees are to be afforded to those men in Cuba. The U.S. government is now addressing those concerns of the district court by starting administrative reviews of the status of each detainee—a long and complex process.

Planners of future combat operations of America in its war against terror should find a solution so the problem of open-ended interrogations and detentions for years as demonstrated in Guantánamo should not arise again.

Conclusion

Hopefully, some facts and some ideas of how America should treat the suspected terrorists have surfaced and will spark dialog and debate among Americans on a subject that is often viewed as a hidden by-product of the war against terrorism.

One of the important factors by which the world will judge the results of this war will not be just the successes won on the foreign battlefields where America fights, but the fairness of justice and punishment that America and its allies give to the enemies captured on these foreign fields.

Fairness has always been a core characteristic of American justice for its citizens. Such a characteristic should be equally available to noncitizens who are captured as suspected terrorists in war.

ENDNOTES

1. Lord Chief Justice Hewart of England in *Rex v Sussex Justices*, 1923.

2. The 10th Annual International Judicial Conference was organized by the Center of Democracy. The Council of Europe was the sponsor of the Conference.

CHAPTER 6

Hearts and Minds in 2025: How Foreign and Domestic Culture Will Shape the Future Battlefield

JOHN HELFERS

Nigeria, 2016:

With the sudden death of President Olusegun Obasanjo in 2012, the political state of Nigeria has weakened considerably during the last four years. The three largest major political groups, the Hausa, the Yoruba, and the Ibo, have moved to consolidate power for themselves, leaving many smaller ethnic groups feeling more marginalized than ever before. Fighting has steadily increased between Christian and Muslim factions in the northern part of this African country, to the point where the entire region is on the verge of a civil and religious war. Wanting to head off a regional conflict before it occurs, a multinational peacekeeping force has been sent in to work alongside the Nigerian Army to help restore order.

One morning, a squad of U.S. Army soldiers—not Special Forces, but regular U.S. infantry—heads into an area populated mainly by the Hausa. They are to meet with a group of local tribal leaders to coordinate security in the region and track down a radical terrorist group that has been attacking villages.

Even before the sergeant gets out of his armored Humvee, he knows much about the region, the politics, and more important, the culture of the people he is about to meet. He has already been educated on the country's politics, religion, history, and culture back in the United States. Entering the second year of a three-year tour of duty in-country, he is already familiar with how the local economic and societal systems operate, and he has a firm grasp of the intertribal alliances and rivalries among the Kanuri, Fulani, Akan, Songhay, and Yoruba peoples in the region. Although he can rely on a sophisticated translation and cultural database program built into the portable computer he wears as part of his uniform, he and the rest of his men are not only familiar with the Hausa language, but also the regional dialect, and each squad member can converse fluently with any native they meet. Equally as important, they also know what not to do, from speaking to certain villagers that may be construed as an insult, to certain gestures that might be misinterpreted; the squad conducts themselves in a manner that is respectful of the indigenous culture.

The meeting goes well; as the sergeant is proficient in the body language and local customs of the Hausa people, he opens a friendly dialogue and acquires the information he needs in order to begin operations against the terrorists in the region. The village chief lets him know that they have seen members of what they believe is part of a terrorist cell moving through the region. Although this is just a reconnaissance mission, the sergeant contacts base command and receives permission to follow up on the information. The group is now being monitored by satellite uplink, so that they are in constant contact with base command.

The squad scouts the area and locates what appears to be not a small cell of terrorists, but a larger, well-organized group that has established a camp several miles away from the village. The insurgents are located in a region that would allow them to target several scattered Muslim villages within a 100-mile radius. Knowing his men are outmatched, the sergeant calls for reinforcements. The base sends another American squad as well as an Italian squad to bring the terrorists to justice. Knowing that the cell might only be *there for a day or so, the three units coordinate their resources and get up-to-the-hour intelligence from their satellite uplink, which gives them the camp layout and an accurate number of the terrorists there, as well as intangibles such as the weather forecast for the next twenty-four hours. They decide to move on the cell just before sunrise the next morning, taking them by surprise and, with the execution of a good plan, capturing the entire group. They post advanced electronic forward scouts that will monitor the area and warn of any hostile activity, then dine with the village that evening.*

In the early-morning darkness, the three squads gear up and head out to their rendezvous point. The flanking squads take their positions, and at the prearranged signal, the three units move into the camp, neutralizing the sentries and catching the rest of the cell by surprise. The operation is a complete success.

The squad processes their prisoners and prepares them for the journey back to the base for interrogation. Before they leave, they drop off drought-resistant grains for planting, owing to the Hausa's primarily agricultural economy, their medic checks the children for mutant strains of the local diseases, and the sergeant makes arrangements for Army engineers to stop by in the next few days and assist with finishing construction of the new well the village needs, as well as ensure that the solar-powered generator they brought here last year is working to capacity. They leave secure in the knowledge that they have opened a fruitful relationship that will help both the peacekeeping forces as well as the local populace in the region, despite the major differences in religion, culture, society, and race between the two groups.

* * *

As the twenty-first century truly gets underway, an examination of the current state of the U.S. military finds a strange juxtaposition. On one hand, it can be said that America's armed forces are the most powerful in the world, able to bring almost unimaginable force to bear anywhere on the planet within a matter of weeks. When properly utilized, as in Operation Just Cause in Panama and leading the multination coalition in Operation Desert Storm, the results are stunningly effective. There is no doubt that when there is a purely military objective to be attained, the U.S. military reigns supreme over any other force in the world.

On the other hand, given its seemingly mediocre effectiveness in environments such as Beirut, Haiti, and Bosnia, and the operational mistakes made after the rapid deployment and offensive into Iraq, it would also appear that the current military is not as effective at defining and executing a wider range of missions, whether that be peacekeeping, tracking down war criminals, or, as in the case in Iraq, working alongside the indigenous populace to help create a new sovereign nation. While the above example may be an idealized vision of the U.S. armed forces' role in future military operations around the world, there is no reason to believe that it cannot happen without infringing on the local cultures that they must interact with on a daily basis.

Although there are many who would argue that this is not, indeed, should not be the U.S. military's goals, the simple fact is that the twenty-first-century battlefield now extends beyond simply defining what objectives need to be attained in a target area, and then sending traditional armed forces in to achieve them. Often, with no one else to maintain order in a war-torn third world nation, the "boots on the ground" are the only hope of maintaining peace after the storm, particularly if all of the enemy forces have not been quelled after the main battles are done.

The ever-growing insurgency in Iraq and the miscalculations about that nation's infrastructure have given rise to a growing concern that today's U.S. armed forces lack the cultural understanding to operate as effectively as possible during combat operations. Lessons that had been learned by some officers during the Vietnam Conflict more than forty years ago have still never been fully implemented. Whereas the last clear enemy, the Communists, was defined in the Korean War, practically all major combat operations (excluding Operation Desert Storm) since then have featured shifting battlefields, guerilla, partisan, and urban warfare, and, with the exception of the two successful operations mentioned above, ill-defined, vague, or incomplete military objectives.

It is clear that future battlefields will range from the mountains and deserts to fighting in urban centers alongside civilian populations where the enemy can blend into the environment, as has been already shown in Iraq. And when the U.S. military is a stranger in a strange land with no clearly defined objective, its effectiveness at anything other than combat is often less than exemplary (though occasionally excellent in isolated incidences) and almost nonexistent as an established working policy.

Throughout history, there have been many examples of American forces meeting indigenous cultures they must work among on their own terms, and adapting to both a different method of operating and a different way of life, which is often in stark contrast to the U.S. military's usual method of doing things. But rather than incorporate these lessons into a broader understanding of how to operate more effectively in foreign environments, the armed forces seems content to rely on its increasingly net-centric and technological-based systems of combat. As a result, the human element is often minimized; left as an afterthought to be utilized by ground forces on the fly, depending on the situation they encounter, if at all. Such decisions lead to poor after-theater planning, such as in Iraq, where the U.S.-led forces were misled as to the organization and strength of the terrorist resistance effort. The civilian planners also made the huge tactical error of disbanding the

Iraqi Army, displacing hundreds of thousands of men, and leaving many with no perceived recourse but to join the resistance.

Although there are several reasons why American military forces are superb at defeating hostile forces but often less effective at working with the local populace both during and after combat operations, this article will attempt to illustrate what may be one of the primary reasons: the reluctance of the U.S. military to account for the effect of indigenous cultures on the target environment in which they are fighting. By examining four areas of culture that need examination and revision in the years to come, it is hoped that a broader understanding of both the successes and failures of considering the impact of culture on warfare can be gained, as well as seeing what role culture will play in military engagements of the future.

First, there is the target culture: the different social mores, customs, history, and lifestyle of the area where military operations are to be staged, and how that affects the soldiers sent there. Second is the military culture itself: the attitude and beliefs of the soldiers themselves in the mission and toward the people they are operating among, and how a broader education can lead to increased tolerance and understanding between widely differing cultures. Third is the culture of America itself: how the nation's perception of the mission and its populace's attitudes toward the goals of military action shape the operating environment for both the soldiers abroad and at home. And finally, there is the culture of the rest of the world: how America's military and political influence and agendas are perceived in other areas of the world is just as important as how its soldiers are perceived in the target culture itself.

Culture: **a**: the integrated pattern of human knowledge, belief, and behavior that depends upon man's capacity for learning and transmitting knowledge to succeeding generations. **b**: the customary beliefs, social forms, and material traits of a racial, religious, or social group. c: the set of shared attitudes, values, goals, and practices that characterizes a company or corporation.[1]

The above quote is just one version of an attempt to define what culture is, and for the purposes of this article, it will serve as a broad definition of a sociological concept that varies widely and is also in a constant state of change around the world.

The challenge of examining the effect of culture on the battlefield is more difficult than looking at future technology, or law, or just about any other aspect of warfare. Although it can be said that culture is a shared experience by a group of people that is transmitted from one group to another over time, not only can the ideals and aspects of a culture change over years or decades, but there is also the aspect of subcultures within a culture to consider, for example, the terrorist sub-culture that has spawned in the past century in the Middle East, and which has gained a greater permanence in that region despite the best (and sometimes not the best) efforts of the free world.

Also, more often than not, examining the future effects of culture means looking back to the past, and seeing just how aspects of culture have taught lessons, right and wrong, and affected how organizations, governments, societies, and nations react and learn as they plan for the future. Several of the cultural aspects listed in the previous section have been profoundly influenced by the conflicts and events of the past sixty years, and it would be remiss to not examine how those experiences have shaped the cultures of today, and, just as important, how the lessons learned will be applied to the battlefield of tomorrow.

The Target Culture

The last time America went to war against a culture that was even remotely similar to its own was during World War II, more than sixty years ago. Having emigrated from the various countries on the European continent to the United States just a few generations earlier, millions of immigrants brought various elements of their own different cultures with them. The general populace then took everyone's separate experiences from each nation, both positive and negative, and blended them into an amalgam that helped create the America of today.

When the United States declared war on the Axis powers, those that went to Europe to fight had an idea of the kinds of armies they would face—determined warriors that fought much like they did. Their shared heritage—despite what Adolph Hitler and the Nazis had done to mold the German people into the Third Reich, accompanied by Mussolini and Italy—meant that there was a common starting point between the two sides. There were atrocities committed in Europe—it is practically impossible to find a war where that has never happened—but the Allied forces storming the French beaches on D-Day had a good idea of what they could expect—an enemy that would fight them head-on, using tactics and technology that both sides were familiar with, and had created and refined themselves in many instances.

The Pacific theater was a completely different matter. The Japanese had combined the Western technology they had gained over the previous ninety years with a blend of cultural, religious, and societal trains of thought that combined ultimate obedience to authority with the idea that soldiers were the sons of the gods themselves, and that death was not the end, but a new beginning, as those killed in battle would ascend to their former divine existence. By indoctrinating new soldiers

133

in the belief that they must make the ultimate sacrifice for their emperor, who was a manifestation of the divine here on earth, in the waning days of the war, they were able to create suicide forces both on land and in the air—the soldiers who would blow themselves up to destroy American troops, and the infamous *kamikaze* pilots. More than any other, the Japanese culture was primed to create these single-minded warriors.

At Okinawa, the clash of these two very separate cultures came to a head. The U.S. forces possibly could have bypassed the 110,000-man army stationed there, but they wanted to utilize the island, only 350 miles away from Japan, as a base of operations (at this time it was assumed that an invasion of Japan would still be necessary). A massive fleet was launched—1,600 ships carrying 250,000 soldiers and support personnel that would use the island once it was under Allied control. Over 12,000 aircraft could be used to assist in the battle if necessary. The commanding officers planned to follow the traditional way of battle: defeat an enemy using superior numbers and technology, force them to surrender, make them realize the futility of continued resistance; in effect, bringing them to heel by force.

The Japanese, however, had a much different plan:

... the Japanese did not realistically hope militarily to defeat the invaders on Okinawa at all! Nor did they worry whether their own army, navy, and air forces would survive the conflict. . .

Instead, by mid-1945 the desperate Japanese military's aims were quite different from all conventional war wisdom. And so their plans were very simple: kill so many Americans, blow up or shoot down so many aircraft, and sink so many ships that the United States—both its stunned military and its grieving citizens back home—would never wish to undergo such an ordeal again. After the butchery to come on

Okinawa, perhaps these rather affluent and soft Westerners would seek a negotiated armistice with Japan—and not tolerate another, greater cataclysm on the mainland in pursuit of an unnecessary unconditional surrender. Okinawa, then, was to offer a suicidal lesson to Americans to stop before they found themselves dying in the millions on the beaches of the Japanese motherland.[2]

Japanese soldiers often sacrificed themselves to accomplish this goal, carrying grenades or explosives and trying to get close enough to enemy soldiers so that the resulting explosion would kill not only him, but anyone in the vicinity as well.

But just like at Pearl Harbor, the Japanese underestimated the resolve of the American forces. Despite losing 12,520 men and suffering 33,631 wounded, along with the destruction of 763 aircraft, and thirty-six ships sunk, the United States sent more men and equipment into that desolate land until they had taken the island completely, annihilating the defending army in the process. Historians have debated as to whether the bloodbath on Okinawa influenced the decision to use the atomic bomb to prevent an even worse slaughter from happening in a ground invasion of Japan. It is not known what part this may have played in the final result, but one can imagine that it had some influence, sacrificing tens of thousands of lives to save hundreds of thousands on both sides.

The American military took lessons away from the Pacific campaign that would not serve them well in future engagements in the area. The official U.S. military history of the campaign perhaps sums it up best:

> The high cost of victory was due to the fact that the battle had been fought against a capably led Japanese army of greater strength than anticipated, over difficult terrain heavily and expertly fortified, and

thousands of miles from home. The campaign had lasted considerably longer than expected. But Americans had demonstrated again on Okinawa that they could, ultimately, wrest from the Japanese whatever ground they wanted.

In one sense, this is true. By throwing virtually unlimited men, weapons, and equipment at the island, the U.S. military had achieved their objective, but at a terrible cost.

Given the fanatical determination of the Japanese defenders, the U.S. commanders assumed that taking and holding land from an Asian enemy was not as important as eliminating the opposing force as completely as possible, thus ending the conflict—a precursor to the disregard for securing and holding territory and an increased emphasis on "body count" in Vietnam. They also assumed that the same tactics that had worked on Okinawa would serve in Vietnam as well—keep throwing men and ordnance at the enemy, and they will eventually capitulate. The flaw in carrying this way of thinking to other wars was that the defenders on Okinawa were cut off from reinforcements. Both Korea and Vietnam were not islands, but the representative faces of conflict in the region, funded and fueled by other nations that kept men and matériel flowing to the front, ensuring an ever-present enemy to fight.

Also, because of the large civilian population on Okinawa—almost 100,000 men, women, and children—that had been forced to serve the Japanese as well, American forces were compelled to treat almost everyone on the island as potential enemies. Twenty years later, when faced with an inscrutable enemy that blended into the local populace so that it was impossible to tell friend from foe, the military's tactics were the same as at Okinawa—shoot first and ask questions later. Only this time, instead of being on an isolated, small Pacific island, they were being filmed by television cameras that broadcast the war around the world, and were involved in trying to win the local populace over to supporting the goals of America in the region.

The Japanese use of suicide attacks also sent messages to the world. While these horrific assaults did have an impact on their enemy, with ships damaged and sunk and thousands of men killed, the Japanese failed to stop the American offensive, and were unable to sink even one Allied aircraft carrier or capital ship. While their *kamikaze* attacks on land and in the air killed thousands, in the end, the tactic did not force America to the negotiating table, and instead may have accelerated the decision to deliver the American version of a "divine wind," the atomic bomb.

Such was the U.S. military's first real experience of using superior numbers and technology against a foe that, when backed into what they considered an impossible situation, used the ultimate weapon they had—themselves. As is so often done by the victors, America committed its version of events into history and turned its attention to helping rebuild the rest of the world, not realizing that what had happened in 1945 was just a terrible foreshadowing of things to come.

* * *

During the Vietnam Conflict, there were isolated suicide attacks, most notably the nineteen-man Viet Cong unit that stormed the U.S. embassy during the Tet Offensive, fighting the American forces there for almost seven hours. When it was all over, only two members were captured alive. Even though both military and civilian agencies knew that the North Vietnamese Army and Viet Cong had been massing troops as a precursor to some kind of large-scale operation, they were still caught by surprise when hundreds of attacks occurred throughout the country on December 31, 1968. The media coverage of the event further increased resistance to the conflict back in America, a favorable by-product of the offensive for the Communists, since it had been a military failure in which the Viet Cong were practically wiped out in much of South Vietnam.

The Tet Offensive characterized the general tenor of the entire conflict, in which America, fielding the best-equipped and -trained army in the world, was forced to fight a war on the terms of a completely foreign culture. Unable to bring their own massive resources directly to bear, the U.S. effort was stymied by incredible restrictions on targets and tactics (North Vietnam was off-limits for invasion or bombing; so were manufacturing plants supplying the enemy) that ensured the North Vietnamese would win, provided they could outlast the Americans.

> In war it is insane not to employ the full extent of one's military power or to guarantee to the enemy that there are sanctuaries for retreat, targets that are off-limits, and a willingness to cease operations any time even the pretext of negotiations is offered.[3]

The American forces never had a chance to prove what they could do. The basic concept of the Vietnam Conflict was to win the "hearts and minds" of the people by providing them an alternative to Communism. Once the people were on the side of the United States and freedom, they were supposed to rise up and defend themselves against the North Vietnamese Army. The U.S. military's planned role was to help the South Vietnamese forces become self-sufficient enough to fend off their enemy, and also provide aerial bombardment that, based on World War II models, should have inflicted enough damage on the enemy that they would be forced to negotiate a truce. Ground troops would be utilized in large-scale operations to locate and destroy the enemy using superior numbers and firepower and luring them into disadvantageous positions.

The U.S. war planners made a critical error by fighting the ground war on the enemy's terms, often in small-scale engagements that ranged from hit-and-run guerilla tactics to full-fledged battles by the NVA and Viet Cong in their terrain and to their advantage. It was directly opposite of what the American armed forces were supposed to do, win by the application of overwhelming force and the best technology in the world. Instead, air power became the military's answer to practically everything, from trying to cut off the supply lines on the Ho Chih Minh Trail to attacking the NVA directly. But since the NVA and Viet Cong had decentralized their forces, there were no obvious targets to attack; the enemy army melted into the jungle and went underground, often literally, leaving only scattered indications of where they might be. Even when the Americans fought and drove off the Communists, such as at "Hamburger Hill" or Khe Sanh, they often ended up withdrawing from the area, so that the NVA or VC could simply move in and refortify; negating any advantage from the victory. Since the American strategy was not based on taking and holding land, but on eliminating the enemy, there seemed to be no progress made anywhere; the military couldn't say "We control this area" or "we've completely destroyed the enemy forces here." Instead, the Vietnam Conflict became a holding action, with no ground gained over several years.

As for trying to change the culture of a two-thousand-year-old society that had been fighting for its freedom during the majority of those two millennia, the programs the U.S. government tried to enact were dismal failures. They attempted to win over the population by applying scientific "nation-building" techniques created in a vacuum, untested, and applied to a people that the scientists did not comprehend from the start:

> Rural pacification, the attempt to bring the vast areas of the Vietnamese countryside under secure government control, was . . . operated by devotees of nation building and systems analysis . . . The counterinsurgency program was unable to defeat the Viet Cong or to separate them from the peasant. In response to the failure of rural pacification, the social planners became even more creative. If the communists could not be removed from the peasants, then the peasants would be removed from the communists. The result was the "strategic hamlets program," which resulted in the creation of artificial villages, usually without an economic and social infrastructure, where peasants were forcibly resettled . . . The rest of the war consisted of attempts at implementing the basic lunacy: the idea that the social structure of a country could be manipulated by outsiders with minimal understanding of the nation or culture.[4]

What the analysts did not understand was that the average Vietnamese peasant had deep societal and spiritual connections to the land they lived on, stretching back for generations, even centuries, unlike Americans, who showed a propensity to pack up and move at a moment's notice. Uprooting them from their homes and fields was like separating them from their heritage, and hardly showed them the respect they deserved, and was destined for failure from the beginning. The clash of cultures engendered by the forcible removal of much of the populace also caused many to turn to the enemy to repel the foreigners that were uprooting them from their homes.

Trying to use the U.S. Army as a tool for social and cultural reform was another critical mistake. How could the indigenous people be persuaded to consider a different way of life if armed soldiers were escorting them to it? The Communists understood this, and promised a "people's republic," which was a lie, of course, but given that American forces were herding up local populations without consideration for where they would end up, the propaganda of the other side must have seemed attractive at the time. These broad-based cultural misunderstandings led to increased hostility between both sides, and increased difficulty in achieving the larger goals of the United States.

And yet, there were those who were able to meet the Vietnamese on their own terms, and learn the best ways to operate and work together in a culture so far removed from their own. The Marine Advisory Unit was one such group:

> Instead of American advisory "teams," as was the usual American practice with Vietnamese units, there would be only two U.S. Marine advisors per infantry battalion, and specialty advisors for communications, medical, motor transport, and senior staff positions. The advisors completely immersed themselves in the units. They and the Vietnamese troops were essential parts of the same command; the Americans couldn't isolate themselves. They wore Vietnamese Marine uniforms, ate their food, spoke their language, and shared their hardships. This forced total integration and dependence, and built mutual trust.[5]

Unfortunately, this kind of deep involvement in the local culture, military or otherwise, seemed to be the province of specialized military units, like the Marine Advisory Group, or the Special Forces, which already had a decade-long history in Vietnam before the United States committed to sending general infantry. General Tony Zinni goes on to recount his experiences traveling throughout the country, seeing all facets of the war in Vietnam, from the mangrove swamps and river complexes in Rat Sung to the rice paddies of the Mekong Delta to the deep jungles near the Cambodian border, and the array of villages and plantations around Saigon itself. One of the first things he learned was that there was no single way to categorize the conflict:

> The geography, the nature of the enemy, the style of fighting, and even the nature of some of the units all added their own particular character to what we might encounter. All tended to create different types of wars, if you will, or different types of the same war.
>
> Because I experienced so many different aspects of the war, I came back with a real understanding that this war was multifaceted; everything was all over the place. There was no clear and simple way to look at it. But most Americans who served in Vietnam had perhaps a year tour and saw only one geographical area. For them it was like the blind man and the elephant. The war they saw was real, but partial.[6]

But to the planners in Washington, D.C. and the majority of the military forces there, the Vietnamese were just that—one homogenous people, in a strange land far away, that was often ambivalent about, or even hostile to accepting American help. And for the majority of the foreign soldiers fighting over there, the indigenous population could either be an excellent asset, as the Montagnard tribes were in the mountains, or a determined enemy, as the local Viet Cong resistance, was. But without a strategy to understand the culture of both hostile and friendly natives, rapprochement was limited, slow, and often on a one-to-one basis. Unlike Mao Zedong's winning over of the Chinese population during his twenty-plus-year-long campaign against Chiang Kai Shek, wherein his army treated civilians with dignity and respect (among his Nine Rules of Conduct were: no confiscations from the peasantry, return borrowed articles, replace damaged items, pay for all purchases, be honest in transactions, be courteous and polite to people and help them when you can), there simply wasn't an organized, concerted effort to win the indigenous people over to the goals that the United States was trying to promote in a way that took their culture into account as a variable. However, the lessons learned by individuals in that conflict would be used to excellent effect in the future, when they became commanders of the armed forces themselves.

* * *

After the morass of Vietnam, the military must have been pleased to return to the more familiar ground of the Cold War: After all, balancing the buildup of nuclear arms with Russia was something that both sides understood; it was a technology-based war, which was all the rage at the time, not one that called for "boots on the ground," possibly in a strange, foreign land. Although plans were created for the possibility of a conventional land war, since the U.S. military's budget was being slashed in the wake of Vietnam, the missile balance and strategic arms talks were what held most of the world's attention. The idea of culture impacting warfare was relegated even further away, not only to the back burner, but just about off the stove entirely. Except for smaller divisions, like the Special Forces, whose province has always been interacting with foreign cultures (and which was also waging its own fight for survival at the time), everyone's eyes were on the "big picture," the prospect of war with the Warsaw Pact. Even popular novels like *Red Storm Rising* by Tom Clancy touted the idea of a conventional, land-based war in Europe, with tanks, armies, and all the trimmings.

The capture of seventy American hostages in Iran, and the appearance of that nation on our threat radar, did little to change our intelligence gathering and cultural analysis of the area in the event that military intervention would be needed later on. During the early 1980s, the United States was working with Saddam Hussein against Iran, and the government apparently felt that they had sufficient coverage of the area at the time, posting only a few soldiers undercover in the country. It was a policy that is still having repercussions to this day, as many military analysts admit that the United States still does not have a clear, fundamental understanding of what is happening in Iran and other nations in the Middle East. Although this is being rectified, the process is slow, and woefully behind the times, leaving the most powerful nation in the world playing catch-up in a region that it is dependent on for the majority of its fuel needs.

* * *

However, when Saddam Hussein invaded and annexed Kuwait in August of 1990, here was the chance for American armed forces to do what they do best; attack and defeat an opponent on a defined, clear field of battle. With the U.S. forces leading the multination coalition, the Iraqi forces were routed and expelled from Kuwait in a staggering five days in 1991. The threat had been neutralized, and the U.S. military saw the reorganization of its structure and training after Vietnam pay off large dividends in the swift execution of Operation Desert Storm.

As part of the coalition, the U.S. military commanders, many of whom had absorbed hard lessons about working with local and foreign cultures in Vietnam and were determined to not repeat that experience, put their knowledge to practical use in planning and preparing for the various missions. Training and information was shared among different branches of the world's militaries.

A major lesson I learned from having been an advisor in Vietnam was how to deal with other cultures. The coalition approach was essential to our success. We simply couldn't ride roughshod over our Arab allies. We had to deal very carefully. And there were significant problems. In their culture they hold back from telling you their real feelings. Especially because Muslims consider Westerners to be "infidels." You will never be part of their brotherhood, no matter what you do.[7] (Lt. General Walter Boomer, USMC)

However, it was not done as part of a set military policy, but here and there as the opportunity came up. Officers read about Arab culture and passed along the knowledge to their men. American officers requested that the local military forces teach their own soldiers about desert survival. The U.S. Marines in particular, perhaps because of their advisory experience with the Vietnamese Marines, were very adept at working with foreign military units of all kinds, rotating their units in to work with the Saudi forces that they would later be fighting alongside. Establishing respect, friendship, and trust with the indigenous forces was an essential part of the success of the overall operation.

A side effect of Desert Storm was to create revolts both in the south by disenfranchised Shiites, and in the north where the Kurdish tribes renewed their revolution against Hussein, cheered on by the American government, but not aided in any other material way. Although the Iraqi Army had been decimated by the recent operations, the beaten dictator was able to mobilize enough armor and troops to crush both rebellions quickly, to the extent of using chemical weapons on the Kurdish tribes. Hundreds of thousands of displaced refugees streamed into the northern mountains toward Turkey and Iran, clinging to life in makeshift camps 8,000 to 10,000 feet above sea level in the mountains. The United States led a multinational effort to provide assistance in an operation named Provide Comfort.

General Tony Zinni describes just how out of depth his Marines were in dealing with the Kurdish culture, and how help arrived in the form of a U.S. intelligence officer who had been based in Turkey:

> The point she repeatedly emphasized: We didn't understand how the Kurds' social system worked. As a consequence, we were trying to connect with them in ways that didn't match their culture . . . picking the wrong people to deal with (a fact that I had already started to realize).[8]

Zinni and his men had been seeking out Western-educated and English-speaking white-collar Kurds: doctors, lawyers, and bankers. They found them, but these people weren't the leaders of the tribes. Then they tried searching out the standard governmental liaisons: mayors, government officials of any kind, to no avail:

> Nell Nesbit made it plain that we had to forget all of that Western thinking and reach out to the tribal chiefs (the Kurds are a tribal society) and figure out how the tribes were structured.
>
> She brought in a Kurdish schoolteacher who answered my questions about social structure and decision-making by mapping out the Kurdish tribal and political structures: how Kurds do things, who makes the decisions, in the society. These were important issues for us as we tried to determine who were the actual leaders in the camps.[9]

Zinni and the rest of the force used their crash course in the local culture to establish relations with the tribes as well as find local merchants that could provide tents, food, and supplies that were less expensive and more acceptable to the refugees than the bulky and less-palatable MREs, which weren't close enough to the standard Kurdish diet. Special Forces teams worked with the tribes in instructing them on basic sanitation and living conditions.

But the camps could not become permanent. The overseeing force was directed to convince the various tribes to return to their homes, where they belonged. A thirteen-nation coalition force had to be mobilized, along with hundreds of thousands of Kurds, and all of them moved back into Iraq, under the noses of seventeen divisions of Iraqi soldiers, many of whom had not fought in Desert Storm, and so were not as fearful of the coalition. It would all be organized and led by the Americans, which had just defeated Hussein's army a few months earlier.

It was a situation ripe for conflict, yet the armed forces achieved its humanitarian and peacekeeping task brilliantly, performing across different military branches, working both with foreign military forces and nongovernment organizations (the Red Cross, Doctors without Borders, etc.), and the indigenous culture to relocate 500,000 Kurds back to their villages when possible, and to new areas in Iraq when that wasn't an option. It was during Operation Provide Comfort where all of the aspects of culture—local, military, and world—came together in a unified effort, and showed what could be accomplished when everyone worked together.

* * *

Then came the events of 9/11, a direct assault on American soil by foreign terrorists that resulted in a massive call to arms against the perpetrators of this heinous attack. Within two months, U.S. forces were mobilized and sent to Afghanistan to seek out and destroy the Taliban, an Islamic religious group that had consolidated its hold on the country after the Soviet withdrawal in 1990. By September 2002, Operation

Enduring Freedom was considered a success: The Taliban's hold on the country had been broken, and the process of installing a new government had begun. Reconstruction has been ongoing, leading to the creation of new governmental, judicial, education, and social systems throughout the country.

However, today there are still problems in Afghanistan. Opium, which had been all but eradicated by the Taliban, is now the country's number-one cash crop again (U.S. forces were actually ordered to ignore the burgeoning Afghan drug trade in the lead-up to the Iraqi invasion). There are various militias totaling 85,000 members still under control of dozens of regional warlords that have been expanding their control in the face of a weakened U.S. and NATO military presence. The American government willfully took money that had been appropriated for rebuilding Afghanistan and shifted it to Iraq for the invasion. At this time, Afghanistan, which was largely seen as the base and training center for many of the 9/11 hijackers, has been relegated to a footnote in history, overshadowed by the invasion of Iraq in 2003. Once again, operating in a foreign culture has led to limited success for the U.S. military, but has not led to fundamental understanding of that culture, which is the first step to bringing about change in a country.

> The first, the supreme, the most far-reaching act of judgment that the statesman and commander have to make is to establish . . . the kind of war on which they are embarking; neither mistaking it for, nor trying to turn it into, something that is alien to its nature.[10]

Currently, U.S. forces are still involved in Operation Iraqi Freedom; and despite what the president said about major military operations being over in 2003, only recently has there been talk of a possible timetable for removing U.S. forces in 2006, despite the recent Iraqi elections. One hopes that the soldiers over there are taking the lessons they are learning right now to heart, since there is a strong likelihood that they will be returning to the Middle East when they are commanders themselves.

Unlike many other operations, the impact of Saddam Hussein's removal from Iraq was actually examined before the mission began. During military operations enacted by the U.S. government in 1998, when the United Nations Special Committee was trying to uncover evidence that the Iraqis were manufacturing weapons of mass destruction, General Zinni realized that Iraq would not be a simple in-and-out mission. After Operation Desert Fox, a heavy bombing run against military and strategic targets in that country, he came to the following conclusion:

> Before Desert Fox, we'd looked at the possibility that we would have to execute the takedown of Saddam; but we always thought that would come after he attacked a nation or Israel, used WMD again on his own people, or committed some atrocity so outrageous we'd have no choice but to go in there and turn over the regime.
>
> "But what if it just collapsed?" I began to ask myself.
>
> It didn't take me long to figure out the answer to that: Somebody would have to go in there to rebuild the country.
>
> "Who?" I asked myself.
>
> As the CINC, I have a plan for militarily defeating Saddam. Doing that isn't going to be hard. But after we defeat him, who takes care of reconstruction and all the attendant problems?
>
> It was clear that we had to start looking hard at this possibility. It didn't take a rocket scientist to see that if we didn't, we could find ourselves in deep trouble.[11]

General Zinni went so far as to create a war game scenario in 1999 to examine the attendant problems that would come up in the wake of deposing the Iraqi dictator:

> The scenarios looked closely at humanitarian, security, political, economic, and other reconstruction issues. We looked at food, clean water, electricity, refugees, Shia versus Sunni, Kurds versus the other Iraqis, Turks versus Kurds, and the power vacuum that would surely follow the collapse of the regime (since Saddam had pretty successfully eliminated any local opposition). We looked at all the problems the United States faces in 2003 trying to rebuild Iraq. And when it was over, I was starting to get a good sense of their enormous scope and to recognize how massive the reconstruction job would be.[12]

But at the time, no one in Washington was interested in actually formulating a "post-invasion" plan in the event of a regime change in Iraq. But General Zinni was, and he assigned his own staff to create a reconstruction plan for that nation, which they worked on until he left Central Command in 2000. After that, the project vanished. And now our nation is faced with the results of not planning for what happens after the mission is supposedly accomplished.

Although the military has applied some cultural lessons from earlier conflicts to this one from a tactical standpoint, including working with local leaders to try to understand the forces arrayed against them, they have been less successful winning the hearts and minds of the general public. Even with the January elections, the majority of the populace still sees the American forces as occupiers, not liberators. American troops and civilian workers are kept from doing their jobs by the insurgent forces that have only grown more powerful during the past three years, and have been unable to make real headway against the terrorists by enlisting the local populace to help uncover the terrorist network. Given that the two sides are separated by the deepest of gulfs—religious, societal, and yes, cultural—it is even more important that time and effort is expended in understanding the culture of the enemy and how and where they operate, not just militarily, but culturally as well, for that is where the battles of the future are going to be fought. The main question in the current "war on terror" is a simple and powerful one: How does one fight an idea? By learning about a people's culture, understanding is gained about the basis of their thought, traditions, and ideas, and only then can a "war" against such an abstract concept be waged as effectively as possible.

This is not to state that it is America's duty to stamp out cultures that embrace terrorist ideology, but rather to learn how to neutralize the aspects of a culture that give rise to that subgroup, and also work with indigenous cultures to improve their situation, and not appear to be benevolently parceling out our help from a position of superiority, as our nation has been wont to do on more than one occasion, such as in Vietnam. Many cultures around the world in areas such as Southeast Asia and the Middle East have thousands of years of history and tradition from which they have drawn to create their current culture, and certainly they must find it disagreeable that a nation that didn't even exist three centuries ago is suddenly coming in and helping the local culture, in many cases without first learning as to whether they want help, and if so, what kind of help is needed. If another country came into America and said, "We're going to help you, no matter what you say or do," the reaction would be righteous indignation, not automatic and humble acceptance.

Despite the lessons that have been afforded to (and sometimes inflicted on) the military during the past sixty-plus years, there has been little change in the overall way of thinking about indigenous cultures.

Even worse, there seems to be a schism occurring among today's military and government leaders, some of whom seem to think that technology will fill the gap, others who still claim that in the end, future battles will still come down to infantrymen hitting the ground and achieving whatever their objective is. Regardless of which method is used, foreknowledge of the culture that they will be operating in will be crucial to effective deployment in the battlefield of tomorrow, whether men or machines are sent to fight.

The conflicts of the future will not be Cold War–era army maneuvers, but limited-scale operations like the ones that happened in Somalia, the Balkans, and what is happening now in Iraq. Future operations, even in places like North Korea and Iran, should that become necessary, will be along the lines of the day-to-day missions that are currently being executed in Iraq and Afghanistan. The battlefront will most likely be in rural and/or urban centers, not against a clearly defined army, but against guerilla troops that are at home in the local populace, and able to strike fast and melt away, whether they go into the neighborhood of their base cities, or the mountains and caves of the surrounding area.

American forces will be the outsiders, and to a certain extent will always be outsiders in foreign cultures, but there is no reason to live down to the role that they may be assigned by the native people. Understanding, manners, and politeness are recognized around the world, and even a military force should be held accountable for not knowing as much as it can about a location and situation before beginning operations in an area, particularly when the facts should be available in the first place. Even something as simple as required language lessons for all personnel, depending on their deployment area, would go a long way toward removing cultural barriers between American soldiers and the native populations.

But steps are currently being taken to improve the U.S. military's understanding of culture and its impact on the battlefield. On January 25–27, 2005, the U.S. Army Training and Doctrine Command hosted a conference to specifically address the concept of culture as part of the Joint Operating Environment. With the idea of both friendly and hostile cultures being realized as a real battlefield variable, steps are being taken to improve the military's understanding of them around the world, and integrate that knowledge into their battle plans.

Perhaps the most significant insight in cultural development is the understanding that most future cultural trends and drivers of social change will come from forces and influences external to a country rather than more traditional internal drivers . . . The access to and awareness of other cultures, either through direct contact with individuals or through technologies that spread the popular culture of others, will increase dramatically by 2020–2030.[13]

The most logical way to accomplish this so that it is ready when needed would be to establish where the logical hot spots around the world are—many of which have existed for years and even decades—and then create an intelligence-gathering network that can accumulate data on any area's different cultures, down to the regional and even tribal level. Since much of this information is already available from studies at universities and anthropologic research, it would not be a difficult task to create a worldwide military database containing all of the important cultural information on every region in the world, whether it is on the various tribes in Nigeria, or the different villages in the Xinjiang province of China. With periodic updates, this would be an invaluable resource in not only identifying possible trouble flare-ups, but also in learning how to effectively deal with indigenous populations from cultural and societal standpoints, rather than simply from the posture of an invading force.

Even more important, this information must be disseminated, and while that will be explored further in the next section, the point that knowledge about another people is useless unless it is shared is very valid, as the lessons that both were and were not taken from World War II and Vietnam show.

There is no place where George Santayana's adage, "Those who cannot remember the past are condemned to repeat it," rings truer than on the battlefield of the future. Even as the enemy, tactics, and terrain changes, often rapidly, the culture they exist in changes at a far slower rate, and studying it provides valuable information on why and how people live like they do, and how the military can work within that environment to achieve their goals.

Military Culture

The war wasn't going anywhere, we weren't winning. We were just losing guys . . . the war had to end. It had to be left behind. It was not only Vietnam that was being lost. We had started to lose America.

In the Army, leadership studies coming out of the War College were saying that the system was busted . . . It's hard to imagine why outrageous behavior was allowed to persist in the Army during that period. In the institution, we had kind of lost our bearings in what was right and what was wrong. And what was appropriate and what wasn't. We had misused some of the psychological stuff that the management theorists were pushing on us. We started to think that we were running some kind of democratic day camp: Generals sitting around coffeehouses talking to troops; troop councils reporting to battalion commanders about what they ought to do. It was a break-down of the command structure. Like inmates had taken over the asylum.

In the 2nd Division, we reinstilled discipline with the attitude: "Let me explain it to you. I'm in charge here and you ain't." That's what the troops needed to hear.[14] (Gen. Colin Powell)

After Vietnam, it could be strongly argued that the entire U.S. armed forces was in a state of disrepair and low morale. The with-drawal from Vietnam was the first time that Americans had left a the-ater of operations without achieving their objective. Disparate elements such as Secretary of Defense Robert McNamara's policy of statistical analysis and ill-conceived programs like "Project 100,000," which had filled the armed services with soldiers that would have otherwise not been able to enlist due to poor scores on the Armed Forces Qualification Test, and the heavy protesting of the conflict by activists at home, had combined to leave the military reeling on all fronts.

Poor policies during the conflict led to breakdowns in efficiency and performance. One of the biggest problems was the one-year rota-tion, which meant that many soldiers were leaving the theater just as they were actually becoming proficient at their assignment. Also, as the date they would go back to "the world" drew closer, soldiers would often become more careful, and thereby cause increased friction on missions, which could jeopardize their teammates. Also, replacing killed or wounded individuals one by one in a particular unit did not help the stability or cohesiveness of the military, as the veterans felt that the new soldiers, who didn't know how to work as part of the team, were a hazard. Due to the need to replenish the command struc-ture due to casualties and the reduction in force after the war, thou-sands of noncommissioned officers had been rapidly promoted, often without the necessary experience. This would cause problems both during the war and in peacetime, as the men who filled positions often did not have the qualifications for them.

The equipment issued to the military was often prone to malfunction or breakdown, with the new M-16 rifle assigned during Vietnam being a prime example (the military switched from the sturdy, hard-hitting 7.62mm bullet to the smaller 5.56mm bullet, and early models of the M-16 had ejection problems and often suffered from carbon buildup in the barrel due to the wrong kind of gunpowder being used). Aircraft flying sorties over targets without proper instruments were, and since the combat zones had been divided up into Air Force and Navy zones of operation, pilots that flew over a zone they weren't cleared to operate in could not attack a target they found there. Just about every branch was hampered by restrictive regulations and rules that limited their effectiveness.

Back in the states, things weren't much better. The government and many in the military seemed to want to forget about the Vietnam Conflict, and turn their attention to the potential European theater. The civil rights movement was dividing the military branches by color, and causing problems with discipline in the ranks. The usual reduction in force that followed a war spread to all aspects of the military, including budgets, vehicles, training, and equipment. The Army Special Forces program was cut in half. The officer core had been eviscerated. There was only one good thing about the post-Vietnam period: There was nowhere to go but up. Retired Army General Carl Stiner sums up what was needed:

> In my judgment, training is the essential element for the readiness of any unit in any service. The very best equipment is great to have, and I'll never turn any down, but well-trained *people* win wars. No im-

personal piece of equipment or technology can ever replace a well-trained soldier, sailor, airman, Marine, or Coast Guardsman.[15]

The turning point, for the Special Forces and the rest of the military, started with the failure of Desert One, the ill-fated attempt to rescue the U.S. Embassy hostages held in Iran in 1980. The operation illustrated the prime weaknesses of the military as a whole, unprepared and unequipped for the mission, and unable to execute a joint operation effectively without running into overwhelming problems that caused the mission to be aborted and lives to be lost.

Although some held it as yet another failed attempt by the military to perform their duty, there were those that had had enough. And officers across all four branches began to do something about it, starting with the troops under their command. They reestablished discipline, weeding out the troublemakers and drug users. They updated the core curriculum of the Army, which was still teaching Korean War tactics in the late 1970s, and began instituting the idea of maneuver warfare, wherein the junior officers and NCOs know the mission plan and objectives, and by working together, execute the mission, staying alert for new and better opportunities to defeat the enemy along the way. Rather than a static, chain-of-command hierarchy that had been promulgated in Vietnam, the military began to both learn from and throw off the past decade, and move forward again. And the officers were leading from the front.

Maneuver warfare began to catch on throughout the armed forces. And with that freedom to execute a mission plan in the best way to accomplish a stated goal, officers in the military began encouraging feedback from junior officers. With respect, of course, but they welcomed commentary, and the potential to make mistakes without being castigated and even more important, learn from them. Soldiers were able to critique their commanding officers, and everyone learned from it. The Marines in particular seemed to take the change to heart, reverting back to their core rule of "every man a rifleman" and instituting an almost open-door policy both up and down the chain of command in the 1980s.

In 1983, the bombing of the U.S. Marine barracks in Lebanon sent shock waves throughout the Corps and the military as a whole. But before they could begin to second-guess themselves or the military's progress, the invasion of Grenada was approved just two days later, and the U.S. forces accomplished its task of suppressing a coup and rescuing American students there. After all the talk, seeing the elements of maneuver warfare in action was a badly needed morale booster. While after-theater reports indicated that there was still work to be done on planning and executing joint service maneuvers and cooperation, it was still an excellent start.

Next came one of the biggest changes in how the military was organized since the Air Force was created—the Goldwater-Nichols National Security Act of 1986. Basically, it removed the top leaders of each branch from operational matters, allowing them to focus on training and preparing their troops for missions that would be decided on by the president and secretary of defense. The Joint Chiefs of Staff could take advice directly to the president and secretary of defense without needing the agreement of the other service chiefs. The idea of joint military operations was strengthened in the bill as well, since each branch was now officially considered a part of the whole U.S. military command under the president and secretary of defense.

Joint education was to be required of all officers; all service schools were now to have a joint war-fighting curriculum approved and accredited by the Joint Staff; prior to promotion to flag rank, officers were required to serve in joint assignments; and those who qualified as CINCs would have to serve in a joint assignment as a flag officer.[16]

The Army Chief at this time, General Carl Vuono, also set about transforming the army into a modern, late-twentieth-century fighting force, emphasizing six key areas: training, force modernization, war-winning doctrine, quality soldiers, leader development, and force structure, or creating the right mix of units to accomplish the missions that would be assigned by the commander in chief.

The emphasis on joint branch training and transformation was soon to pay off. First, in Operation Just Cause, the mission to remove dictator Manuel Noriega from power in Panama in 1989. The military used psychological operations to effectively speak to the local populace and reassure them that the U.S. military was there to truly help them. Along with causing Noriega's surrender and extradition to America, the military removed the entire corrupt Panamanian Defense Force, and paved the way for a democratic government. During the first real joint operation between different branches of the military, things did not always progress as smoothly as planned, such as the SEAL raid on Padilla airfield that left four men dead and eight wounded, but overall the four branches worked well together to complete their mission.

All of this led up to the largest war since Vietnam—Operation Desert Storm, where the U.S. military firmly regained their poise and ability, and executed the concepts of maneuver warfare in a stunning 100-hour blitz of the Iraqi forces that effectively destroyed the enemy's fighting force. Along the way, the U.S. military not only adapted to the desert environment, an area that they had never really prepared for, in record time, but the commanders also fielded and managed a multinational force with unparalleled skill and diplomacy, making sure that practically every unit, foreign or domestic, worked together and knew what their assignment would be.

Desert Storm also used psychological operations, or psy-ops, to attempt to destabilize the Iraqi army, expose Iraqi propaganda, and strengthen coalition support for the war. The operation was primarily aimed at setting the record straight, especially in the countries and cultures around Iraq, countering Hussein's propaganda and illustrating just what an evil dictator he truly was. One of their greatest coups was suggesting to prominent Muslim leaders that Saddam's attack on Kuwait was a violation of Islamic law that prevented a Muslim from attacking a fellow Muslim. Saddam had even called for a justified jihad, which was even more wrong. Using the aspects of local culture in Cairo, a media center in the region, and blanketing the airwaves and newspapers, recognized and respected Islamic sources were soon denouncing Saddam's false claims.

Also, the leaflet campaign was very successful at causing desertions among the Iraqi army. B-52s would drop information actually telling the enemy when and where they were going to strike. They would then bomb the area, and afterward drop more leaflets warning of future strikes. Group defections were common in the days following the bombing runs that were preceded and followed by information warfare. Leaflets also were carefully constructed to illustrate the common Iraqi soldier in a positive light, telling them that they had been misled by their leaders, but that they would be treated with respect and dignity upon surrendering to the coalition forces (serving its dual purpose of informing and persuading, the two main functions of psy-ops). Coalition soldiers—the supposed enemy of the Iraqis—were shown in unthreatening ways. The tactics of one military culture were used to undermine another, and it was a stunning success. Over 98 percent of Iraqi prisoners of war claimed to have seen a leaflet, with 80 percent saying afterward that they had been influenced by it, and 70 percent saying that a leaflet had been instrumental in convincing them to surrender. Even allowing for inflated claims by prisoners wishing to comply with their captors, the fact remains that the Iraqi Army's morale and discipline was so weak that the psy-ops assault on the military culture had the desired effect.

Of course, for every success, there are those operations that do not work as effectively as they should due to breakdowns in military planning and execution. One of these was Operation Anaconda, the U.S.-led mission against Taliban elements in the Shah-I-Kot valley near the eastern border of Afghanistan. Although the reports after the battle hailed it as a success, with more than 450 Taliban soldiers killed while only losing eight allied soldiers, in reality the mission was a hodgepodge combination of different units thrown together with no clear chain of command and two generals running around on the ground. The information gathered about the enemy force was inaccurate, there was no artillery backup and unreliable air support, and the plan enacted was poorly thought out in the first place, leading to confusion and miscommunication among the various task force elements. In particular, one of the Special Operations Groups had formed an alliance with a local Afghan militia force on the condition that there would be an almost hour-long aerial bombardment of the target area before the ground units moved in. However, there never had been an air strike planned for the mission in the first place, indeed, the airfield at Bagram couldn't even muster enough firepower to make that happen. Also, while the Afghan forces were being referred to as "the main effort" in the operation, later on it was revealed that that reference appeared to be more for propaganda purposes; to have the appearance of an Afghan leader and unit in the battle rather than realistically use his knowledge and experience. The problem was that no one had informed the Special Forces liaisons working with the locals that that was the case, leading to more confusion among the units. Finally, when reconnaissance revealed a sizable enemy force parked right on the spot that the Advance Force Operations units wanted to take and hold to open up the valley for troop off-loading, the intelligence failures came to light too late, leading to some of the fiercest fighting of the war in Afghanistan, and what was worse, the unnecessary casualties that may have gone along with it. Failures in the military culture of information sharing and cooperation were in large part responsible for the disappointing execution of the operation, and despite its final successful outcome overall, follow-up reports indicated that other Taliban soldiers in the area had probably escaped.

Current Operations

At the time of this book's publication, there are approximately 130,000 U.S. soldiers in Iraq, and although the president claims to be working on beginning graduated withdrawal of these soldiers, at the same time, other units in the U.S. are being activated for duty. Three years after the successful invasion of Iraq and the removal and subsequent capture of Saddam Hussein, there is still no clear path out of the country for either the military or America.

Instead, what's left of the coalition forces are struggling to adapt their primarily third-generation warfare tactics to an opponent that is using fourth-generation warfare principles of combat:

> . . . this kind of warfare is neither new nor surprising. It has been evolving around the world during the past seven decades. An evolved form of insurgency, fourth-generation warfare uses all avail-

able networks—political, economic, social, and military—to convince the enemy's decision makers that their strategic goals are either un-achievable or too costly for the perceived benefit.

It is rooted by Mao Zedong's fundamental precept that superior political will, when properly employed, defeats greater economic and military power. However, unlike the campaigns waged by Mao in China, 4GW does not attempt to win by defeating the enemy's military forces. Instead, via diverse networks, 4GW directly attacks the minds of enemy decision makers to destroy the enemy's political will. And fourth-generation wars are often long—measured in decades rather than months or years.[17]

Everything stated above is exactly the type of warfare that the United States would rather not fight, preferring instead to bring over-whelming firepower and technology to the battlefield and defeat the enemy through straight-up, unit-to-unit combat. Although Desert Storm was a success in 1990, it was the last gasp of third-generation warfare, and some generals were already realizing this:

The next influential event was Desert Storm, which, as far as I am concerned, was an aberration. Though it seemed to work out okay for us—indeed proved beyond doubt how enormously powerful our Cold War military really was—it was the final salute of the Cold War military. It left the impression that the terrible mess that awaits us abroad can somehow be overcome by good clean soldiering, just like in World War II. In reality, the only reason Desert Storm worked was because we managed to go up against the only jerk on the planet who was stupid enough to challenge us to refight World War II—with less of everything that counted, including the moral right to do what he did to Kuwait. In the top-level war colleges, we still fight this type of adversary, so we can always win. I rebelled at this notion, thinking there would be nobody out there who would be so stupid as to fight us that way. Then along came Saddam Hussein, and "good soldiering" was vindicated once again.[18] (Gen. Tony Zinni [ret.])

The truly disappointing part of all this is that America's military should have already grasped the basic principles of fourth-generational warfare years ago, having had ten years of experience with it during the Vietnam Conflict. Despite the January 2005 elections in Iraq, the parallels between that war and the current operation in Iraq are unmistakable: The U.S. forces are fighting a holding pattern, dictated by the goals and tactics of their enemies, who have patience and all the time in the world to keep the Americans occupied until public sentiment begins to turn against the war. They are willing to keep fighting for years, until the United States is gone, and the Iraqi government is left on its own to try and put down the insurrection without coalition support. Whether this will be possible against such a determined enemy that follows the tenets of fourth-generation warfare is unclear at this time.

Indeed, it seems that the "coalitions of the willing"; loosely affiliated groups of people with political or ideological differences that ally together to drive the invaders from their county, have adopted fourth-generation tactics wholeheartedly. They create guided munitions through the use of suicide bombers, once again utilizing the same tactics of the Japanese Imperial Army on Okinawa in World War II. They attack civilians and infrastructure, willing to accept casualties even among their own people to advance their cause. They also use religious sites and civilian neighborhoods both as staging points and places of refuge. They send messages to their supporters that their cause is just, a threat to the uncommitted to stay out of the fight or suffer the same fate, and a warning to their enemies that they are involved in a fight they cannot win. If pressed or possibly in danger of losing a city or area, they open up negotiations with the enemy, allowing them more time to bring in reinforcements and equipment, all the while wearing down their enemy's political will and motivation to fight.

This is the enemy of the future, a low-tech, networked group without a defined base of operations, whose soldiers are adept at fighting unconventionally, and are driven by ideological fanaticism to do whatever they feel it will take to defeat their enemy. How, then, do armed forces deal with this threat?

Future Military Culture

Although the U.S. armed forces are in the middle of a transformation of both its soldiers and its technology, there is still a basic disagreement on which direction the military should go in the future: technology-oriented or individual-oriented.

Shortcomings demonstrated by the American effort in Iraq are human rather than technological: cultural awareness, information operations, civic action, and, above all, intelligence from strategic to tactical. During the present cultural phase of the war, intimate knowledge of the enemy's motivation, intent, will, tactical methods, and cultural environment have proven to be far more important than smart bombs, aircraft, and expansive bandwidth. Success in this phase rests with the ability of leaders to think and adapt faster than the enemy, and for soldiers to thrive in an unfamiliar environment of uncertainty, ambiguity, and unfamiliar cultural circumstances.

The greatest advantage can be achieved by outthinking rather than out-equipping the enemy. Today, wars are won by creating alliances, leveraging nonmilitary advantages, reading intentions, building trust, converting opinions, and managing perceptions—all tasks that demand an exceptional ability to understand people, their cultures, and their motivations.

Yet the transformation effort remains wedded to the premise that success in war is best achieved by creating an overwhelming technological advantage over the enemy. A fixation on big programs continues to shape how the transformation community looks at future war. A human view of warfare is woefully lacking. Where are the initiatives that promise to create better-educated and more culturally aware soldiers? How will the Defense Department increase the ability of its soldiers to interact with indigenous peoples and gain their allegiance in future wars? How is the Defense Department ensuring that our forces will be as effective at stability and peacekeeping as they are at killing? These are the first questions that the transformation team must answer.[19]

Major General Scales's words best illustrate the direction that future warfare is headed. While there will always be a need for the best technology, those weapons and equipment should not become the end-all of tactics and strategy for an operation. Against an enemy that uses irregular methods and equipment, all the technology in the world is not going to stop them, as evidenced by the improvised explosive devices that the insurgency has been using with terrible effectiveness in Iraq. Most reactive wartime technology is based on neutralizing a known threat; which is exactly what terrorists work to avoid; the gathering of knowledge about their organization, their operations, their tactics, and their true ideology. This is the sorely needed intelligence that will help to combat an enemy whose goals are based on a religious tenet, not the desire for territory or sole gain of power.

One of the primary goals of the future military should be to create a World Culture College, similar to the War College, but examining both civilian and terrorist cultures and societies to learn how they operate and then find ways to work both with the indigenous cultures, and against the external ones that threaten the local society. With the inclusion of the proposed world cultural database mentioned earlier, this would be an effective tool in identifying the cultural aspects of a region and population that would affect military operations there, and whether those factors would be worked with, around, or straight through if necessary.

Every branch of the military also needs to take a hard look at the operations of the last fifty years, and recognize that every soldier—not just the Special Operations groups—will need a basic understanding of the foreign culture that they will be operating in from the very first day a theater of war is established. In fact, although there has usually been an arms-length agreement between the SOGs and the mainstream army, it would be hard to think of a better group to help train soldiers quickly and effectively to deal with indigenous populations and understand various cultural barriers and traditions around the world, and learning how to deal with them. This is not a suggestion that the SOGs should be done away with; on the contrary, they fulfill a unique role that an infantryman should not be expected to handle. A group of trained, dedicated soldiers that can operate in the field on their own for long periods of time and function among native groups with relative ease will be needed more than ever in the future. But in accordance with the military's current requirement of Joint Operations, what better way to teach the soldiers of tomorrow about cultural awareness than from those who do it every day? Not only would this give the regular soldiers an understanding of how foreign language and culture plays their individual roles on the battlefield, but it would also reduce the distance that is often seen between the SOGs and the rest of the military, accomplishing two goals at once. Utilizing the resources that the military already has in place should be a key component of more effective armed forces in the future.

One example of this could be creating an offshoot of the SOG Robin Sage Field Training Exercise that is part of the Special Forces training at Camp McKall, part of Fort Bragg in North Carolina. Special Forces candidates undergo a nineteen-day training exercise to create and train a guerilla force from the local population, many of whom are played by Americans. There is no reason that this program could not be re-created in different areas of the nation to reflect different cultures. In fact, shuttered military bases across the country could be reopened and repurposed to train every branch to work in various cultures around the world. Need a Middle Eastern setting and curriculum? Send your units to Fort Huachuca in Arizona. Plan on sending soldiers to Central America? The jungles and swamps of Florida would be an ideal lowland training ground, while soldiers that are scheduled to be stationed in mountainous nations like Korea or elsewhere can train in the Rockies or Appalachians. By simulating the foreign environment and culture as closely as possible, one- to two-week intensive training courses can be created that would immerse American soldiers in the other world that they will be living and working in for the next few years, and better prepare them to operate there during times of both peace and war.

The other aspect of the military that should be overhauled is how it distributes its troops. First, the military should look at extending tours for all branches around the world to a minimum of two years, and perhaps even longer in certain areas. An important lesson from Vietnam that was cited as a main reason why American forces couldn't get a handle on the situation was that a one-year tour was barely long enough to get an idea of what was going on, then, just when a soldier was becoming truly effective at his assignment, he was removed from it, and the learning cycle had to begin all over again with a new person, hampering relationships and understanding of the dynamics of the conflict. Extended tours of duty would enable both sides to learn from each other, and allow for the introduction and continuation of far-reaching operations under one commander, so that someone else wouldn't have to take over and learn and create relationships from scratch, possibly jeopardizing the progress that had been made up to that point.

The military should also extend the idea of joint operations to not just the branches of the U.S. armed forces, but also include civilian law enforcement divisions as well. The CIA, FBI, DEA, Department of Homeland Defense, and the rest of the federal units fighting any enemies of America must become as networked as their opponents, able to disseminate information and pool resources quickly and without rancor. Future operations will depend on the military and other organizations being as cohesive as the enemy they will be fighting against.

Technology will still play an important role in the future military, as it always has. One of the key components of the effective utilization technology is making sure that the military has the right tools to do their job. Secretary of Defense Donald Rumsfeld's infamous quote, "You go to war with the army you have, not the army you might want or wish to have," his off-the-cuff response to a soldier's question as to why the men in Iraq weren't getting armored Humvees more quickly, is a prime illustration of the incredible lack of awareness of this basic concept. But Rumsfeld's answer is indicative of a long history of the military's cycle of inflation during wartime and reduction afterward. Ever since America was founded, it seems that the armed forces have suffered from inadequate peacetime budgets, manpower, and training and equipment until a war comes along. Then the government seems to panic, take a look at the state of the military at the time, and throw them everything but the kitchen sink, at which time the armed forces usually advance to the forefront of technology and ability among all the armies of the world. When the war is over, the cuts begin again, whittling away at the military's effectiveness until the cycle begins all over again with the next conflict. It happened after Vietnam, with the end of the Cold War, and it happened again between Desert Storm and Enduring Freedom/Iraqi Freedom. The current army alone, the backbone of the "boots on the ground" philosophy, which is expected to fight on the ground anywhere in the world, stands at about 500,000 men, less than half the size it was in 1990. The top brass says they think this is enough, yet the military's numbers are stretched in Iraq (giving rise to the number of "Stop Loss" orders in 2004, basically preventing soldiers that had already served their stated time from leaving the armed forces), and it doesn't take into consideration what might happen if a second war started in Iran or North Korea. Military recruiters across the country are under tremendous pressure from their superiors to enlist more soldiers—why is that if we have enough troops already? The fact is that America's armed forces are undermanned for the tasks expected of them today.

A better idea would be to keep a permanent level of troops always enlisted and ready for any situation that might come up instead of the feast-or-famine cycle that has come to represent how the armed forces go from one conflict to the next. Along with a fixed, sustainable troop level, commanders should make sure that all of the armed forces have the basic equipment they need to carry out their missions, such as properly armored vehicles and body armor for every soldier on the ground in a hostile environment, whether they are on the front line or not. When the U.S. Army doesn't have enough bullets for training its soldiers, something is seriously wrong with the policies for obtaining equipment. Congressional budgets for military items, which are often larded with pork-barrel projects, should be decided on exclusively as they pertain to the military, without other bills being tacked on in an endless stream of special-interest projects for the nation's representatives. The research and development, procurement, and logistics systems all need to be streamlined so that new technology and equipment isn't being tested on the battlefield, but beforehand, so that the soldiers have the best equipment available when they are deployed, not receiving it after the fact—or after it is too late.

Finally, and this is something that today's military forces have embraced in the past few decades, the continuing need for feedback by soldiers who have actually faced combat, who know what it's like, and know what they require to do their job effectively is a vital component of knowing how to deal with challenges the military will face in the future. As Major General Robert Scales says about the future of the transformation process:

> If soldiers and Marines are doing virtually all of the fighting and dying, then it seems logical that some of these men should be playing pivotal roles in deciding how wars should be fought in the future. This isn't the case. Instead, the transformation team consists mostly of academics and officers from the air and sea services. I know many of these men. All are exceptional individuals—patriotic and selfless. But knowing the true nature of war demands more than good intentions. Wisdom comes from study and practice. The future of war cannot be divined without the ability to understand, well, war—specifically war on the ground.
>
> If future enemies have chosen to fight us on land, then surely someone with experience in that dimension might be the thought leader of

the transformation team. The war of ideas that will guide us into the future should be moderated by those with a record of proven performance in fighting the unplugged, human-centered, unconventional campaign that will most certainly confront us generations into the future.[20]

To better examine the questions of culture and transformation that will come up, the military should also reexamine the mandatory retirement age. Many of the authors quoted in this article are the military leaders of the past decade, men with unparalleled experience in warfare and, as shown by their ideas here, excellent thoughts on how to move the transformation of the military forward effectively. Yet the majority of them are already retired, forced out of the military just when their skills and knowledge are most needed. Many civilian executives reach the peak of their administrative power at age sixty and beyond, and still have anywhere from ten to twenty years of excellent service ahead of them. Military commanders nearing the mandatory retirement age are in exactly the same position—still willing to serve their country, but unable to due to current policy. The military is limiting its operational effectiveness by not utilizing one of its best assets—the men who have served in combat and seen the changes that have happened over the past forty years, and who are best qualified to speak as to what can be done to avoid the mistakes of the past and move forward with confidence that the military is truly ready to handle any challenge it might face.

One would hope that the military will not repeat the mistakes of Vietnam and cull some of the best men, those with the experience to adapt the armed forces to the new battlefield that looms on the horizon, out of the service before they can really put their hard-earned experience to work in preparing for the next war. As General Carl Stiner commented, nothing replaces training, and in the same vein, one would imagine that nothing replaces the experience of real combat, and the lessons learned from that experience. At the very least, the operations in Afghanistan and Iraq will at least serve the next generation of military commanders in knowing how to work more effectively with the indigenous cultures in a nation to accomplish their goals on the future battlefield.

American Culture

Q: But don't you believe that the threat that bin Laden posed won't truly be eliminated until he is found either dead or alive?

The President: Well, as I say, we haven't heard much from him. And I wouldn't necessarily say he's at the center of any command structure. And, again, I don't know where he is. I-I'll repeat what I said. I truly am not that concerned about him. I know he is on the run. I was concerned about him, when he had taken over a country. I was concerned about the fact that he was basically running Afghanistan and calling the shots for the Taliban.

But once we set out the policy and started executing the plan, he became—we shoved him out more and more on the margins. He has no place to train his Al Qaeda killers anymore. And if we—excuse me for a minute—and if we find a training camp, we'll take care of it. Either we will or our friends will. That's one of the things—part of the new phase that's becoming apparent to the American people is that we're working closely with other governments to deny sanctuary, or training, or a place to hide, or a place to raise money.

And we've got more work to do. See, that's the thing the American people have got to understand, that we've only been at this six months. This is going to be a long struggle. I keep saying that; I don't know whether you all believe me or not. But time will show you that it's going to take a long time to achieve this objective. And I can assure you, I am not going to blink. And I'm not going to get tired. Because I know what is at stake. And history has called us to action, and I am going to seize this moment for the good of the world, for peace in the world and for freedom.[21]

The attack on the two World Trade Center towers on September 11, 2001, finally drove the idea home to America that this country was not immune to terrorist attack. Why the government didn't take the idea of a massive assault on American soil more seriously after the 1993 bombing of the same buildings is still a subject of much debate. Also, the fact that the government did not appropriately investigate the leads it had in the months and even years leading up to 9/11 seems to indicate a strange unwillingness to believe information about potential attacks even when evidence that they might happen was right under agents' noses. In 1995, when Philippines police captured terrorist Abdul Hakim Murad, they learned something very interesting about his education:

All those years in flight school, he confessed, had been in preparation for a suicide mission. He was to buy, rent, or steal—that part of the plan had not yet been worked out—a small plane, preferably a Cessna, fill it with explosives, and crash it into CIA headquarters. There were also secondary targets that terrorist cells wanted hit: Congress, the White House, the Pentagon, and possibly some skyscrapers—Youssef [Ramzi Ahmed Youssef, the mastermind behind the World Trade Center bombing] had made it clear that they had unfinished business with the World Trade Center. The only problem, Murad complained, was that they needed more trained pilots.[22]

Six years later, they apparently found a way to get those pilots trained—in American flight schools—and then fly two fully fueled airliners into the World Trade Center towers. Despite a fairly lengthy list of intelligence briefings and even government scenario plans that utilized the idea of airplanes being flown into buildings, the U.S. government is on record as saying it had no conceivable idea that an attack of this magnitude could have been perpetrated and carried out, much less during the watch of several national and international American law enforcement agencies.

The quote by President George Bush above illustrates a fundamental flaw in American thinking—that nowadays, once the United States steps in anywhere and makes progress against a foe, that foe is automatically on his way to being defeated. He still believes in the tenets of third-generation warfare, which have already been left behind. It hasn't happened in Afghanistan, a country now responsible for three-quarters of the world's opium production and still populated by oppressive regional warlords, the reforming Taliban, and possibly by Osama Bin Laden himself. And, despite the capture of Saddam Hussein, and the elections in Iraq, that nation is still under daily attack by an established and growing insurgency movement aimed at destabilizing the government that is under construction, and driving the United States and coalition forces out as soon as possible.

This idea also pervades American thought in general—that our military will conquer any foe it faces; after all, they did in Desert Storm, right? But that is not the kind of war that is being fought today, and once again, the wrong people are being sent in who are using the wrong methods to fight it. And at the same time, the nation is slipping back into complacency about threats to our own country. America in general needs to realize that it is extremely vulnerable to a terrorist attack among a broad spectrum of avenues, and to protect against that will require many changes in how its citizens live everyday.

> In the new threat environment, the United States has 600,000 bridges to protect and 14,000 small airports from which terrorists can wreak havoc. There are 4 million miles of paved roadways and 95,000 miles of coastline for extremists to escape on. Eighteen thousand separate law enforcement bodies need to be synchronized in any counterterror response. In addition to Boston Harbor, there are 361 other ports just as exposed. The United States boasts a network of 260,000 natural gas wells and 1.3 million miles of pipeline that terrorists can blow up. In New York City alone, the subway system has an astonishing 1.2 billion riders annually. Seventy-seven million passengers use its three airports annually. More than 16 million commercial cargo containers arrive by air, sea, and land every year, and all it would take for a catastrophic disaster would be for one of the steel crates to contain a nuclear device. . .
>
> The grim task of cataloguing the nation's vulnerabilities was the necessary first step toward insuring that our imagination would never fail us again and that we would not find ourselves in a predicament where even residents of a small Midwestern town would fear for their safety. As former assistant FBI director Stephen Pomerantz explained to me: "We have to acknowledge our weaknesses to take corrective action. And we have to recognize that we are far behind other countries in this regard."[23]

The above words are not fearmongering, they are simply the truth.

One might ask, but what does this have to do with culture and the future battlefield? Everything, if terrorists decide to bring their war across our very porous borders again. The United States cannot stop the multibillion dollar drug trade that flows into our nation from seemingly every direction, yet it expects to somehow prevent a well-organized terrorist cell from smuggling nuclear material or a dirty bomb into the country? America itself must take many harsher steps to prevent another attack like the one on the World Trade Center.

So how should today's American culture adapt to the realities of the current situation that it finds itself in?

First, the American government should be as candid as possible about the reasons that it chooses to go to war, particularly with its own population. Operation Enduring Freedom in Afghanistan practically sold itself; our nation was going after the terrorist organization that had attacked our country and killed 3,000 people on American soil. It would have been hard to find an American who wasn't for that.

Operation Iraqi Freedom, however, wasn't nearly so easy. Despite all the purported "evidence" bandied about before the invasion, there haven't been any weapons of mass destruction discovered in Iraq. Although Al Qaeda has operated in Iraq previously, there has still been no firm evidence linking Saddam Hussein to their terrorist operations. And the reasoning that the United States had to step in because the dictator was brutalizing his own people doesn't hold up, either; after all, he had been doing that for the previous twenty years, and America wasn't very interested in stopping him earlier. Our nation had even worked with him during operations against Iran in the 1980s when it suited our purposes. (There is a film that can be found on the Internet that shows then-special envoy to Iraq Donald Rumsfeld shaking hands with Saddam Hussein in 1983.) Even President Bush's claims that the liberation of Iraq has started movements in other countries can be argued. The Palestinian government was only able to start realistically negotiating for a true peace accord with Israel after the death of

Yasser Arafat, and the movement to remove the Syrian presence from Lebanon began with the assassination of former Prime Minister Rafik Hariri. Even the new relations established with a suddenly peaceful Libya have their roots in the Clinton Administration's handling of that nation's involvement in the Pan Am 103 bombing, and incentives from the American government to drop sanctions against the country in exchange for their forswearing terrorist and WMD program support. However, the changes in the current political conditions of any of these countries cannot be attributed to an outside event, like the liberation of Iraq, as the single biggest cause.

During World War II, the fight was against totalitarianism—good versus evil. Vietnam was a misunderstood conflict that polarized the nation into two sides. Judging by the hundreds of antiwar protests that marked the second anniversary of the Iraq invasion, there is a large part of the nation that feels the justifications for this war were false. Meanwhile, more than 2,000 U.S. soldiers have died, and more than 15,000 soldiers have been injured, while the country has spent more than 250 billion dollars to fund the reconstruction effort that the government had said would be financed by the sale of Iraqi oil. Not since Vietnam has such a policy of blatant falsehood and dishonesty been used to gather support for a war. Although there is always going to be antiwar activists, if the U.S. government wants the general support of the American people, as well as the rest of the world, it has to start by being honest with them from the beginning.

Second, the country should make sure to finish what it starts. Just nine days after 9/11, President George W. Bush delivered a speech to Afghanistan in which he demanded: "Deliver to United States authorities all the leaders of Al Qaeda who hide in your land." Yet in the quote at the beginning of this section, barely six months later, he practically dismissed bin Laden as "out on the margins" and stated "he has

no place to train his Al Qaeda killers anymore." Once the ruling Taliban infrastructure was dismantled to Bush's satisfaction, he conve-
niently shifted money, troops, and support to the pending invasion of
Iraq, leaving the mastermind behind the deadliest attack on U.S. soil
still alive and able to plot more assaults on America. Like a child with
attention-deficit disorder, Bush committed to the Afghanistan invasion
until he got what he wanted, then moved the majority of the soldiers
to Iraq and left a skeleton force of American troops there to work with
a German-led NATO contingent to clean up what's left.

In Iraq, there is talk about partial troop drawdown as early as 2006,
but that is dependent on the small Iraqi military's ability to fight the insurgency themselves, which at this time is still in doubt. All of which
means that there will still be thousands of American troops in the country for the next several years, manning the permanent bases that have
been created there. It is very doubtful that the insurgency will be destroyed by the time the military pulls out, leaving both Americans and
Iraqi civilians still at risk from terrorist attacks. Once again, the government, led by the president, will leave the job they set out to do half-
finished. If America is to maintain its status as a superpower, it needs to
back up its claims of spreading democracy in regions by actively continuing to work with those nations it claims to have helped long after the
headlines about freedom and liberation are just a memory.

The American people are partially at fault here as well; given that
before Vietnam, the longest time that America was involved in a declared war was four years, the general populace seems to think that the
military should be able to go anywhere and mop up any opposing
force quickly. This is another third-generation concept of warfare that
has been indoctrinated into the American psyche, particularly after
Desert Storm, and it is an idea whose time has passed. Future conflicts
will most likely be engagements that may last for years at a minimum,

but if the American people are not promised a quick solution, and instead told what the probable time line will be, the majority will most likely be more accepting of that situation. But this will only work if the government doesn't try to withhold information or spin the reasons for combat in the first place.

Another thing the American government can do is to let the military run its own operations. In the buildup to Operation Iraqi Freedom, Army Chief of Staff Eric Shinseki said that the coalition would need approximately 300,000 men to effectively occupy Iraq after combat operations were over, and he also called for thousands of armored vehicles to be sent as well. Civilian planners such as Secretary of Defense Donald Rumsfeld refuted or ignored his advice. More than 2,000 deaths later, the Army is still scrambling to both fight the insurgency and get enough armored Humvees for the soldiers, while officers that try to fight for the protection and safety of their men are removed from service. Although Goldwater-Nichols allows the president and his staff to decide what missions the armed forces should be sent on, the execution of those missions should be left to the commanders of the military, not civilians with little to no experience in the military. Mistakes such as the dissolving of the Iraqi Army, the shortsighted idea of L. Paul Bremer (another man who has not served one day in the military), the ongoing lack of fundamental equipment and armor for our soldiers, and having to mobilize the National Guard, civilians who are completely unsuited for overseas combat operations, can all be traced to decisions made by civilian planners, not by the men who run the military. While the president and his staff can and should decide what missions the U.S. military should embark on, it is the men and women with years and decades of experience in the military, who know what they and the soldiers under their command need to best execute the mission, who should be in charge of defining how it should be carried out. Under

Bush's administration, the military's logistics and pre-invasion planning has been revealed to be severely deficient, leading to many deaths in Iraq that may have been prevented with proper forces and equipment in place. A first-world country should not be equipping its soldiers with civilian equipment or less.

Finally, American citizens need to realize that our country is vulnerable to another terrorist attack, and allow steps to be enacted to protect ourselves. The government should work with companies at risk, such as chemical plants and energy companies, to modernize their security. U.S. law enforcement agencies must put aside their turf wars and partisanship and realize that there is a bigger problem facing this nation, and that everyone's efforts are needed to fight it effectively. Like the military, the agencies charged with defending our nation must be streamlined (why does our nation need more than a dozen separate security organizations in the first place?) networked with each other so that they can fight enemies of the state as effectively as possible. Programs like a national identity card should be given serious consideration, along with the civil liberties problems that they may entail, so that we may find a suitable compromise that will help keep our citizens secure while not trampling over their civil rights any more than we already have. Security at the ports and borders of our nation must be strengthened immediately, otherwise it is not a mater of whether there will be another terrorist attack on American soil, it will only be a matter of when and where.

World Culture

Security chiefs on both sides of the Atlantic repeatedly turned down the chance to acquire a vast intelligence database on Osama bin Laden and more than 200 leading members of his Al Qaeda terrorist network in the years leading up to the 11 September attacks, an *Observer* investigation has revealed.

They were offered thick files, with photographs and detailed biographies of many of his principal cadres, and vital information about Al Qaeda's financial interests in many parts of the globe.

On two separate occasions, they were given an opportunity to extradite or interview key bin Laden operatives who had been arrested in Africa because they appeared to be planning terrorist atrocities.

None of the offers, made regularly from the start of 1995, was taken up. One senior CIA source admitted last night: "This represents the worst single intelligence failure in this whole terrible business. It is the key to the whole thing right now. It is reasonable to say that had we had this data we may have had a better chance of preventing the attacks."[24]

As the United States looks to the future, the president and key members of his staff have flown around the world, trying to mend fences and build support for future endeavors, military or otherwise. This new posture is a far cry from his "bring 'em on" cowboy mentality displayed at the beginning of Operations Enduring Freedom and Iraqi Freedom. With coalition members pulling out of the Iraq theater as the occupation goes on with seemingly no end in sight, it seems that America, having started the war against Iraq practically by itself, will be trying to finish it that way as well, with a scattering of smaller countries still providing a few thousand troops in the rebuilding effort.

Of course, ever since the end of World War II, America has often had blinders on with regard to seeing which threats are real, and which threats are passé. In Thomas Barnett's book *The Pentagon's New Map*, which details the Pentagon's plan for world relations in the coming century, he postulates that the Cold War was effectively finished by

1973, as that was when the two superpowers had reached détente, even if neither of them had quite realized it at the time, and the collapse of the Soviet Union was a foregone conclusion:

> Why is it important to realize that the Cold War really ended in 1973 and not in 1989? Because the world we are dealing with today largely emerged between those two dates. Between 1973 and 1989, the world evolved dramatically. We just did not notice it because America was still so focused on the superpower rivalry with the Soviets. During these years, the Middle East shifted from being a strategic backwater to the main focus of U.S. military responses around the world, China began its amazing evolution from Mao Zedong's isolated society to Deng Xiaoping's emerging market, and globalization expanded beyond the Old Core of the United States, Western Europe, and Japan to include the "new globalizers": in Latin America and Developing Asia. By staying so fixated on the Soviet threat for so long, we missed a global security order long in the making. When America finally woke up from the Cold War, we found that new strategic environment so unfamiliar that we experienced brain-lock, retreating from the grand strategy of containment to a fearful reliance on "chaos" as our guiding principle.[25]

As the U.S. military had been forced to do so often in the past two centuries, now the Pentagon and the U.S. government were playing catch-up with much of the rest of the world in regard to globalization and the emergence of new nations as economic powers—or dangerous threats to peace.

As the quoted newspaper article states at the beginning of this section, America was, for whatever reason (the article goes on to state that the Clinton Administration snubbed Sudan's offer because they had classified the African nation as a terrorist state) unwilling to review the information the Sudan was offering, as was Great Britain. Perhaps so, but if that particular state was still willing to hand over dossiers on one of the premier terrorists of the last twenty years, one would think the Americans would have at least investigated the offer instead of so casually dismissing a treasure trove of information, and then reaping the whirlwind on 9/11. Could the intelligence the Sudanese were offering have led to stopping the World Trade Center attacks? Perhaps. The point is, America wanted to do things its way, and felt it wasn't subject to another culture's efforts regarding a dangerous criminal, and therefore passed up a prime opportunity to head a terrorist off before he could do very real damage.

In any future scenario, particularly in regions where the United States still doesn't have accurate intelligence (like Iran), it cannot afford to discount intelligence from other sources. Indeed, Secretary of State Condoleezza Rice traveled to Europe and the Middle East to meet with regional leaders and strengthen ties to allies. From a cultural standpoint, one wonders how she would fare in either Iran or North Korea, two countries that view women in subservient roles, and would most likely be offended by the notion of sitting down with one to discuss matters of state. One would think that the president would be personally involved in talks with either country, but to have a woman issuing demands to Iran may not be the best way to win over the government there. This is not a sexist statement, however, but a difference in cultures that makes it pertinent. Ms. Rice may be the world's best negotiator, but when faced with a cultural divide to bridge that she may not even be aware of, the possibility of her achieving anything of import in certain nations is unlikely indeed.

Nevertheless, the important thing that your nation must realize is that although it is at the forefront of leading the world, it is also still a part of the world, and must operate as such. America needs to maintain cultural relations in areas where its own intelligence resources are lacking until it has the capability to create its own networks. For example, the nation's intelligence agencies still do not have a true Arabic education program to understand the fundamental mind of the terrorist and the culture of the area in general. There is no reason not to pick the brains of civilians in those areas, to learn from the locals, so to speak. Then, once a clearer picture can be obtained, the government, or the military can begin to apply that information to whatever scenarios they wish.

Diplomacy among friendly and not-so-friendly nations will be a key component of future warfare. As the United States found out in Iraq, shouldering the burden of a war is not an easy task, even for a nation that is supposed to have the best military in the world. But military force is just one part of the future battlefield, which has already shifted to a more culturally defined role. In the future, there won't be a "field of battle," but a battle of cultures does seem very likely.

America has embarked on an ambitious mission to continue to spread its message of peace and freedom to more places around the world, but that mission will only be effective if it first takes the time to understand how that message will be heard, interpreted, and understood by the cultures it is addressing. Along the way, America must remain sensitive to not only the nations near possible trouble areas, but also to the reaction of the global community at large to its own actions. Scandals like the travesties in the prisons in Abu Ghraib and Guantánamo Bay, and even in the Unites States after 9/11, where American citizens were held without being charged with a crime and denied their legal rights, have not done anything to help the United States in its relations around the world. Indeed, the government's "do as we say, not as we do" policy toward holding and interrogating suspected terrorists is something that this nation would never put up with if Americans were being subjected to the same kinds of treatment that our government, and yes, our military, has visited on others. Yet we as a country apparently expect those people, foreigners or citizens, to accept the abuses that are heaped on them whether they are guilty or (as in many cases) innocent, and go on their way without complaint, assuming they survive the process in the first place, all as a process of protecting ourselves. When America has to stoop to the tactics shown in the images taken from Abu Ghraib, it is hard to hold ourselves up as examples for the rest of the world to follow. The idea of shipping terrorism suspects off to foreign countries with less stringent interrogation laws is equally repugnant, yet our government is condoning that practice as well. For America to truly lead the world, it must do so by example, and an excellent way to do that would be by the simple expedient of treating its captured prisoners, no matter what their nationality or suspected crimes, humanely.

The fact remains that, although the United States is still the lone superpower in the world, the status of countries and regions on the planet are constantly changing. With the advent of technology and education around the globe, combined with the steady decline of America's educational system, it is a possibility that we as a nation may eventually find ourselves on par with other countries or regional communities in the world, and may have to rely on them for intelligence and other indirect means of assistance before and during a military operation. However, if the government and various intelligence agencies work with their counterparts in other nations, even if at one time they regarded them suspiciously (as was the case with Sudan), the payoff can be much greater for everyone involved, and much worse for the terrorists that threaten every free country.

Summary

Language skills and cultural knowledge are vital combat multipliers. A single officer fluent in the local language and aware of cultural nuances can be far more effective to our military than entire squadrons of FA/22s.[26] (Ralph Peters)

As the world heads further into the twenty-first century, it is obvious that the planet is poised on the brink of massive changes. Advances in technology have already created a global community, one that will only grow larger, more diverse, and closer with each passing year.

But for all that reach and integration, there is still a surprising lack of insight about other nations that America seems to be content with, and more particularly, other cultures within those nations. If our military is to effectively fight conflicts in the future, it must continue the steps that have been initiated in understanding foreign cultures, and the role their views, customs, and lifestyles play in their villages, their regions, their nations, their races, their continents. Only then can our soldiers effectively enter an area with up-to-date knowledge of cultural awareness about both their allies and their enemies, know both what to expect from the indigenous people, and how to best work with them to achieve their shared goals.

It is highly unlikely that war will ever be abolished on this planet; somewhere, sometime, there will always be a person or group that is willing to use deadly force to achieve their goals. However, by taking the time to understand that person, group, or society, how they live and operate, and how they can be dealt with either from a platform of peace or, if necessary, a position of force, our military and nation can hope to truly exhaust all other methods before resorting to force.

Knowing the culture that a soldier or diplomat is going to be operating in is the key first step, for without it, we are left with an unthinkable and sole alternative, resorting to the outdated tactics of World War II; throwing men and equipment at the enemy until they are wiped out, and suffering unnecessary casualties in the process. This is a price that is too high to pay in our modern age, and one that can also be alleviated with proper preparation; namely, asking questions and learning about where our country plans to send its men to fight and die, so that they are as prepared as possible to accomplish their mission alongside, not against the cultures of the rest of the world.

ENDNOTES

1. *Merriam-Webster Online Dictionary.* http://www.merriam-webster.com, 8 March 2005.

2. Victor Davis Hansen, *Ripples of Battle: How Wars of the Past Still Determine How We Fight, How We Live, and How We Think* (New York: Doubleday, 2003) 21.

3. Victor Davis Hansen, *Carnage and Culture: Landmark Battles in the Rise of Western Power* (New York: Doubleday, 2001) 430.

4. George and Meredith Friedman, *The Future of War: Power, Technology, and American Dominance in the Twenty-first Century* (New York: Crown Publishers, Inc., 1996) 65.

5. Tom Clancy with Gen. Tony Zinni (ret.) and Tony Koltz, *Battle Ready* (New York: Putnam Publishing Group, 2002) 33.

6. Clancy, Zinni, and Koltz, op. cit., 36.

7. Lt. Gen. Walter Boomer, USMC, "Up Front" from *Leading the Way: How Vietnam Veterans Rebuilt the U.S.: An Oral History* by Al Santoli (New York: Ballantine Books) 214.

8. Clancy, Zinni, and Koltz, op. cit., 207.

9. Clancy, Zinni, and Koltz, op. cit., 207–8.

10. Carl von Clausewitz, *On War*, 1873

11. Clancy, Zinni, and Koltz, op. cit., 19.

12. Ibid., 20.

13. "The Joint Operational Environment—Into the Future," United States Joint Forces Command, January 2005.

14. Gen. Colin Powell, "Fixing the System" from *Leading the Way*, Santoli, 101–2.

15. Tom Clancy, Gen. Carl Stiner (ret.), and Tony Koltz, *Shadow Warriors* (New York: Putnam Publishing Group, 2002) 123.

16. Tom Clancy with Gen. Fred Franks Jr. (ret.), *Into the Storm* (New York: Putnam Publishing Group, 2002) 121.

17. Col. Thomas X. Hammes, USMC, "4th-Generation Warfare," *Armed Forces Journal*, November, 2004, 41.

18. Clancy, Zinni, and Koltz, op. cit., 423.

19. Maj. Gen. Robert Scales, U.S. Army (ret.), "Transformation," *Armed Forces Journal*, March 2005, 24–5.

20. Scales, op. cit., 26–7.

21. Transcript of presidential press conference, 13 March 2002, http://www.white house.gov

22. Matthew Brzezinski, *Fortress America* (New York: Bantam Books, 2004) xix.

23. Ibid., 8–9.

24. David Rose, "Resentful West Spurned Sudan's Key Terror Files," *The Observer*, 30 September 2001.

25. Thomas P. M. Barnett, *The Pentagon's New Map: War and Peace in the Twenty-first Century* (New York: Putnam Publishing Group, 2004) 38–9.

26. Ralph Peters, "A Grave New World: 10 Lessons from the War in Iraq," *Armed Forces Journal*, April 2005, 35.

CHAPTER 7

The Eye of God—The Finger of God

WILLIAM R. FORSTCHEN, PH.D.

Terrorist Leader Mysteriously Struck Dead Before Followers
(A.P. Report: September 11, 2018)

Terrorist mastermind Abdulla, a.k.a. the Butcher, was mysteriously slain to-day in Kafiristan while extolling a crowd of followers in front of a mosque.

Several eye witnesses declare that there seemed to be a flash from the heav-ens, Abdulla then collapsed, head bursting into flames.

The crowd quickly dispersed in terror. Abdulla, yet another in a long line who had declared himself to be the Mahdi or Revealed One had risen to promi-nence for his role in the devastating dirty-bomb attack on Hollywood three months ago. Of the "Unholy Twelve," the ringleaders of the attack, nine have thus died mysteriously, the most recent being Abdulla's brother while sitting in an outdoor bistro in Paris. The death is similar to the fate of the late presi-dent of Kafiristan, who died yesterday while sitting in a secured courtyard in-side his palace. Just hours before his death, President Zarif denied any knowledge or support of the attack on Hollywood.

The secretary of defense, when questioned today on CCN about this latest incident denied all knowledge then shrugged, saying "perhaps it is the finger of God," a term now in wide use throughout the Middle East for this rash of mysterious deaths that has paralyzed several terrorist cells. There are reports of over fifty such deaths in the last two months.

* * *

General George Patton often lamented the passing of what was supposedly an old tradition of warfare, the contest of champions to decide the outcome of battle, thus sparing the lives of thousands of soldiers, many of them most likely more than glad to have the situation thus resolved.

Since the ending of the Thirty Years War in 1648, a tradition evolved in Western European warfare that armed conflict was to be contained to uniformed soldiers in the ranks. Officers and civilian leaders were, in fact, to be exempt from any deliberate attempts at killing since the nobility on both sides, limited in numbers, believed that the role of the officer was not only to lead, but also to control his own rabble from engaging in excessive violence. Though obviously self-serving, this concept, evolving during the Age of Enlightenment was truly intended to in some degree contain the violence of war, a violence that had spun out of control during the religious wars of the sixteenth and seventeenth centuries.

It became so codified and accepted, at least by Western European combatants that in one famous encounter, after English and French troops had marched to within effective killing range, the two sides halted, officers saluted each other, with the English making the generous proposal, "Gentlemen of France, you may fire first," and then of course stepping behind their enlisted men, the peasant rabble whom officers often feared more than their supposed enemies.

Thus the dismay and official protests when, at Saratoga, an American marksman armed with a Pennsylvania long rifle took out a Hessian officer, with a deliberate shot, at over two hundred yards, an action perceived by one side at least, as not cricket and terribly unfair.

Even into World War II, at least on the western front, certain rules were observed, with officers receiving better treatment as POWs, and in the surrender of large formations, the right to retain side arms, again as a means of controlling their enlisted men, but also as a badge of honor.

What evolved as well was an absolute taboo against assassination of enemy leaders or the deliberate targeting of a leader for death. It was felt that such actions might only serve to destabilize an opponent, and there was also the clear understanding that such actions might trigger a quid pro quo.

Such rules were repeatedly codified at various conventions and conferences throughout the nineteenth and into the twentieth century.

At Waterloo, it is reported that a British gunner spotted Napoleon and approached Wellington with the suggestion that they try a shot at "old Boney." Wellington, horrified, replied "Good God, man, generals have better things to do than to be taking potshots at each other."

A raid by British commandos to kill Rommel, which went terribly wrong, resulted in the execution of the commandos as terrorists, an action accepted within the rules of war when it was clearly evident that the raid's intent was not just to disrupt the Afrika Korps headquarters but to kill Rommel as well. In the Pacific war, where the Japanese denounced the Geneva conventions, the Americans' killing of Yamamoto in a daring intercept was defined as the shooting down of a plane, which just happened to have Yamamoto inside.

This mentality survived, at least in the West in relationship to other Western opponents across the twentieth century. Even when it came to Desert Storm, this rule was still in place. By the Western rules of war, to directly target Saddam Hussein for death was deemed unacceptable, but to kill him as collateral damage, such as the bombing of a headquarters or the blowing up of a Winnebago, would be acceptable. A fine rhetorical distinction but a clear one nevertheless, even if the end result was the same for the person in question.

That all changed on 9/11.

Assassination of key leaders has almost without exception been deemed as underhanded and unacceptable by Western standards of warfare, filtering down even to generals and officers in the field. Yet in the Middle East and Far East, such logic is seen as unbalanced and even immoral.

By the Western rules of war, first there must be a formal declaration of hostilities, a formal notice that a killing match is about to begin, and in so doing providing the opportunity for the opponent to kill more of your own people. Second, and far more important though, it is soldiers who then die, sometimes in the millions, young men, and now women, who literally had nothing to do with the creation of the conflict, but who are then sent to kill others who also had nothing to do with the creation of the conflict.

The Eastern view of such rules is that it is an ultimate absurdity. The primary issue of war is to bend an opponent to one's will. If killing the leader, either one who has acted aggressively toward you, or who denies what you seek, will lead to a speedy conclusion, so much the better. There is, in such a view, no immunity in war.

That view, is again open for debate in the West in light of 9/11, the obvious intent of terrorists to decapitate our government that day and by our own changing of the rules during operations in Afghanistan and Iraq.

How might technology, but ten to fifteen years off, affect this profound shift in the contemplation of war, the sanctity of leaders, and, as well, the psy-ops opportunities available? Thus the potential and acceptability of what could be called "The Finger of God," a combination of space-based systems, computers, and microweapon technology, a concept evolving from a weapons program known as "Rods from God."

"Rods from God," is a weapons system that has been discussed for years, the concept being a bolt or arrow of tungsten or depleted ura-nium, several meters in length. It is intended primarily as a fast-reaction bunker buster or specific target hitter that can be deployed on extremely short notice, as long as the orbiting system is within range.

A launch platform, in space, might carry dozens of such rods. Upon the decision to launch, the rod would be "dropped" from its car-rier in space and accelerated up to hypersonic speeds by a booster pack that would punch it through the atmosphere and on to its target. It is strictly a kinetic energy weapon, not unlike nonexplosive armor-piercing bolts in use today in ground warfare.

Hitting at speeds in excess of 8,000 miles per hour, the bolt vapor-izes on contact, the energy thus discharged having far more destruc-tive impact than any conventional explosive, capable of taking with it a fair-size building, vehicle, and even reinforced underground struc-tures up to fifty feet deep.

The drawback to this upscale weapon concept is cost effectiveness relative to the amount of damage inflicted, also the need to have nu-merous orbiting platforms to ensure that a weapon is available at any given moment. Why spend billions of dollars to launch and maintain such a system when cruise missiles or, as recently demonstrated, a hellfire missile dropped from a drone can achieve the same results?

A scaled-down version, "The Finger of God," however, might very well be in order if accepted rules of war are changed, linking this weapons system to what I call "The Eye of God."

Remarkable advances have been made in just the last few years on computer-enhanced surveillance and individual identification. Hun-dreds of different factors for identification of an individual can be cata-loged, ranging from the usual height, weight, and eye color categories to more subtle identifiers, which shortly might include DNA sampling; social and life-habit categories, such as locations frequented, profiles and locations of close associates and friends, and on down to favorite locations for a walk or a rendezvous.

This profiling can then be placed into a receiving database that is linked to next-generation surveillance satellites and high-altitude stealth drones that can hover over target areas for days, even weeks, along with standard human intel and next-generation microdrones.

Of course, the obvious example for this need is the hunting of bin Laden, which as of this writing, is approaching four years. His general location, at times to within a few hundred square miles, has been known, and there are rumors of a number of escapes only minutes ahead of his hunters, and yet still he remains at large, and in so doing creates a role model for future terrorists and rogue leaders.

The Eye of God can end that.

A search for a particular individual can be launched and handed over to a fully remote system. A suspected area for a target is continually monitored. Next-generation computer-enhanced sweeps could literally scan a crowd of hundreds of thousands, through hovering drones zeroing in on potential suspects and then pinpointing them in real time.

Once acquired, it would be all but impossible for that individual to effectively elude tracking, as the remote database on him is uploaded with an infinite number of additional data points such as clothing, those observed around him, method of movement, and patterns of behavior. Smaller drones, birdsize, could swing down for a closer look, dropping microtrackers. These microtrackers, sophisticated microchips with some ability at propulsion for a limited distance, would attach to vehicles in use, or perhaps even the individual himself, and if successfully placed would activate a signal.

Even an individual who knows he is hunted, such as bin Laden or Saddam would eventually find it impossible to elude this Eye of God.

A prime example of this potential was Saddam in the last days of the 2003 offensive to Baghdad, when Saddam made several outdoor public appearances to boost morale. In a next-generation environment of remote sensing systems and complex databases, his presence would have been detected within minutes. Even if he then fled to a building or underground location, successful deployment of a host of micro-trackers could continue to yield information and track his every move.

Once located, the lidless eye of remote sensing would be relentlessly on target until the decision was made as to the next step, a decision that might already be preprogrammed.

Step two then would be the termination.

There has been speculation by sci-fi writers for generations about death beams from the sky that could eliminate targets, even entire cities, but for the purpose needed here, the amount of energy that would have to be generated would make the profile of the launch platform far too large. Also, lasers don't work unless the sky is clear, and a hunted target, if fearful of lasers would definitely avoid the sunny outdoors.

The Finger of God could rely upon nothing more than gravity and a small propulsion and navigation system. A ceramic fléchette is all that is necessary. The entire "package" would be the fléchette, a microguidance and tracking system and a small, detachable, directional control and boost system.

It could actually be launched from space, if the target is remote or an opponent has effective means of preventing drones from gaining their airspace (an area of research that will most likely trigger a microarms race in the twenty-first century: the development of microdrones versus measures to block or take them out.)

The cheaper, easier route would indeed be from a stealth drone hovering ten to twenty miles over the intended target. Once the target has been acquired and locked in, the Finger is dropped and free-falls toward the target. Ceramic, it would be all but undetectable. In the final seconds of free fall, the fléchette receives a final boost from a small rocket pack, just a couple of pounds of propellant would be needed. The rocket and guidance pack detaches as it approaches the last few hundred feet and veers off, self-destructing well clear of the target while the Finger races down at near supersonic speed, striking the target and penetrating his skull. An small explosive charge would disintegrate the fléchette once it is inside the head, bursting the victim's skull. Even if the target is inside a room, as long as a "tracker" has a lock on him, the package can still be delivered through a window.

The war is over.

An even more exotic approach, still perhaps a couple of generations off, would actually depend on the microtrackers. Deployed from a birdsize drone, the mosquito-size tracker would lock onto the target, land on him, and then deliver a "sting," with a potent poison, fast or slow acting. After stinging, the tracker would fall off and self-destruct, with the destruction of the targeted individual following shortly thereafter.

This actually conjures images of the "seekers" in Frank Herbert's *Dune*, miniature assassin machines that could be preprogrammed to hit but one target, and could float in the air or hang onto a wall or ceiling, and wait to strike.

Again the war is over.

A third potential, in the event of a traditional twentieth-century-type battlefield environment, is for hundreds, perhaps thousands of such fléchettes and microtrackers hitting enemy forces on the front line, or hundreds of miles to the rear, perhaps even while parading before their leader as Saddam's army did prior to 2003, or upon Taliban forces gathered in a soccer field to enjoy an afternoon.

Psy-ops has always been a crucial element of warfare, and at times, its effectiveness is not fully grasped by the West as it is in other cultures. The Mongols, upon declaration of war, often declared "the Hunt," assigning a division of their elite troops the single task of bringing back the head of the enemy ruler. In at least one famous case, advance word of this decision caused the ruler to flee in panic, a true decapitation of command before the act was even completed.

The power of combining the Eye of God and the Finger of God is potent. It is a statement on several levels. First, the obvious one that individuals responsible for terrorism will now be hunted down individually and terminated without warning.

The termination without warning is the second and perhaps far more debilitating aspect of this weapon, in many ways destroying the target before he is even dead. If known or even suspected to be in place, it cannot help but eventually create a crippling paranoia. Any appearance outside, for more than a few moments, might lead to detection. Once detected, a walk outside of even but a minute or two on that day, or six months later will result in death.

Fear becomes a constant companion. There is no longer even a certain legendary "romance" with the chase, the fox eluding the hounds to the delight of followers. This type of chase has an almost archetypical appeal, of the lone hero always outwitting his pursuers, such as Robin Hood, the frontiersman Simon Kenton and Daniel Boone eluding scores of pursuers for weeks, gangsters of the 1930s, and, yes, today with bin Laden. With the Eye of God, it will become cold, remorseless, and unbeatable. In the end, the Eye will eventually locate, and the Finger destroy.

All normal activities must cease, there is no longer a safe place anywhere on the planet to hide . . . even if the system is not operative at the moment, the mere knowledge that it "might" be out there will have the desirable impact of instilling fear, altering behavior, and creating a paranoid mind-set and lifestyle.

In its most dramatic usage, as in our earlier fictional story, the striking down of a leader before his followers, knowing that the delivery system is literally in the heavens, untouchable, would be terrifying. A silent strike, but one man dead, no collateral damage to be used for propaganda, and in each who witnesses it, the question of whether they are now marked as well.

If done at night, in the dark, with the body found at dawn, the concern will be the same for those standing around the remains . . . are we being watched . . . are we next?

Across 2,500 years of armed conflict, there have been numerous claims that a new technology will make war so frightful that peace will reign. Such claims were made for the catapult, the machine gun, airplanes, and even nuclear weapons. But perhaps there might be at least some potential with this one. If those who create war, especially terrorist war, know that the moment they act, or even before they act, that "God" is watching, waiting, and will indeed strike . . . what then?

CHAPTER 8

Weapons of the Next War

KEVIN DOCKERY

Future Small Arms

Introduction

Almost without regard to who a specific opposition is, or where a future conflict might take place, the final outcome will only be decisively reached through the use of an age-old military axiom with a new name—boots on the ground. No matter how a conflict is prosecuted, through the use of air assets, naval support, space platforms, or even political or economic means, it is the soldier who stands and holds the ground who establishes the final victory. The final domination of the combat arena will require the presence of the armed individual soldier. This is the person who the U.S. military today calls the Warfighter.

The individual soldier is the person who will have to enter and clear a building, room-by-room, door-by-door, to eliminate an enemy presence without simply leveling the structure. Even through the use of small robots and unmanned aerial vehicles, it is the individual who will have to finally confirm that the information that has been received is correct. The capture of Saddam Hussein and the elimination of his regime did not come about through the use of high technology, boats, planes, or satellites, though all of those assets contributed greatly to his final downfall and seizure. It was a small group of soldiers armed with individual weapons and hand grenades who drew the ousted despot from his spider hole and took him into custody.

The tools of the individual warrior have maintained their basic concepts over the centuries while seeing their greatest technological advancements during the last hundred years. It may be difficult to imagine just what the next hundred years may bring in the way of personal armament, but just the last fifty years have shown the most changes in the way firearms are made, how they are used by the soldier, and what they can do to the enemy.

New advances in small arms are being made that result in weapons that are lighter, stronger, and more destructive to the enemy than any that were known before. The goal of today's ordnance engineers is to develop durable weapons that are easy to use while able to fire faster, farther, and with more accuracy, than those in use today. To accomplish these goals, weapons are being designed as part of a whole system that works together in order to complete the mission successfully. The firearm itself is only going to be one part of that whole. Both on the weapon and on the operator, will be electronics that make up the balance of the system. They will allow the war-fighter to operate in the dark, in smoke, in the open, or in heavily built-up areas with much greater efficiency and in greater safety than experienced now. And the systems will be able to be combined, a squad of multiple soldiers being linked together to operate as a single coordinated element, an element that will be much stronger and more effective than just the sum of its parts.

In the age of the terrorist and the guerrilla, the individual soldier will take on an even greater importance as the final arbiter of victory. The challenge for the future is to take that individual and protect him, hide him, inform him, and effectively arm him.

Side Arms

Small arms are considered only part of the future Warfighter, the term now being used to describe the soldier as part of an overall weapons system. The immediate direct-action component of the Warfighter is his personal weapon, whichever small arm he may be assigned to complete his mission. Except perhaps for a knife, there is no weapon more personal to an individual soldier than his side arm. The weapon can be easily carried in a holster on the thigh, waist, or chest, and is always available for immediate defense without getting in the way of other duties as a shoulder arm can.

The short length and one-handed use of the average side arm gives it an advantage in close-quarter situations or combat where a shoulder weapon could be too long and cumbersome for quick use. Lastly, a side arm is a quick, immediate, personal defense that can be drawn and employed when a primary weapon has run out of ammunition or suffered a stoppage. These factors make obtaining a side arm very desirable for many soldiers who may not be issued one as a normal part of their equipment. Just because they aren't authorized one does not mean the average American troop won't go well out of his or her way to obtain one. The added weight is often accepted as the cost for the reassurance that comes with a side arm always being available.

The advantages of a side arm do not come without a price. Most are pistols that are held in one hand, often braced with the non-firing hand, when in use. Extensive and valuable training time has to be spent for the individual user to develop any real proficiency with a hand weapon. Even with laser-aiming devices and white-light illuminators, it takes considerable practice to reach any real degree of skill with a handgun.

Terminal ballistics, the "stopping" power that a handgun can put onto a target, is also limited by practical considerations. Powerful pistols, those chambered for large-caliber, heavy bullets, have a correspondingly higher recoil. This makes the weapons even more difficult to use, especially by smaller-statured troops. Learning to properly control recoil also takes increased amounts of training time for the users.

The longest-serving side arm in the U.S. military has been the M1911A1 .45 ACP automatic pistol. Adopted in 1911 and modified to the A1 configuration in 1926, the venerable ".45" has seen continuous U.S. service for seventy-four years. The heavy bullet and rugged John Browning design of the M1911A1 has proven itself in every fighting theater in the world during two World Wars, Korea, Vietnam, and countless smaller conflicts. Modifications to the M1911A1 to increase its accuracy and ease of use has resulted in the weapon still being used by limited special operations units.

In January 1985, the M1911A1 was finally officially replaced with the Beretta 92SB-F semiautomatic pistol, type classified as the Pistol, M9. The M9 is a lightweight design with an alloy frame and steel slide, chambered for the 9x19mm round, a much more internationally used round of military ammunition than the .45 ACP. The double-action trigger system of the M9, along with its increased number of safeties, makes the weapon faster and easier to use than the earlier M1911A1. In addition, the lighter recoil of the 9x19mm NATO round also decreases training time while the increased magazine capacity (fifteen rounds as compared to the M1911A1's seven rounds) is suggested to be able to make up for the lower terminal ballistics of the 9mm.

In spite of some difficulties in use, the M9 has remained the standard service pistol among all U.S. forces for the last twenty years. Some special operations units, most notably the Navy SEALs, replaced their M9 Berettas with the Sig-Sauer P-226 pistol. During testing for the new service weapon, the P-226 came in second to the Beretta, primarily in price. Other aspects of the weapons, such as magazine capacity, reliability, and construction, were generally the same. The design of the P-226, as well as other advantages in the design, especially in the locking system, made the weapon the preferred choice of the Navy SEALs in the early 1990s. Since that time, the Sig P-228, a slightly smaller version of the P-226 with a thirteen-round magazine capacity, has been adopted as the M11 pistol by the armed services for use where a more compact side arm is needed.

The terminal ballistics of the 9mm round, especially when used in suppressed handguns, was considered unsatisfactory for use by special operations units. In 1996, the Mark 23 offensive handgun was adopted for use. The frame of the Mk 23 is the first adopted into the U.S. armed services to be made of a metal-reinforced polymer material. The polymer plastic is considered tough enough for very heavy use while remaining completely corrosion-resistant. This pistol has a twelve-round magazine capacity and a double-action trigger mechanism that allows the hammer to be cocked back for accurate single-action fire, or the trigger pulled back double-action to cock the hammer back and release it. A secondary decocking lever allows the hammer to be lowered safely on even a chambered round without touching the trigger. The Mk 23 is chambered for the .45 ACP round and comes equipped with a screw-on sound suppressor. In addition, the Mk 23 was the first U.S. military handgun to come with a laser and visible light–aiming module that can be attached underneath the front of the frame, ahead of the trigger guard.

The increased caliber of the .45 projectile gives the Mk 23 effective terminal ballistics, even when fired through the suppressor. A patented recoil-reduction system mitigates the use of the heavy round of .45 ammunition, even when the pistol is loaded with higher-velocity loads, a requirement put forward by the Special Operations Command. The laser-aiming module gives both visible light to illuminate a target as well as an infrared (invisible except through night-vision goggles) or red laser target designator. This use of a laser indicator and reduced recoil increases the quick accuracy of the Mk 23, even while the operator is wearing a swimming or gas mask.

Some future developments in military-style handguns can be seen in the FN design of the Five-seveN tactical pistol. Though not yet adopted by any major military group, aspects of the Five-seveN pistol stand out. The semiautomatic weapon is made primarily of composite materials, both in the frame and the slide, resulting in a very lightweight design. The use of composites and polymers throughout the Five-seveN also reduce the chances of the weapon malfunctioning due to corrosion. The double-action-only trigger mechanism prevents there being a need for a secondary, manual safety, though the company has stated that one is available if a user so desires. Normally, only by pulling the trigger intentionally and over a long distance, can the weapon be made to fire. On the front of the frame, ahead of the trigger guard, are mounting rails formed into the frame for the securing of a laser-aiming device or illuminator.

Using the relatively small 5.7x28mm round, the Five-seveN holds twenty rounds in its polymer magazine while still weighing only 1.36 pounds when empty. The 5.7mm ammunition gives the Five-seveN pistol effective terminal ballistics while the light high-velocity bullet results in low recoil to the operator. The Five-seveN is not prone to overpenetration of a target, and the ammunition is designed to have a relatively short maximum range, minimizing the danger area of a miss. The weapon is intended to be a companion side arm for people armed with the P90 submachine gun, presently the only other weapon being chambered for the FN-proprietary 5.7x28mm ammunition.

Even with careful selection of calibers and design, pistols still remain difficult to master and a training-time problem. Increasing the hit probability of an operator using a handgun is one of the reasons for the adoption of the laser-aiming device. Another method for increasing the hit probability of a handgun is to fire multiple projectiles from a single pull of the trigger. Use of multiple-projectile ammunition, like a modern miniature shotgun shell, would have very poor terminal effects on a target. The use of full-automatic fire, such as found in the relatively rare true machine pistols, has never proven practical because of its making the weapon uncontrollable. The recoil from a single round is difficult to control in a hand weapon, the recoil from multiple rounds would cause an operator to spray fire indiscriminately, and most of that fire would be wasted into the air.

The controlled burst, a full automatic weapon mechanically limited to fire a set number of rounds for each pull of the trigger, is a practical way to increase hit probability in a hand weapon while minimizing wasted ammunition. The first handgun to fully realize this potential increase in hit probability, and lethality, was the German Heckler and Koch VP70M (*M* for *military*) pistol of the mid-1970s. The 9mm VP70M operated as a standard semiautomatic pistol, though one with a very large (eighteen-round) magazine capacity. To keep the weight down, the VP70M was one of the first weapons mass-produced with a polymer frame.

In addition to its unusual magazine capacity, polymer frame, and double-action-only trigger, the VP70M had an unusual accessory, a clip-on hollow polymer stock that could also act as a holster for the weapon. The upper front of the stock had a mechanism that allowed the VP70M to be switched over to fire full-auto in three-round bursts only. The cyclic rate of fire for the pistol on full automatic was very high, on the order of 2,200 rounds per minute. That allowed the full three rounds to be fired while the operator was still moving from the recoil of the first round. When fired with 9x19mm tracer projectiles, a clear image of a group of rounds can be caught photographically when looking over the operator's shoulder.

This group of rounds being fired quickly significantly increases the chance of a target being struck by at least one of the projectiles. The requirement of the stock being attached to the VP70M makes the pistol more of a limited submachine gun that any other weapon. The idea of a compact submachine gun being used as a side arm has since developed into the Personal Defensive Weapon, or PDW concept. With further work, the ideal military side arm of the future might well be a small automatic weapon that can be used with one hand if necessary, rather than a pistol.

Submachine Guns

Less than one hundred years old, the submachine gun was one of the first practical, one-man automatic weapons. Originally intended for use in the close-quarters combat of the trenches of World War I, the submachine gun has proven itself a compact piece of devastating firepower for the right situation. The classic definition of the submachine gun is a hand or shoulder weapon chambered for a pistol-caliber cartridge and capable of full-automatic fire. The demise of the submachine gun has been predicted several times over the decades, and those predictions have been proven wrong as the flexible weapon has reestablished its value as combat situations have changed.

The most commonly seen submachine gun in both military and police hands at present is the German-designed Heckler and Koch MP-5 series. Developed in the mid-1960s, the MP-5 is a very accurate weapon that has been adopted by special operations units all over the world. This adoption has allowed the weapon to constantly undergo upgrades as the users have made suggestions. Most commonly seen chambered in 9x19mm NATO, the MP-5 was adopted by the German military in the 1970s, resulting in its being named the Machine Pistol model 5. Flexibility in design and the addition of various accessories have resulted in their being over 120 variations of the basic MP5 to address almost any tactical need.

The basic operating system of the MP5 is a roller-locked, delayed-blowback system that gives the weapon a very good first-round accuracy. This initial accuracy, combined with the firepower allowed by the full-automatic capability of the weapon, is what has made the MP5 series so popular with the world's special operations, police, and counterterrorist organizations. One series of the MP5 is referred to as the K model, (*K* for *kurz*, German for *short*). The MP5K series is very compact, little larger than a big pistol, normally found without a stock, and in use for security and other missions where concealability is a need.

When fitted with a side-folding stock, the MPK becomes the PDW (personal defense weapon) model. An optional suppressor, which fits in a pocket that can hold a normal 30-round MP5 magazine, can be screwed onto the barrel of the MP5-PDW, helping to conceal the location of the weapon when it is fired. All of the standard MP-5 weapons can be fitted with suppressors, and there is a special series, the SD models, that come with a suppressor attached as part of the weapon.

In the MP5SD series (*SD* for *schalldämpfer*, German for *silencer*), the barrel of the MP5 is surrounded by a suppressor tube with internal parts to slow down the escape of propellant gases. In addition to the tube extending past the muzzle of the weapon, there are a series of small ports, gas escape holes, drilled around the barrel of an SD model. These ports allow the propellant gases to escape before they push the bullet past the speed of sound, eliminating a sonic crack when the weapon is fired. Though the gas-porting system lowers the terminal ballistics of the 9mm round significantly, the MP5SD series is very popular for its very quiet firing characteristics.

The standard MP5 submachine gun can be fitted with either a fixed stock, a sliding stock, or a simple cap that goes over the rear of the receiver, eliminating a stock completely. Different trigger housings can be placed on the weapon to allow semiautomatic fire only, semi and full automatic, two- or three-round controlled bursts, in addition to full automatic fire, different styles of forearms, some of which include built-in tactical lights, and a wide variety of sights, both optical and electronic. An optional Modular Rail System forearm with a removable vertical foregrip has been built for the MP5 so that the wide variety of laser designators and other accessories designed for the U.S. SOPMOD kit (see *Rifles* for a description) can be mounted on the submachine gun. The suppressor used with the MP5 PDW model can also be mounted on the standard MP5 fitted with the correct barrel.

All of these characteristics make the MP5 series a very flexible weapon for a wide variety of applications. U.S. forces have been less than pleased with the 9x9mm chambering of the MP5, as well as its overly complex roller-locking system. The development of the 10mm MP5/10 was primarily intended for the law enforcement market, as that is where the 10mm automatic pistol round has seen widespread use. This model of MP5 also has been chambered for the .40 Smith and Wesson cartridge. But these MP5/10 variations were not completely acceptable to the U.S. military.

The Heckler and Koch UMP (Universal Machine Pistol) was designed with the intent of matching the needs of the modern and future user. Chambered for the .45 ACP round, the UMP has noticeable terminal ballistics. The standard military loading for the .45 ACP, the 230-grain M1911 ball round, is subsonic when fired, even from the longer barrel of the UMP. This means there is no sonic crack heard when the round is fired through a sound suppressor, significantly reducing the sound signature of the UMP. The bulk of the parts for the UMP are made of glass-reinforced polymers, including the twenty-five- or ten-round box magazines. Military standard rails are available for the weapon, allowing it to mount the standard range of sighting and target indication devices.

The operating system of the UMP is much simplified over that of the earlier MP5, yet it can still safely fire both standard and special high-velocity loadings of the .45 ACP. A version of the UMP chambered for the 9x19mm round has also been developed.

The extent to which the MP5 has been modified and upgraded, as well as the development of the UMP, shows how much a submachine gun can be changed to meet changing requirements. The high rate of fire of a submachine gun (the cyclic rate of the MP5 is 800 rounds per minute, the UMP is 580 rounds per minute, and the small MP5K models, including the PDW, cycle at about 900 rounds per minute) means it can saturate a target area with rounds, increasing the hit probability of a moving target at close range. The submachine gun, much like the pistol, does require additional specialized training so that it can be used effectively in the proper situation. Compact models of standard assault rifles have made inroads into the tactical arena where the submachine gun has tended to rule. But a new form of submachine gun, the personal defense weapon, is providing a new market.

The MP5K-PDW has proven popular with a wide range of users due to the weapon's small size and accuracy. But the recoil of even the 9x19mm round has proven difficult to control, especially in such a compact weapon, even with it having a folding stock. New lower-impulse rounds have been developed for weapons that are intended to bridge the gap between the true submachine gun and the pistol. These new weapons are able to be carried with the same ease that a military pistol is holstered, but include the firepower of a submachine gun in a controllable package.

First among this new class of weapons is the Fabrique Nationale Herstale (FNH) P90 submachine gun. A "bullpup" design where the main action of the weapon is behind the trigger assembly, the P90 is a very compact weapon, much larger than a pistol but still smaller than a standard machine gun. Chambered for the 5.7x28mm round, the P90 has a special magazine that rotates the round 90 degrees from how it is carried in the magazine to where it can be chambered in the weapon. This ammunition rotation system allows the magazine of the P90 to lay across the top of the weapon, eliminating any protusions and giving very sleek lines to the gun. The horizontal magazine design also allows the P90 to have a fifty-round magazine capacity and still remain compact. The magazine is made from a translucent plastic so the operator can immediately see how much ammunition is left by just glancing at the top of the weapon.

The idea behind the P90 was to give operators of heavy weapons, vehicle drivers, and vehicle crewmen, a weapon they could constantly carry without it getting in the way of their normal duties. When slung diagonally across the chest, no part of the P90 extends past the shoulders of the average soldier. A driver can work the controls of a vehicle without the P90 getting in his or her way, and an armored vehicle crewman can move through a hatch without having to leave the weapon behind.

The bullpup design of the P90 gives the weapon a built-in shoulder stock while still keeping a short overall length, with a fairly long barrel length for a good muzzle velocity. Most of the body of the weapon, as well as a number of internal parts, are made of high-impact plastic, keeping the P90 light as well as corrosion-resistant. The unusual front grips of the P90 give the weapon a very solid two-handed hold and futuristic lines. The weapon is fast and easy to handle, with the necessary controls being duplicated on both sides of the P90 so that is can easily be used by right- or left-handed shooters. Ejection of empty brass is out of the bottom of the weapon, also increasing its ambidextrous use.

The recoil of the special 5.7x28mm ammunition is light, making the 900-round cyclic rate of fire of the P90 controllable. The small 5.7mm bullets have a very high muzzle velocity, on the order of 2,300 feet per second and can penetrate more than forty-eight layers of kevlar armor at up to two hundred meters. The round has proven interesting enough that a number of manufacturers will be producing it, and additional weapons chambering it are being considered in addition to the Five-seveN pistol.

Officially adopted by the German military is another example of a future personal defense weapon. This is the Heckler and Koch MP7-PDW, chambered for their 4.6x30mm round. The short length of the MP7 makes it compact enough to be carried in a holster like a normal handgun. The MP7A1-PDW has a folding front grip as well as an extending buttstock. Even with the front grip folded and the buttstock collapsed, the weapon can be fired one-handed like a handgun. Additionally, it can be shouldered and gripped with both hands and fired like a submachine gun. Accessory rails are on the outside of the receiver of the MP7A1 to allow the mounting of various laser designators and illuminators. A rail across the top of the weapon can be used to mount optical or electronic sights.

With the stock retracted and flash hider removed, the overall length of the MP7A1 is less than fifteen inches. The usual twenty-round magazine fits flush into the grip of the weapon, and an extended forty-round version is also available. The 4.6x30mm round has half the felt recoil of a standard 9x19mm round, and the MP7A1 can controllably fire these rounds at a cyclic rate of 950 rounds per minute. In spite of the small size of the 4.6x30mm round, the projectile can penetrate a 1.6mm titanium plate and twenty layers of kevlar armor out to two hundred meters. Made of carbon-fiber reinforced polymers with embedded metal parts, the MP7A1 has a weight of only 3.8 pounds, including a loaded twenty-round magazine. A wide range of ammunition types, including tracer, blanks, hollow-points, and various weights and styles of ball rounds, have been developed for the MP7A1.

Rifles

The final effectiveness of the soldier on the ground is based on his primary weapon, the most basic of these being his rifle. A modern small arm, those developed since the adoption of smokeless powder, has a service life of normally between twenty to thirty years—some more, some considerably less. Since the adoption of the bolt-action Krag-Jorgensen magazine-fed repeating rifle in 1892, the U.S. military has issued five major infantry shoulder rifles, the Krag, the M1903 Springfield, the M1 Garand, the M14, and the M16 rifle. The first four of these weapons, respectively, served as frontline weapons for eleven, thirty-four, twenty-one, and seven years. The M16 and its variations have served in the military for forty-plus years. It is still the main infantry weapon of all of the U.S. armed services. Several of these rifles saw continuous use after being replaced as the Standard A infantry arm. The versions of the M1903 Springfield, M1 Garand, and M14 rifles that had the longest service life were primarily the specialized sniper models. In that mission, the M14 is still being issued today as the M25 sniper rifle as well as in other variations.

When the M16 first became available in the early 1960s, there was a great deal of reluctance on the part of the military ordnance community to adopt the new weapon. Many of the high-ranking officers in ordnance, and elsewhere in the military, saw no need for the very futuristic-appearing weapon. The general consensus among the military leadership was for the long-range, aimed, single-fire philosophy of military firepower. In general, this is referred to as the "gravel-belly" view, that of a soldier laying prone in the gravel and picking off a target at long range, five or six hundred yards away or more, with slow, methodical marksmanship. That philosophy is conserving of ammunition and considered the traditional measure of a soldier. The idea of a standard issue, individual, full-automatic shoulder arm, directly runs against this view of a soldier. Even when the Germans developed the assault-rifle concept during the latter years of World War II, and successfully fielded such a weapon, the U.S. military was very slow, or reluctant, to take note.

By 1944, the Germans were issuing the MP 44, a selective-fire rifle capable of firing in either semiautomatic or full-automatic modes. This gave it the heavy, immediate firepower that fit in very well with the German Blitzkrieg form of warfare. It had greater lethality than the submachine gun and more volume of fire than the standard-issue bolt-action rifle. What was very notable about this weapon was the smaller round it fired rather than the standard German 8x57mm. The 8x33mm Kurz round fired by the MP 44 was shorter than the standard rifle round and launched a lighter bullet. This made the MP 44 much more controllable in full-automatic fire. The shorter maximum effective range of the 8x33mm Kurz round was not considered a drawback by the Germans, who had years of combat experience. Referred to as the Sturmgewehr (Storm or Assault rifle) the weapon did not have a great deal of impact on the U.S. forces, who did not face it in very great numbers. By the end of World War II, the U.S. military had the M2 carbine, firing a light .30

caliber round and select-fire. Troops who had the light M2 carbine enjoyed its firepower, but didn't care for the light round it used.

The Soviets, who did see a large number of the MP 44s facing them on the Eastern Front, were very much impressed. Its influence helped lead to the development and adoption of the AK-47.

No other weapon will probably ever be able to match the production numbers and distribution of the basic AK-47 design. This weapon and its derivatives will remain seen on the battlefields of the world for decades to come. With an estimated 70 million weapons produced in a number of countries, predominately the AKM-47 rifle chambered in 7.62x39mm, the AK will long be a favorite of the guerrilla and terrorist alike. The primary appeal of the weapon's design is its simplicity of use, heavy firepower for its size, and extreme ruggedness. Though not as accurate as a number of other weapons of the same type, the basic AK-47 will continue to operate in severe environments and is maintainable by native populations with little technology available to them.

For the U.S. military, the individual use of automatic fire was not considered valuable, or even desirable, on the modern battlefield. The uncontrolled use of full automatic fire would cause the troops to waste ammunition when they "sprayed" an area. In the first years of the Vietnam conflict, American troops armed with mostly semiautomatic M14 rifles (the weapon could be changed to select-fire by the addition of a part at the order of the commanding officer) faced the AK-47 for the first time in numbers and felt badly outgunned. The adoption of the select-fire M16 was pushed forward.

Introduced in large numbers in the early 1960s, the M16 rifle was built of aluminum alloy and plastics instead of the machined steel and wood of earlier small arms. To minimize weight, only the parts that would directly receive the heavy stress and pressures of firing were made of steel. Whenever possible, lightweight materials replaced traditional ones. The new construction materials and design made the M16 light and easy to carry. It was also the first effective U.S. assault rifle to reach wide issue; the classic assault rifle being a shoulder-fired weapon chambered for a mid-sized cartridge and capable of full-automatic fire.

The small, high-velocity round fired by the M16 was one of the reasons that the weapon met such resistance to its adoption by the military command. The 5.56mm projectile was two-thirds the weight of the 7.62mm projectile fired by the M14. But the high velocity of the round made it far more destructive to tissue. Troops in the field did tend to fire on full-automatic a great deal with their M16s, the technique was referred to as "reconnaissance by fire" or more generally "spray and pray." Ammunition was expended in great quantity, but troops did not tend to run out of ammunition as a result, they simply carried more of the lightweight 5.56mm rounds and aluminum magazines.

Modifications to the basic M16 resulted in the final adoption of the M16A1. There was still resistance to the adoption of such a small weapon by everyone except the troops that had to carry it. The weapon proved the combat effectiveness of the high-velocity, small-caliber concept. And the use of high technology in the form of alloy forgings and plastics established a precedent that has been followed today and will continue into the foreseeable future.

Experience with the M16A1 caused suggestions to its design to be made by several services, notably the U.S. Marine Corps. A modified version of the weapon was adopted in the early 1980s as the M16A2. In this weapon, there were a number of cosmetic and practical changes that gave the weapon a greater effective range at the cost of some terminal lethality. The full-automatic feature was dropped in favor of a trigger system that allowed only for controlled three-round bursts to be fired. The thought was again to prevent ammunition wastage and increase the hit probability of the weapon. The three-round burst was considered optimum for a rifle-caliber weapon to ensure that at least one projectile from a burst would strike a target before recoil forces drove the muzzle up and away from the line of sight.

In 1989, the U.S. Army announced the details of the prototype rifles for the Advanced Combat Rifle program. These weapons were to be tested in simulated combat conditions for an extended length of time to try and establish weapons technology that was greatly improved over that of the M16A2. The Colt ACR rifle was a basic M16 action with modifications to make it more lethal and easier to hit with. Additionally, the Austrian Steyr-Mannlicher company designed a bullpup rifle that fired a type of fléchette ammunition. The fléchette is a long, fin-stabilized "arrow" projectile that has been proven to be very destructive to tissue when it is fired at high velocities. The AAI corporation also produced a fléchette-firing rifle for the ACR program. The discrete fléchette, a single projectile fired a round of ammunition, was considered a highly desirable project goal during the 1960s in the Special Purpose Individual Weapon (SPIW) program. The light recoil of the fléchette combined with its high-velocity lethality could not be combined with an effective, economical weapon/ammunition package during the SPIW program. It didn't prove to be much more successful during the ACR tests. The fourth weapon tested was the German G11 rifle, a revolutionary new design that utilized caseless ammunition.

All of the designs were considered technology demonstrators for the ACR program, and none proved sufficiently advanced over the M16A2 to justify their further development and eventual adoption. One aspect of the Colt ACR version of the M16 that did impress the testers and users was the flat-topped receiver that could easily accept various sighting devices. This would prove valuable in a later weapon.

Another variation of the basic M16 design that has seen greater and greater use is the shortened carbine model known as the M4. The M4 has a sliding stock and a shorter barrel than the rifle. These characteristics make the weapon smaller and more maneuverable in close quarters. It also makes an already light rifle even lighter and easier to carry—something very valuable to special operations troops who have to work well behind the lines and need to carry everything they'll need for a mission on their persons. Adopted in 1994, the M4 carbine has the standard three-round burst mechanism of the M16A2. For the firepower demands required by the Special Operations Command, the M4A1 is capable of full-automatic fire. In addition, the M4A1 has the flat-topped standard mounting rail on the top of the upper receiver.

The M4A1 carbine has quickly become the standard shoulder weapon for U.S. special operations forces. The military standard mounting rail (the well-known Picatinny rail) provides an interface that secures a removable upper carrying handle with a standard iron sight (resembling that of the M16A2 rifle) that causes the weapon to resemble a standard M4 carbine. In place of the carrying handle, a wide variety of sighting systems are normally installed on the upper rail of the carbine. To extend the capabilities of the M4A1 to securely mount accessories, the Rail Interface System (RIS) was adopted.

The RIS replaces the standard handguards of the M4/M4A1 with a set of Picatinny rails that match the top of the receiver for the M4A1. Four of these flat, grooved rails cover the top, bottom, and sides of the RIS, allowing standardized mounts to be used to attach accessories to the weapon. To supply a set of these materials to the operators, the Special Operations Peculiar Modification Accessory Kit for the M4 (SOPMOD M4) was developed. The SOPMOD M4 kit includes such items as the:

ACOG Reflex sight

ACOG 4 power Day Optical scope

AN/PEQ-5 Carbine Visible Laser

AN/PVS-17A Mini Night-Vision Sight

Visible light Illuminator

Backup Iron sight

AN/PEQ Infrared painter/illuminator

Combat Sling assembly

Universal Pocketscope (AN/PVS-14) mount

Forward vertical handgrip

M203 40mm Grenade Launcher mount

M203A1 9-inch barrel assembly

40mm Grenade Launcher Leaf sight

Quick detachable muzzle sound suppressor

Additional accessories, such as a removable 12-gauge shotgun for door-breaching (the Enhanced Shotgun Module—ESM), thermal sight, and laser range finders, are added to the kit as they become available.

The success of the M4A1 and the SOPMOD kit proved the usefulness of many of the accessories and established their value Army-wide. This aided the development of the M16A4 in 1994. The A4 model of the M16 shares most of the characteristics of the M16A2, but it has the flat-topped Picatinny rail upper receiver and removable carrying handle/rear sight assembly. The M16A4 retains the three-round-burst fire capability of the M16A2 rifle, but it can accept a number of the sighting systems used with the M4/M4A1 as well as additional accessories. To fulfill a Navy requirement, the M16A3 was developed returning the full-automatic fire capability to the weapon. Limited numbers (less than 8,000) of the M16A3 have been produced, and presently offered models of the weapon include the flat-topped Picatinny rail upper receiver.

The adoption of the M16A4 has become part of what is called the Modular Weapon System, where different stocks, accessories, and upper receivers of differing barrel lengths can be added to the basic weapon's receiver as mission requirements dictate. Some of these upper receivers include the 10-inch-barreled Close Quarters Battle Receiver (CQBR). The short-barreled versions of the M16, such as the M4/M4A1 and the CQBR make the M16 a faster-to-handle weapon that takes up less room than a full-sized rifle. But, the shorter barrels (14.5 inches for the M4/M4A1) lower the velocity of the 5.56mm round significantly. The short-barreled carbine versions of the M16 and other weapons have supplanted the submachine gun in many cases, but the lower muzzle velocities of such weapons have dropped the lethality of the round to an almost unacceptable level. The basic 5.56x45mm round is presently considered limited, with little room left for any further practical improvement.

Combat experience has shown that the 5.56mm round, even in its improved versions and new weapons, has reached the upper limit of its effective range and terminal ballistics at those ranges common for some special operations missions. Operations in mountainous areas often had to be held up while heavier caliber small arms were brought forward to deal with dug-in positions. The M14, with its heavier 7.62x51mm round, has been brought back into frontline use primarily to add to the ranges where small units can effectively engage the enemy while providing a greater volume of fire than offered by a standard sniper weapon. The greater penetration of the 7.62mm projectile has also proved more effective in urban operations within towns and cities. Modifications to the M14, including rail mounting systems, shorter barrels, and collapsible stocks, have increased the useful life of the original weapon. But a replacement for the M14 battle rifle, as well as the M16 family, has been sought out for future operations.

New calibers and weapon designs are required, particularly by the special operations community, to satisfy their evolving operational requirements. Being a smaller, more specialized, military community than the larger services, special operations can streamline their adoption process and quickly get the newest weapons into the hands of their operators in the field.

For a replacement of the M4/M4A1 carbine, Special Operations Command solicited a proposal for a weapon that could be used for close-quarter battle as well as having improved long-range capabilities and penetration. The ability to use standard calibers of foreign military ammunition with minimum modification to the basic weapon would increase the value of the new weapon, making resupply easier for troops operating behind enemy lines. The new weapon that meets these criteria, among others, is the Special Operations Forces Combat Assault Rifle (SCAR). Both a light (SCAR-L) and a heavy (SCAR-H) version are planned.

The SCAR-L is coming on-line presently and has an all-metal receiver for an extended service life and increased strength. Chambered for the 5.56x45mm round, the SCAR-L is capable of being changed to use different calibers based on the original 5.56mm round by simply switching out barrels and other parts. These changes can be done on the unit level. Originally planned to be issued in 7.62x51mm, the SCAR-H will be a replacement for the M14 rifle. Intentions are for the SCAR-H to also be changed over to other calibers, such as the 7.62x39mm round used in the AK-47 family.

Army desires for a replacement of the M16 rifle family has led to the extensive development and testing of the XM8 design. The XM8 is a single-caliber design chambered for the 5.56x45mm round. Internally, the weapon is generally based on the German G36 design, already a proven weapon adopted by the German military. Utilizing a common receiver, the XM8 can be assembled into a compact, sliding stock carbine with a 9.0-inch barrel, a baseline carbine with a 12.5 inch barrel, or a 20-inch long-barreled Designated Marksman/Automatic Rifle (DMAR) version. The quickly detachable XM320 40mm grenade launcher can also be added to the baseline carbine by simply changing over the hand guard.

The large number of polymer components of the XM8 system can be easily cleaned with just water, without harming the material in any way. The parts also keep the overall weight of the weapon low, only 6.4 pounds for the prototype baseline carbine. The fiber-reinforced polymer material can be produced in different colors such as green, tan, brown, and white, for additional camouflage effects.

A particular feature of the XM8 that was taken from the G36 is the weapon's capacity to accept an advanced sighting system from the outset. The standard Integrated Sight Module (ISM) contains both a red-dot reflex sight that is very quick to use, as well as backup iron sights. The module also utilizes an infrared laser illuminator/pointer as an integral part of the system. For the DMAR version, the sight is a 4 power Advanced Magnified Optic (AMO) with a red-dot reflex and a ranging reticle etched on the lens. The AMO also includes the infrared laser capabilities of the ISM sight.

The XM8 and SCAR-L are advanced versions of the original weapon concept envisioned by Eugene Stoner in the late 1950s when he was designing the AR-15, which became the M16 rifle. That concept was for a lightweight automatic weapon that would give an individual soldier accurate, high-volume firepower far greater than that of the average weapon of the day. Fifty years later, that basic idea has not changed, and it will take an evolutionary leap in firearms technology to really grow beyond the present state of the art.

The only weapon presently available that represents a great leap forward in firearms technology is the G11 rifle, with its revolutionary caseless ammunition. The 4.73x33mm round of the G11 is made up of a square, cross-sectioned, rectangular chunk of propellant surrounding the conventional projectile and consumable primer. The propellant is a strong, hard solid made up from a modified high-explosive (HMX) to give it temperature resistance. The entire round of 4.73x33mm caseless ammunition weighs 80 grains with a 52-grain projectile. The savings in weight are obvious between the caseless round and the comparable M855 ball 5.56x45mm with its overall weight of 187 grains and a 62-grain projectile. That gives the 4.73x33mm round a 233 percent weight savings over the standard 5.56mm ball round.

The 4.73mm caseless round does not lose much in the way of efficiency against the 5.56x45mm rounds. Both ball rounds launch their projectiles at a nominal muzzle velocity of 3,000-plus feet per second. The advantages of caseless ammunition are not just in the weight of the round, but also in the relative mechanical simplicity of the action needed to fire it. There is no fired case to be extracted or ejected, eliminating those functions from the weapon cycle.

The mechanism of the G11 takes advantage of the greater simplicity of operation. The gas-operated system of the G11 is designed to slide inside the polymer casing of the weapon. When fired on normal full-automatic, the G11 operates at a cyclic rate of approximately 450 rounds per minute. Set to fire in mechanically limited three-round bursts, the G11 fires at a cyclic rate of over 2,000 rounds per minute. At that high cyclic rate, the G11 discharges the third round of a burst in 55 milliseconds. The time required for the transfer of recoil to the shoulder of the operator is 120 milliseconds. The last round of a burst has left the barrel before the firer can feel, and respond to, the recoil from the first round.

The sliding mechanism and fast cyclic rate of the G11 gives it a very high hit probability, even at combat ranges. The short (under thirty inches) weapon is almost completely sealed against mud or dirt getting inside of the receiver casing. The fifty-round magazine of the G11 lays horizontally along the top of the barrel, adding to the streamlining of the weapon. A 1-to-1 power optical sight makes up the carrying handle of the G11, aiding the overall fast handling and aiming properties of the weapon.

* * *

Science fiction is growing closer to being science fact. The weapons of the military are becoming more and more like those previously seen only on the pages of books and in popular entertainment. A combination of the technology that resulted in the G11 and the XM25 could be combined to make in reality the M41A Pulse Rifle, a 10x28mm caseless assault gun with an underbarrel repeating 30mm grenade launcher as popularized in the science fiction movie *Aliens*.

Grenade Launchers

One of the ultimate packages of firepower for the individual small arms user is the combination of a point-fire weapon (rifle/carbine) with an area fire weapon (grenade launcher). The area fire weapon would launch an explosive projectile that would spread fragmentation over a target zone. That would make such a weapon more effective for targets that cannot be easily seen, such as those behind cover, in a vehicle, or in a room, as well as those in groups. The point-target weapon would be used for directly firing on a target that could be seen.

The premium example of a successful combination weapon of this type has for years been the M16/M203, and M16-family weapon with a 40mm M203 grenade launcher mounted underneath the barrel. The tremendous influence of this weapons system is clearly shown by the concept having been duplicated around the world. A number of countries now produce their own versions of the 40mm grenade launcher, in different calibers as combination and stand-alone (dedicated) weapons.

One of the reasons for the success of the 40mm grenade launcher is the wide variety of effective ammunition that is made for it. Utilizing the high-low pressure system for ballistic stability, the 40x43mm grenade cartridge can launch a large payload while keeping the recoil manageable and the weapon weight low. A marvel of miniaturization when first introduced in the 1950s, the 40mm high-explosive grenade is both effective and accurate from about thirty meters out to a maximum range of four hundred meters. This allows the 40mm grenade launcher to cover the ground from between the maximum distance a grenade can be hand-thrown to the minimum range of most first-support weapons.

The first 40mm grenade launcher to see wide use was the M79, a short, stubby, weapon resembling a fat, sawed-off, single-barreled shotgun. The grenadier who was normally armed with an M79 also carried a side arm for personal protection and close-in fighting. To give the 40mm grenadier additional firepower, the M203 grenade launcher was developed and type-classified in 1968. With the M203 mounted underneath the barrel of an M16A1 rifle, the user could choose to fire either weapon just by switching his hand to a different trigger. When later mounted underneath the barrel of an M4/M4A1 carbine, the M203 or shorter-barreled M203A1, became one of the favorite shoulder-weapons of the special operations troops.

For all of its popularity, the M203 suffers from a number of drawbacks. The 40x43mm round is large and heavy, with a single M406 HE grenade weighing a half-pound. The adoption of the M433 High Explosive Dual Purpose (HEDP) round with its shaped-charge warhead capable of penetrating over two inches of armor while still spreading fragmentation, made the weight of the ammunition much more acceptable. But most 40mm grenade launchers are still limited to single-shot capability, and require a trained skill in range estimation for maximum effective use.

For special operations use, the Enhanced Grenade Launcher Module (EGLM) has been proposed. Suggested as an interim weapon until new technology has been proved out, the EGLM will be a lightweight 40mm grenade launcher that can be mounted underneath the barrel of a variety of host weapons, such as the M4A1 or SCAR-L. Addition of a shoulder stock will also make the EGLM usable as a compact stand-alone weapon. Improvements in design and sights will aid the EGLM in being easier to use and capable of firing a wider range of ammunition than the M203.

The adopted design for the EGLM is the Heckler and Koch AGC grenade launcher. The weapon was accepted for issues in 2005. The AGC uses a side-opening barrel system, as compared to the slide-forward action of the M203. The side-opening barrel makes the AGC easier to load with longer munitions as well as being simpler and faster to load while the operator is in the prone position. The addition of a retractable stock and sight assembly allows the AGC to be used as a stand-alone launcher for special applications. The H&K AGC is also the basis for the XM320 40mm grenade launcher suggested for the XM8 lightweight modular weapons system.

Suggested as a potential replacement altogether for the 40mm grenade launcher/rifle family is the Objective Individual Combat Weapon (OICW), given the designation XM29 Selectable Assault Battle

Rifle (SABR). The XM29 combines a semiautomatic 20mm grenade launcher with a six-round magazine with a "kinetic projectile" weapon firing the 5.56x45mm round.

Advancements in ammunition fusing, fire control, and weapon systems have made the XM29 possible, if not presently practical. Improved fragmentation of the 20mm projectile increases its effective lethality over that of a 40mm grenade. The lighter projectile can also be launched up to 1,000 meters downrange while still remaining accurate and effective.

The lethal effectiveness of the 20mm grenade centers on its advanced fuse system. Set electronically by the sight system while still in the chamber, the 20mm fuse detects and counts the rotations of the projectile as it spins through the air to the target. Once the set number of rotations has been reached, the round detonates as an airburst explosion.

Identified as the XM1018 round, the 20mm High Explosive Air Burst (HEAB) munitions for the XM29 is practical because of the development of the computerized, laser range-finding, ballistic computer sight developed as part of the XM29 system. The sight will automatically determine the range to a selected target when activated by the operator. Simple controls on the weapon allow the operator to add or subtract meters from the computed range, and this information is fed into the fuse of the chambered round. Additionally, the sight puts up a secondary ballistically calculated aiming point in the sight reticle. By placing the aiming point on the target, the gunner can accurately fire the grenade, which can be set to explode just beyond a wall or other cover to attack a hidden target.

The drawback that has prevented the XM29 SABR from being fielded is the excessive weight of the system (eighteen-plus pounds). Reductions in ammunition capacity and range from 1,000 meters to 500 meters and an increase in caliber to 25mm have not solved the difficulties in perfecting the weapon. The kinetic energy aspect of the XM29 has been spun off into the XM8 program. The grenade launcher aspect of the XM29 has been changed to a stand-alone system, the XM25.

The prototype XM25 25mm weapons were delivered to the U.S. military in the spring of 2005. The weapon has a 500-meter effective range and uses the same sight technology as the XM29. The 25mm ammunition to the XM25 has a reported 500 percent increase in hit-to-kill performance over existing 40mm systems. Given improvements in technology, the grenade launcher may return to being a part of the XM29 combination weapon concept.

* * *

One of the problems with microprocessors and computers is that the more things that are going on while a device is being operated, the more chances you have that things can go wrong. With the present flow of technology, the eventual marriage of the firearm and the electronic computer is inevitable. Electronic sights have been in use for decades, as have laser range finders. Combinations of optical sights, laser range finders, and ballistic computers have been made for sighting systems. But these devices are still limited in numbers and applications.

Computerized ammunition is already here and is being reduced in size for use in ever-smaller munitions. Eventually, smart ammunition and weapons will remove the human factors from the equation except for the final decision to pull the trigger.

Directed Energy Weapons

The popular image of a future weapon remains that of some form of directed energy device. The hand-phaser or blaster of popular entertainment and science fiction have not yet come about, but the possibilities for their existence are on the horizon. Lasers, charged particle beams, microwaves, electromagnetic launchers, and other exotic technologies all are being developed with different degrees of success. Advances in power supplies and even basic building materials need to be made before the potential for these technologies can be fully reached—though some of these devices are already reaching certain levels of success in the field.

Only having existed since about 1960, the laser (for Light Amplification by the Stimulated Emission of Radiation), is presently the most advanced of the directed energy systems. It is the high-energy lasers that grab the imagination when it comes to beam weapons, it is the low-energy laser (LEL) that has solidly established its value in the field. Besides their use in laser range-finding systems, the LEL has shown a value not foreseen by its proponents. By the mid-1980s, low-energy visible lasers had been developed that could effectively be mounted on small arms and used as aiming devices. The civilian and law enforcement markets were the first to sell such devices, which drove the development of even smaller and more rugged laser systems.

The bright, straight beam of the laser-aiming light on a weapon would place a usually red dot on a target, a dot that indicated where the projectile would strike when the weapon was fired. It was quickly realized that being targeted by such a laser dot was a very good reason for a perpetrator to quickly give up. There was not much of a question that if the laser could mark the target, a lethal projectile could quickly follow just as easily.

Both visible, such as the U.S. Military Carbine Visible Laser (CVL), or the invisible infrared AN/PEQ-2A and AN/PAQ-4C laser-aiming lights, are issued to be mounted on individual and crew-served direct-fire weapons. The visible laser produces a beam from an electronic diode system that places a distinct aim spot on a target over 600 meters away from the weapon. The infrared systems produce the same distinct aim spot, but by using an IR laser diode system, the spot can only be viewed though night-vision devices. Through the use of either night-vision goggles worn by the operator, or a night-vision device mounted directly on the weapon, the IR laser can clearly indicate a target both to the operator and any members of his element or additional observers.

In 1994, during Operation United Shield in Somalia, U.S. Marine forces utilized low-energy lasers as a spotting system. When opposing gunmen or snipers drew too close to Marines or U.N. assets, they were illuminated with the laser systems. Not a round had to be fired by the Marine marksmen as the Somali gunmen would withdraw or stand still when they saw they were marked by a laser. The psychological value of an LEL target-marking system had been established. The laser-aiming light, both visible and infrared, will remain an asset in the U.S. weapons inventory well into the future.

The antipersonnel use of the laser as a weapon of war has already become the focus of international regulation and protocols. The problems of energy transfer and supply, cooling, and other technological hurdles to lethal-level, high-energy, man-portable laser weapons have yet to be solved. "Medium" energy laser weapons, those able to have a biological effect other than death, have been developed and tested. The drawback to these laser weapons is that their primary antipersonnel effect is to cause blindness, either temporary or permanent.

Depending on a number of factors including wavelength, time of exposure, and output energy, lasers that emit a beam of less than a milliwatt are considered eye-safe (Class I). Military lasers in the 50-milliwatt-and-up range are listed as an acute direct-exposure hazard to the skin and eyes (Class IIIb). Many military range finders and target designators, especially those that are vehicle or aircraft mounted, are dangerous. But they are no more dangerous than many other battlefield hazards. Most important, they were not designed to be used as direct weapons. The United States has officially prohibited the development of antipersonnel laser weapons intended to dazzle or blind opposing forces troops.

Because of this prohibition, some U.S. laser devices were suspended from further development. The Dazer is a man-portable, shoulder-fired, rifle-like Class IV tactical laser weapon. The battery-powered system consists of a ten-pound laser rifle, a twenty-three pound electronics package, including the battery pack, and mounted with an electronic sighting system such as the Simrad KN200 or KN250. Intended for special operations use only, the Dazer can fire up to 1,000 times before reaching the end of its battery life. The near-infrared beam from the Dazer is considered to be effective (though the definition of that term is not released) at up to 1,000 meters. The Dazer system operates at a peak power load of 1,600 amps at 1,450 volts, though the specific power output remains classified. The device does not fire a continuous beam but is capable of single shot or "bursts" of up to fifty shots per minute.

The Dazer is reported to be a fielded system with the U.S. Special Operations Command since the mid-1990s. Two other pieces of laser ordnance were also developed in the 1990s and are more along the lines of laser-ammunition than weapons in and of themselves. These are the Saber 203 Laser Intruder Countermeasures System and the Perseus Optical Munition. Both of these devices use the M203 40mm grenade launcher as their primary support weapon.

The Saber 203 is reported to be an Air Force development as a "laser system that can temporarily blind or impair the vision of enemy soldiers." The laser device itself is a grenade that is chambered in a standard M203 as a round of ammunition would be. A small, electronic control box mounts underneath the grenade launcher to operate the laser diode in the munition. According to Air Force reports, the laser operates well below the maximum permissible exposure levels at its intended range of 50 to 250 meters. The maximum range of the Saber 203 is listed as 300 meters. The effect of the Saber 203 is compared to being exposed to a flashbulb at night, temporarily dazzling an opponent and impairing their ability to operate. This was one of the new laser devices successfully used by the U.S. Marines in Somalia during Operation United Shield. Further use of the device is now listed as being restricted to the Special Operations Command.

The Perseus Optical Flash laser is also a round of ammunition intended to be fired from the 40mm grenade launcher. The Perseus uses an explosive shock wave to pump a compact laser device into firing a single burst of coherent light. Once used, the expended round is simply ejected and the grenade launcher is ready for use again. No specific data is available on the output of the Perseus round, but the effect is reported to be an intense flash of white light and laser light bright enough to temporarily blind both people and sensors.

Though the United States has suspended development of such laser devices that would simply blind opposing troops, other countries have not shown the same restraint. In 1994, the Chinese government displayed the ZM-87 Portable Laser Disturber for international sale. A tripod-mounted weapon, the ZM-87 system weighs seventy-three pounds with its battery power supply. Marketed as a weapon that can be used against both soldiers and sensor systems, the power output of the ZM-87 is more than capable of causing permanent blindness in individuals. During an arms exhibition in the Philippines in March 1995, one of the system's primary functions was suggested to be the cause of eye damage in soldiers.

The limited specifications available on the ZM-87 state that the effective range for eye damage for the laser is 2,000–3,000 meters. If the eye is looking through a telescopic sight or device of 7 power magnification, that eye-damage range is increased to 5,000 meters. The ZM-87 is listed as being able to fire 15-megawatt laser pulses at either of two different frequencies. That gives the weapon a flash blinding (dazzle) range of 10,000 meters. Firing in at least one green-range laser frequency, the ZM-87 is reported to have been sold to a number of countries, and even some terrorist and political groups, before sales were said to have been halted. It is the first tactical laser to have been fielded specifically for use against human targets.

The most commonly mentioned targets for laser weapons are incoming ballistic and tactical missiles. This type of target requires a high-energy laser (HEL), and these are the weapons that have been receiving the bulk of available funding for development. Primary among these laser weapons is the airborne laser or ABL system, designated the YAL-1A by the Air Force. Mounted onboard a highly modified Boeing 747-400F cargo plane, the heart of the ABL is a chemically pumped oxygen-iodine laser (COIL).

Developed in 1977, the COIL uses turbine-pumped atomized hydrogen peroxide and potassium hydroxide along with chlorine gas to create singlet delta oxygen (SDO). The SDO gas so created is used to excite molecular iodine gas into releasing photons. The photons are collected and amplified by a pair of mirrors framing the laser cavity. The whole reaction vessel and laser cavity is held in what is called an individual laser module, six modules linked in series are presently what are being used in the development state for the ABL. Each module is the size of a panel van and weigh nearly as much as a loaded one (4,500 pounds for each module). Even though the mixing chemicals are very reactive, the by-products of a "shot" are water, heat, potassium salt, and oxygen.

The laser tube for the system runs much of the length of the huge aircraft, terminating in a nose-mounted rotating mirror. The megawatt-range COIL system is intended to be able to destroy theater ballistic missiles, such as the Scud, during the boost-phase of their launch. As soon as the missile passes through any cloud layer (usually at 10,000 feet), the tracking lasers and computers in the flying ABL aircraft lock onto and track the target. The aircraft normally will be flying at an altitude of about 40,000 feet. Once locked on and tracking, the COIL of the ABL can be fired to a range of several hundred miles. Future plans have the ABL mounting as many as twenty-six COIL modules, allowing it to defend against a host of missile launches. The present schedule for building and development has a fleet of seven Boeing 747 ABL platforms being airborne before 2010.

Another COIL system intended for battlefield use is the Airborne Tactical Laser (ATL). A self-contained system, the ATL is a roll-on/roll-off system of modules that can be mounted on any large aircraft, such as a V-22 Osprey or CH-47 Chinook helicopter. Installed in under four hours, the ATL is expected to operate at altitudes from sea level to 10,000 feet. It will have a lethal range against cruise missiles of about 20,000 meters, while leaving no exhaust from the sealed laser modules or any IR signature beyond the momentary laser beam itself.

Presently, HEL can be as small as several-meter-long tubes weighing hundreds of pounds, along with their immediate support equipment. Power supply requirements are in the 20,000-volt, 15,000-watt range and greater. Weapons of this class have already been tested and have destroyed ex-Soviet artillery rockets in flight. Mounted in something as small as a HUMV infantry vehicle with the power supply in a follow-on trailer, these laser systems make up the Mobile Tactical High Energy Laser (MTHEL). Since June 2000, advanced concept technology demonstrators of the MTHEL have shot down twenty-eight single and multiple launched rockets as well as five 152mm artillery projectiles.

The next most advanced form of directed energy weapons fall in the electromagnetic class, commonly referred to as "rail guns." So named because of the conductive (usually copper) rails that the projectile travels along, rail guns use neither a traditional barrel nor chemical propellants to drive their projectiles. Much smaller, more compact, and of a higher lethality than chemically depended weapons, the rail gun utilizes a huge pulse of electric current to magnetically drive a projectile down the rails and toward the target.

Envisioned for use as a replacement for the main gun in tanks and other armored vehicles, the state of present rail-gun technology centers around a launcher with rails of about ten feet in length and weighing several hundred pounds. The entire weapon and its power supply takes up the space of a small residential house. Using up to 4.5 million amps at 5 kilovolts per "shot," the rail gun can drive a fin-stabilized, discarding-sabot, long-rod, heavy metal penetrator at velocities of 2,000 meters per second. The penetrators drive themselves into and through heavy steel armor by simple kinetic energy, actually causing the metal to turn plastic and flow away from the penetrator. Future long tungsten rod or depleted uranium penetrators will be launched at targeted velocities of 2,500 meters per second, (over 6,800 feet per second) or greater. This compares very well to the present 1,680 meters per second (4,600 feet per second) of the 120mm M829A2 armor-piercing, fin-stabilized, discarding-sabot, tracer (APFSDS-T) round presently used in the M1A2 Abrams tank. Conceivable developments in high-temperature superconductors and power supply/generation could reduce the size of an electromagnetic rail gun to the size of a shoulder-fired anti-armor weapon of the two-meter class, much like the old M20 3.5-inch bazooka.

Much more important than just the soldiers and their weapons systems will be the targets of future conflicts. The electronic computer brains of sophisticated systems, as well as the power supplies that feed them and the communications nets that connect them, have specific weapons being developed to attack them. In the 1990s, the power grid of Baghdad, and later Bosnia, came under attack by a specialized payload carried in aircraft-delivered ordnance and cruise missiles. Instead of fragmentation and blast, the warheads of these weapons were loaded with carbon fibers. The exploding munitions sprayed the conducting and hard-to-see fibers across power grids and generating systems, shorting them out and eliminating power transmission throughout the immediate conflict arena.

The effectiveness of such attacks is still being evaluated. But the munitions intended to deliver such power-grid-attack payloads are further being reduced in size and increased in efficiency. Carbon-fiber-loaded grenades and hand-placed demolition charges are ready to be optimized and placed in troops' hands with the finalization of the requirement.

An additional electronic-equipment attack that has unquestioned effects is the nonnuclear electromagnetic pulse. Discovered during testing of nuclear weapons, the electromagnetic pulse, or EMP, generates destructive voltages in all forms of sophisticated electronic materials. Proper shielding can minimize these effects, but such protection is prohibitively expensive and heavy for many applications. Rather than being produced only by a nuclear explosion, EMP has been successfully created electronically. Diehl Munition Systems of Germany has already marketed the DS 110 High-power Radio Frequency system (suitcase version), effectively an electronic satchel charge. The wideband, electromagnetic pulse from the system can disrupt or destroy targeted telephones, PC computers, PC networks, Global Positioning

System (GPS) receivers, alarms, and surveillance equipment. Weighing twenty-eight kilograms in a suitcase measuring 500 x 410 x 200 millimeters, the self-contained battery in the DS 110 can power the system for thirty minutes continuously or for three hours in controlled bursts. With an external power supply, the device can run for twenty-four hours or more. Even sophisticated electronic fusing of projectiles can be disrupted by the DM-110. Further developments of the EMP weapon can only be expected to increase with the greater and greater dependence on electronics on the battlefield.

Appendix

An excerpt from the original text of Shock and Awe: Achieving Rapid Dominance, *by Harlan K. Ullman and James P. Wade, from whence the theory was coined.*

Shock and Awe

The basis for Rapid Dominance rests in the ability to affect the will, perception, and understanding of the adversary through imposing sufficient Shock and Awe to achieve the necessary political, strategic, and operational goals of the conflict or crisis that led to the use of force. War, of course, in the broadest sense has been characterized by Clausewitz to include substantial elements of "fog, friction, and fear." In the Clausewitz view, "shock and awe" were necessary effects arising from the application of military power and were aimed at destroying the will of an adversary to resist. Earlier and similar observations had been made by the great Chinese military writer Sun Tzu around 500 B.C.E. Sun Tzu observed that disarming an adversary before battle was joined was the most effective outcome a commander could achieve. Sun Tzu was well aware of the crucial importance of achieving Shock and Awe prior to, during, and in ending battle. He also observed that "war is deception," implying that Shock and Awe were greatly leveraged through clever, if not brilliant, employment of force.

In Rapid Dominance, the aim of affecting the adversary's will, understanding, and perception through achieving Shock and Awe is multifaceted. To identify and present these facets, we need first to examine the different aspects of and mechanisms by which Shock and Awe affect an adversary. One recalls from old photographs and movie or television screens, the comatose and glazed expressions of survivors of the great bombardments of World War I and the attendant horrors and death of trench warfare. These images and expressions of shock transcend race, culture, and history. Indeed, TV coverage of Desert Storm vividly portrayed Iraqi soldiers registering these effects of battlefield Shock and Awe.

In our excursion, we seek to determine whether and how Shock and Awe can become sufficiently intimidating and compelling factors to force or otherwise convince an adversary to accept our will in the Clausewitzian sense, such that the strategic aims and military objectives of the campaign will achieve a political end. Then, Shock and Awe are linked to the four core characteristics that define Rapid Dominance: knowledge, rapidity, brilliance, and control.

The first step in this process is to establish a hierarchy of different types, models, and examples of Shock and Awe in order to identify the principal mechanisms, aims, and aspects that differentiate each model as unique or important. At this stage, historical examples are offered. However, in subsequent stages, a task will be to identify current and future examples to show the effects of Shock and Awe. From this identification, the next step in this methodology is to develop alternative mission-capability packages consisting of a concept of operations doctrine, tactics, force structure, organizations, and systems to analyze and determine how each form or variant of Shock and Awe might best be achieved. To repeat, intimidation and compliance are the outputs we seek to obtain by the threat of use or by the actual application of our alternative force package. Then the mission capability package is examined in conditions of both MRCs and OOTW.

For discussion purposes, nine examples representing differing historical types, variants, and characteristics of Shock and Awe have been derived. These examples are not exclusive categories and overlap exists between and among them. The first example is "Overwhelming Force," the doctrine and concept shaping today's American force structure. The aims of this doctrine are to apply massive or overwhelming force as quickly as possible on an adversary in order to disarm, incapacitate, or render the enemy militarily impotent, with as few casualties and losses to ourselves and to noncombatants as possible. The superiority of American forces, technically and operationally, is crucial to successful application.

There are several major criticisms and potential weaknesses of this approach. The first is its obvious reliance on large numbers of highly capable (and expensive) platforms such as the M-1 tank, F-14, -15, and -18 aircraft and CVN/DDG-51/SSN-688 ships designed principally to be used jointly or individually to destroy and attrite other forces and support capability. In other words, this example has principally been derived from force-on-force attrition relationships, even though command and control, logistical, and supporting forces cannot be disaggregated from this doctrine.

The other major shortcoming of a force-on-force or a platform-on-platform attrition basis is that with declining numbers of worthy and well-enough equipped adversaries against whom to apply this doctrine, justifying it to a questioning Congress and public will prove more difficult. While it is clear that "system of systems" and other alternative military concepts are under consideration, for the time being, these have not replaced the current platform and force-on-force attrition orientation. It should also be noted, there will be no doctrinal alternatives unless ample effort is made to provide a comprehensive and detailed examination of possible alternatives.

Second, this approach is based on ultimately projecting large amounts of force. This requires significant logistical lift and the time to transport the necessary forces. Rapidity may not always follow, especially when it is necessary to deliver large quantities of decisive force to remote or distant regions. Third, the costs of maintaining a sufficiently decisive force may outstrip the money provided to pay for the numbers of highly capable forces needed. Finally, at a time when the commercial marketplace is increasing the performance of its products while also lowering price and cycle time to field newer generations systems, the opposite trends are still endemic in the defense sector. This will compound the tension between quality and quantity already cited. None of these shortcomings is necessarily fatal. However, none should be dismissed without fuller understanding.

Certainly, Rapid Dominance seeks to achieve certain objectives that are similar to those of current doctrine. A major distinction is that Rapid Dominance envisages a wider application of force across a broader spectrum of leverage points to impose Shock and Awe. This breadth should lead to a more comprehensive and integrated interaction among all the specific components and units that produce aggregate military capability and must include training and education, as well as new ways to exploit our technical and industrial capacity. It is possible that in these resources, technical, and commercial industrial areas that Rapid Dominance may provide particular utility that otherwise may constrain the effectiveness of Decisive Force.

The second example is "Hiroshima and Nagasaki." The intent here was to impose a regime of Shock and Awe through delivery of instant, nearly incomprehensible levels of massive destruction directed at influencing society writ large, meaning its leadership and public, rather than targeting directly against military or strategic objectives even with relatively few numbers or systems. The employment of this capability against society and its values, called "counter-value" in the nuclear deterrent jargon, is massively destructive strikes directly at the public will of the adversary to resist and, ideally or theoretically, would instantly or quickly incapacitate that will over the space of a few hours or days.

The major flaws and shortcomings are severalfold and rest in determining whether this magnitude and speed of destruction can actually be achieved using nonnuclear systems to render an adversary impotent; to destroy quickly the will to resist within acceptable and probably unachievably low levels of societal destruction; and whether a political decision would be taken in any case to use this type of capability, given the magnitude of the consequences and the risk of failure.

It can be argued that in the bombing campaign of Desert Storm, similar objectives were envisioned. The differences between this example and Desert Storm are through the totality of a society that would be affected by a massive and indiscriminate regime of destruction and the speed of imposing those strikes as occurred to those Japanese cities. This example of shock, awe, and intimidation rests on the proposition that such effects must occur in very short periods of time.

The next example is "Massive Bombardment." This category of Shock and Awe applies massive and, perhaps today, relatively precise destructive power largely against military targets and related sectors over time. It is unlikely to produce an immediate effect on the will of the adversary to resist. In a sense, this is an endurance contest in which the enemy is finally broken through exhaustion. However, it is the cumulative effect of this application of destruction power that will ultimately impose sufficient Shock and Awe, as well as perhaps destroy the physical means to resist, that an adversary will be forced to accept whatever terms may be imposed. As noted, trench warfare of World War I, the strategic bombing campaign in Europe of World War II (which was not effective in this regard), and related B-52 raids in Vietnam and especially over the New Year period of 1972–73, illustrate the application of massive bombardment.

Massive Bombardment, directed at largely military-strategic targets, is indeed an aspect of applying "Overwhelming Force," even though political constraints make this example most unlikely to be repeated in the future. There is also the option of applying massive destruction against purely civilian or "counter-value" targets such as the firebombing of Tokyo in World War II when unconditionality marks the terms of surrender. It is the cumulative impact of destruction on the endurance and capacity of the adversary that ultimately affects the will to resist that is the central foundation of this example.

The shortcoming with this example is clear and rests in the question of political feasibility and acceptability, and what circumstances would be necessary to dictate and permit use of massive bombardment. Outright invasion and aggression such as Iraq's attack against Kuwait could clearly qualify as reasons to justify using this level of Shock and Awe. However, as with Overwhelming Force, this response is not time sensitive and would require massive application of force for some duration as well as political support.

Fourth is the "Blitzkreig" example. In real Blitzkreig, Shock and Awe are not achieved through the massive application of firepower across a broad front nor through the delivery of massive levels of force. Instead, the intent is to apply precise, surgical amounts of tightly focused force to achieve maximum leverage but with total economies of scale. The German Wehrmacht's Blitzkreig was not a massive attack across a very broad front, although the opponent may have been deceived into believing that. Instead, the enemy's line was probed in multiple locations and, wherever it could be most easily penetrated, attack was concentrated in a narrow salient. The image is that of the shaped charge, penetrating through a relatively tiny hole in a tank's armor and then exploding outwardly to achieve a maximum cone of damage against the unarmored or less protected innards.

To the degree that this example of achieving Shock and Awe is directed against military targets, it requires skill, if not brilliance, in execution, or nearly total incompetence in the adversary. The adversary, finding front lines broken and the rear vulnerable, panics, surrenders, or both. Hitler's campaign in France and Holland and the seizure of the Dutch forts and the occupation of Crete in 1940 are obvious illustrations. The use of special operations forces in significant numbers is an adjunct to imposing this level of Shock and Awe.

Desert Storm could have been a classic Blitzkreig maneuver if the attack were mounted without the long preparatory bombardment and was concentrated in a single sector—either the "left hook" or the Marine attack "up the middle," and with total surprise. The major differences between the operation in Kuwait and Germany's capture of France in 1940 were that the allies in Saudi Arabia had complete military and technical superiority unlike the Germans and that, once under attack, Iraq's front line collapsed virtually everywhere, giving the coalition license to pick and choose the points for penetration and then dominate the battle with fire and maneuver. The lesson for future adversaries about the Blitzkreig example and the United States is that they will face in us an opponent able to employ technically superior forces with brilliance, speed, and vast leverage in achieving Shock and Awe through the precise application of force.

It must also be noted that there are certainly situations such as guerrilla war where this or most means of employing force to obtain Shock and Awe may simply prove inapplicable. For example, the German Blitzkreig would have been performed with the greatest difficulty in the Vietnam War, where enemy forces had relatively few lines to be penetrated or selectively savaged by this type of warfare.

The shortcomings of Blitzkrieg ironically rest in its strengths. Can brilliance and superiority be maintained? Is there a flexible enough infrastructure to ensure training to that standard, and can the supporting industrial base continue to produce at acceptable costs the systems to maintain this operational and technical superiority? Rapid Dominance requires a positive answer to these questions, at least theoretically.

The fifth example is named after the Chinese philosopher-warrior, Sun Tzu. The "Sun Tzu" example is based on selective, instant decapitation of military or societal targets to achieve Shock and Awe. This discrete or precise nature of applying force differentiates this from Hiroshima and Massive Destruction examples. Sun Tzu was brought before Ho Lu, the King of Wu, who had read all of Sun Tzu's thirteen chapters on war and proposed a test of Sun's military skills. Ho asked if the rules applied to women. When the answer was yes, the king challenged Sun Tzu to turn the royal concubines into a marching troop. The concubines merely laughed at Sun Tzu until he had the head cut off the head concubine. The ladies still could not bring themselves to take the master's orders seriously. So, Sun Tzu had the head cut off a second concubine. From that point on, so the story goes, the ladies learned to march with the precision of a drill team.

The objectives of this example are to achieve Shock and Awe and hence compliance or capitulation through very selective, utterly brutal and ruthless, and rapid application of force to intimidate. The fundamental values or lives are the principal targets, and the aim is to convince the majority that resistance is futile by targeting and harming the few.

Both society and the military are the targets. In a sense, Sun Tzu attempts to achieve Hiroshima levels of Shock and Awe but through far more selective and informed targeting. Decapitation is merely one instrument. This model can easily fall outside the cultural heritage and values of the United States for it to be useful without major refinement. Shutting down an adversary's ability to "see" or to communicate is another variant but without many historical examples to show useful wartime applications.

A subset of the Sun Tzu example is the view that war is deception. In this subset, the attempt is to deceive the enemy into what we wish the enemy to perceive and thereby trick, cajole, induce, or force the adversary. The thrust or target is the perception, understanding, and knowledge of the adversary. In some ways, the ancient Trojan Horse is an early example of deception. However, as we will see, the deception model may have new foundations in the technological innovations that are occurring and in our ability to control the environment.

The shortcomings with Sun Tzu are similar to those of the Massive Destruction and the Blitzkreig examples. It is questionable that a decision to employ American force this ruthlessly in a quasi- or real assassination will ever be made by the United States. Further, the standard to maintain the ability to perform these missions is high and dependent on both resources and on supporting intelligence, especially human intelligence—not an American strong point.

Britain's Special Air Service provides the SAS example and is distinct from the Blitzkreig or Sun Tzu categories because it focuses on depriving an adversary of its senses in order to impose Shock and Awe. The image here is the hostage rescue team employing stun grenades to incapacitate an adversary, but on a far larger scale. The stun grenade produces blinding light and deafening noise. The result shocks and confuses the adversary and makes him senseless. The aim in this example of achieving Shock and Awe is to produce so much light and sound or the converse, to deprive the adversary of all senses, and therefore to disable and to disarm. Without senses, the adversary becomes impotent and entirely vulnerable.

A huge "battlefield" stun grenade that encompasses large areas is a dramatic if unachievable illustration. Perhaps a high-altitude nuclear detonation that blacks out virtually all electronic and electrical equipment better describes the intended effect, regardless of likelihood of use. Depriving the enemy, in specific areas, of the ability to communicate, observe, and to interact is a more reasonable and perhaps more achievable variant. This deprival of senses, including all electronics and the substitution of false signals or data to create this feeling of impotence, is another variant. Above all, Shock and Awe are imposed instantly, and the mechanism or target is deprivation of the senses.

The shortcomings of the SAS approach mirror in part shortcomings of other approaches. Technological solutions are crucial but may not be conceivable outside the electromagnetic pulse (EMP) effects of nuclear weapons. Intelligence is clearly vital. Without precise knowledge of who and what are to be stunned, this example will not work.

The sixth example of applying Shock and Awe is the "Haitian" example (or to the purist, the Potemkin Village example). It is based on imposing Shock and Awe through a show of force and indeed through deception, misinformation, and disinformation, and is different from the U.S. intervention in Haiti in 1995. In the early 1800s, native Haitians were seeking to extricate their country from French control. The Haitian leaders staged a martial parade for the visiting French military contingent and marched, reportedly, a handful of battalions repeatedly in review. The French were deceived into believing that the native forces numbered in the tens of thousands and concluded that French military action was futile and that its forces would be overwhelmed. As a result, the Haitians were able to achieve their freedom without firing a shot.

To be sure, there are points of similarity between the Haitian example and the others. Deception, disinformation, and guile are more crucial in this regime. However, the target or focus is the will and perception of the intended target. Perhaps the Sun Tzu category comes closest to this one, except that while Sun Tzu is selective in applying force, it is clear that imposing actual pain and shock are essential ingredients, and deception, disinformation, and guile are secondary. Demonstrative uses of force are also important. The issue is how to determine what demonstrations will affect the perceptions of the intended target in line with the overall political aims.

The weakness of this form of Shock and Awe is its major dependency on intelligence. One must be certain that the will and perceptions of the adversary can be manipulated. The classic misfire is the adversary who is not impressed and, instead, is further provoked to action by the unintended actions of the aggressor. Saddam Hussein and the Iraqis' invasion of Kuwait demonstrate when this Potemkin Village model can backfire. Saddam simply let his bluff be called.

The next example is that of "The Roman Legions." Achieving Shock and Awe rests in the ability to deter and overpower an adversary through the adversary's perception and fear of his vulnerability and our own invincibility, even though applying ultimate retribution could take a considerable period of time. The target set encompasses both military and societal values. In occupying a vast empire stretching from the Atlantic to the Red Sea, Rome could deploy a relatively small number of forces to secure each of these territories. In the first place, Roman forces were far superior to native forces individually and collectively. In the second place, if an untoward act occurred, the perpetrator could rest assured that Roman vengeance ultimately would take place. This was similar to British "Gunboat Diplomacy" of the nineteenth century when the British fleet would return to the scene of any crime against the crown and extract its retribution through the wholesale destruction of offending villages.

There were several vital factors in Rome's ability to achieve Shock and Awe. The invincibility of its legions, or the perception of that prowess, and the inevitability of retribution were among the most significant factors. In other words, reprisals and the use of force to exact a severe punishment, as well as the certainty that this sword of Damocles would descend, were essential ingredients. The distinction between this category and the others is the ex post facto nature of achieving Shock and Awe. In the other categories, there is the need for seizing the initiative and applying contemporaneous force to achieve Shock and Awe. With the Roman example, the Shock and Awe have already been achieved. It is the breakdown of this regime or the rise of new and as yet unbowed adversaries that leads to the reactive use of force.

The major shortcoming is the assumption of the inevitability of reprisals and the capacity to take punitive action. That is not and may not always be the case with the United States, although we can attempt to make others believe it will be. The takeover of the U.S. Embassy in Tehran by dissident "students" in 1979 and American impotence in the aftermath are suggestive of the shortcoming. That aside, the example or perception of the invincibility of American military power is not a bad one to embellish.

The next category for achieving Shock and Awe is termed the "Decay and Default" model and is based on the imposition of societal breakdown over a lengthy period but without the application of massive destruction. This example is obviously not rapid but cumulative. In this example, both military and societal values are targets. Selective and focused force is applied. It is the long-term corrosive effects of the continuing breakdown in the system and society that ultimately compels an adversary to surrender or to accept terms. Shock and Awe are therefore not immediate either in application or in producing the end result. Economic embargoes, long-term policies that harass and aggravate the adversary, and other types of punitive actions that do not threaten the entire society but apply pressure as in the Chinese water torture, a drop at a time, are the mechanisms. Finally, the preoccupation with the decay and disruption of society produces a variant of Shock and Awe in the form of frustration collapsing the will to resist.

The significant weakness of this approach is time duration. In many cases, the time required to impose such a regime of Shock and Awe is unacceptably long or simply cannot be achieved by conventional or politically acceptable means.

The final example is that of "The Royal Canadian Mounted Police," whose unofficial motto was "never send a man where you can send a bullet." The distinction between this example and the others is that this example is even more selective than Sun Tzu and implies that standoff capabilities as opposed to forces in place can achieve the required objectives. There should not be too fine a point, however, in belaboring differences with the other examples in this regard over standoff. A stealthy aircraft, bombing unimpeded, is not distinct from a cruise missile fired at 1,000 miles, regarding the effect of ordnance on target.

A few observations about these examples offer insights on which to test and evaluate means of applying Rapid Dominance. It is clear that the targets in each category include military, civilian, industrial, infrastructure, and societal components of a country or group. In certain cases, time is the crucial consideration in imposing Shock and Awe, and in most of the examples, emphasis is on a rapid or sudden imposition of Shock and Awe. However, in several examples, the effects of Shock and Awe must be and are cumulative. They are either achieved over time or achieved through earlier conditioning and experiences. Not all of these categories are dependent on technology or on new technological breakthroughs. What is relatively new or different is the extent to which brilliance and competence in using force, in understanding where an adversary's weak points lie, and in executing military operations with deftness, are vital. While this recognition is not new, emphasis is crucial on exploiting brilliance and therefore on the presumption that brilliance may be taught or institutionalized and is not a function only of gifted individuals.

There is also a key distinction between selective or precise and massive application of force. Technology, in the form of "zero CEP" weapons, may provide the seemingly contradictory capability of systems that are both precise and have the net consequence of imposing massive disruption, destruction, or damage. This damage goes beyond the loss of power grids and other easily identifiable industrial targeting sets. Loss of all communications can have a massively destructive impact even though physical destruction can be relatively limited.

In some of the examples, the objective is to apply brutal levels of power and force to achieve Shock and Awe. In the attempt to keep war "immaculate," at least in limiting collateral damage, one point should not be forgotten. Above all, war is a nasty business or, as Sherman put it, "war is hell." While there are surely humanitarian considerations that cannot or should not be ignored, the ability to Shock and Awe ultimately rests in the ability to frighten, scare, intimidate, and disarm. The Clausewitzian dictum concerning the violent nature of war is dismissed only at our peril.

For a policy maker in the White House or Pentagon and the concerned member of Congress with responsibility for providing for the common defense, what lessons emerge from these examples and hierarchies? First, there are always broader sets of operational concepts and constructs available for achieving political objectives than may be realized. Not all of these alternatives are necessarily better or feasible.

However, the examples suggest that further intellectual and conceptual effort is a worthwhile investment in dealing with national security options in the future.

Second, time becomes an opportunity as well as a constraint in generating new thinking. In many past cases, time was generally viewed as an adversary. We had to race against several clocks to arrive "firstest with the mostest," to prevent an enemy from advancing, or to ensure we had ample forces on station should they be required. Rapid Dominance would alleviate many of these constraints, as we would have the capacity to deploy effective forces far more quickly. Therefore, in this case, we can view time as an ally. The political issue rests in longstanding arguments to limit the president from having the capacity to deploy or use force quickly, thereby involving the nation without conferring with full consultation with Congress. While this is an obvious point, it should not eliminate alternative types of force packages, derived from Rapid Dominance, from full consideration and experimentation. Indeed, our experience with nuclear weapons and emergency release procedures shows that delegating instant presidential authority can be handled responsibly.

Responding to the precise, rapid, and massive criteria of several models, it is clear that one capability not presently in the arsenal is a "zero-CEP" weapon, meaning one that is precise and timely. It is also clear that, while deception, guile, and brilliance are important attributes in war, there are no guarantees that they can be institutionalized in any military force.

Another capability that Rapid Dominance would stress relates to the Sun Tzu example. Suppose there are "EMP-like" or High Powered Microwave (HPM) systems that can be fielded and provide broad ability to incapacitate even a relatively primitive society. In using these weapons, the nerve centers of that society would be attacked rather than using this illustrative system to achieve hard-target kills because there were few hard targets. To be sure, HPM and EMP-like systems have been and are being carefully researched.

Finally, to return to the idea that deception, disinformation, and misinformation are crucial aspects of waging war, Rapid Dominance would seek to achieve several further capabilities. By using complete signature management, larger formations could be made to look like smaller and smaller formations made to seem larger. At sea, carrier battle groups could be disguised, and smaller warships could be made to appear as large formations. This signature management would apply across the entire spectrum of the senses and not just radar or electronic ranges. Indeed, gaining the ability to regulate what information and intelligence are both available and not available to the adversary is a key aim. This is more than denial or deception. It is control in the fullest sense of the word.

The next step is to match the four significant characteristics that define Rapid Dominance—knowledge, rapidity, brilliance, and control—with Shock and Awe against achievable military objectives in order to derive suitable strategies and doctrines, configure forces and force packages accordingly, and determine those integrated systems and innovative uses of technologies and capabilities that will provide the necessary means to achieve these objectives in conditions that include both the MRC and OOTW.

Future Directions

At this stage, Rapid Dominance is an intellectual construct based on these key points. First, Rapid Dominance has evolved from the collective professional, policy, and operational experience of the study group covering the last four decades. This experience ran from Vietnam to

Desert Storm, and from serving with operational units in the field to being part of the decision-making process in the Oval Office in Washington, D.C. It also included immersion in technology and systems from thermonuclear weapons to advanced weapons software.

Second, Rapid Dominance seeks to exploit the unique juncture of strategy, technology, and innovation created by the end of the Cold War and to establish an alternative foundation for military doctrine and force structure.

Third, Rapid Dominance draws on the strategic uses of force as envisaged by Sun Tzu and Clausewitz to overpower or affect the will, perception, and understanding of the adversary for strategic aims and military objectives. But, in Rapid Dominance, the principal mechanism for affecting the adversary's will is through the imposition of a regime of Shock and Awe sufficient to achieve the aims of policy. It is this relationship with and reliance on Shock and Awe that differentiates Rapid Dominance from attrition, maneuver, and other military doctrines, including overwhelming force.

Shock and Awe impact on psychological, perceptual, and physical levels. At one level, destroying an adversary's military force, leaving the enemy impotent and vulnerable, may provide the necessary Shock and Awe. At another level, the certainty of this outcome may cause an adversary to accept terms well short of conflict. In the great middle ground, the appropriate balance of Shock and Awe must cause the perception and anticipation of certain defeat and the threat and fear of action that may shut down all or part of the adversary's society or render its ability to fight, useless, short of complete physical destruction.

Finally, in order to impose enough Shock and Awe to affect an adversary's will, four core characteristics of a Rapid Dominance–configured force were defined. First, complete knowledge and understanding of self, of the adversary, and of the environment are essential. This knowledge and understanding exceed the expectations of dominant battle-field awareness and DBA becomes a subset of Rapid Dominance.

Rather like the wise investor and not the speculator who is only familiar with a particular company and not the stock market in general, the Rapid Dominance force must have complete knowledge and understanding of many likely adversaries and regions. This requirement for knowledge and understanding will place a huge, new burden on the military forces and necessitate fundamental changes in policy, organization, training, education, structure, and equipage.

Second is rapidity. Rapidity combines speed, timeliness, agility, and the ability to sustain control after the initial shock. Rapidity enables us to act as quickly as needed and always more quickly than the adversary can react or take counteractions. Rapidity is also an antidote to surprise. If we cannot anticipate surprise, or are surprised, rapidity provides a correcting capacity to neutralize the effects of that surprise.

Third, and most provocatively, is setting the standard of operations and execution in terms of brilliance. The consequences and implications of setting brilliance as the standard and achieving it are profound. Reconfiguration of command authority and organization, possibly to decentralization down to individual troops, must follow. Allowing and encouraging an operational doctrine of the "first to respond" will set the tempo, provided that effective deconfliction of friendly-on-friendly engagements has been assured.

This, of course, means that complete revision of doctrine, training, and organization will be required. The matter is not just "fighting smarter." It is learning to fight at even higher standards of skill and competence.

Fourth is control of the environment. Control is defined in the broadest sense: physical control of the land, air, sea, and space, and control of the "ether" in which information is passed and received. This requires signature management throughout the full conflict spectrum—deception, disinformation, verification, information control, and target management—all with rapidity in both physical and psychological impact. By depriving an adversary of the physical use of time, space, and the ether, we play on the adversary's will and offer the prospect of certain destruction should resistance follow.

The next step in this process must be specifically defining this Rapid Dominance force in terms of force structure, capabilities, doctrine, organization, and order of battle. We have begun this effort and are focusing on a joint task force sized somewhere between a reinforced division and a full corps (i.e., a strength of 75,000–200,000). We also have the aim of being able to deploy this force within five to ten days of the order to move and, of course, will be able to send smaller force packages on a nearly instantaneous basis. We appreciate the mobility and logistical implications of this requirement.

Once we design this "paper" force and equip it with "paper" systems, we must evaluate it against five basic questions and tests.

The first test of this Rapid Dominance force will be against the MRC. The comparison, in the broadest sense, must be with the programmed force and whatever emerges from the Quadrennial Defense Review of 1997. We will need to examine closely how and where and why Rapid Dominance and Shock and Awe work, and where they do not. At the very least, we expect that this will help strengthen the current force and improve current capabilities. Of course, it is our hope that this test will validate Rapid Dominance as a legitimate doctrine.

Second, the Rapid Dominance force must be tested across the entire spectrum of OOTW. These are the most difficult tests because, in some of them, no force may be suitable and no force may work.

Third, the test of determining the political consequences of Rapid Dominance must be conducted. On one hand, if this force capability can be achieved and Shock and Awe administered to affect an adversary's will, can a form of political deterrence be created? In the most approximate sense, and we emphasize approximate, the analogy with nuclear deterrence might be drawn. An adversary may be persuaded or deterred from taking action in the first instance. On the other hand, this capacity may be seen as politically unusable, and allies and others within the United States may not be fully trusting of the possessor always to employ this force responsibly.

Fourth is the test of the implications of Rapid Dominance for alliances and for waging coalition warfare. Our allies are already concerned that the United States is leaving them far behind in military technology and capability. If we possess this force and our allies or partners do not, how do we fight together? Our view is that this can be worked out through technology sharing and perhaps new divisions of labor and mission specialization. However, these are important points to be considered.

Finally, what does all this mean for resource investments in defense?

It is also likely that because Rapid Dominance will cause profound consequences, the iron grip of the political bureaucracy will make a fair examination difficult. It is no accident that other attempts at change, especially those that ask for or are tainted with reform, have had a short life span. It is interesting to note in this regard that the President's Commission on Intelligence and its fine report that recommended changes and refinements to the U.S. intelligence community, despite a very positive initial reception, led to only a few meaningful actions.

This discussion leads to two final points. We are all too well aware that any strategy and force structure will have vulnerabilities and potential weaknesses. The experiences that this study group collectively had in Vietnam makes this concern very strongly held. We observe that in the private sector, the vulnerability of information systems is real and is being exploited. A former director of the FBI has told us that in New York, for example, the number-one recruiting target for organized crime is the teenage computer whiz. We think that this "hacking," writ large in the private sector, must be assumed as part of the defense problem. Hence, sensitivity to vulnerabilities must be even greater, perhaps ironically, than it was during the Cold War, because exploitation can come from many more sources in the future.

Second, wags may criticize Rapid Dominance as attempting to create a "Mission Impossible Force." To be sure, we emphasize and demand brilliance as the operational goal. However, we also know that the military today is seen as a leading example of the best American society has to offer. We wish to build on this reality. We note the experience and the performance, albeit under highly unusual circumstances, of Desert Storm. We see no reason why that level of performance cannot be made a permanent part of the fabric of the American military.

Because we have entered a period of transition in which we enjoy a dominant military position and a greatly reduced window of vulnerability, this is the right time for experimentation and demonstration. Rapid Dominance is still a concept and a work in progress, not a final road map or blueprint. But the concept does warrant, in our view, a commitment to explore and an opportunity that could lead to dramatically better capabilities.

We believe that through Rapid Dominance and the commitment to examine the entire range of defense across all components and aspects, a revolution is possible. If Rapid Dominance can be harnessed in an affordable and efficient way and an operational capability fielded to impose sufficient Shock and Awe to affect an adversary's will, then this will be the real revolution in military affairs. We ask those who are intrigued by this prospect to join us.

About the Authors

Eric Haney, author of *Inside Delta Force* is a founding member of Delta Force, and an expert commentator concerning Special Forces operations as seen on CNN, FoxNews, and MSNBC.

William Terdoslavich is a contributor to *History in Dispute* and author of *The Jack Ryan Agenda—Politics and Policy in the Novels of Tom Clancy: an Unauthorized Analysis.*

James Campbell is a career army officer, and has served in infantry assignments around the world. He is also a lecturer in History at the University of Maine. His research specialties are British and U.S. military history, the British Empire, and the history of sport.

Paul A. Thomsen is a contributor to *History in Dispute*, *American History* and *Military History* magazines as well as *The Journal of Military Intelligence*. He is also the author of *Rebel Chief—The Motley Life of William Holland Thomas.*

Eugene Sullivan is a graduate of West Point and a Vietnam veteran. He has served as an Army Ranger instructor, a White House lawyer for President Nixon, and the General Counsel of the U.S. Air Force and the supersecret spy agency NRO. Now on senior status with the U.S. Court of Appeals for the Armed Forces, Judge Sullivan also heads a judicial consulting firm that includes three former heads of the FBI who are also former judges (William Webster, William Sessions, and Louis Freeh).

ABOUT THE AUTHORS

John Helfers is the author of the *Alpha Bravo Delta Guide to the U.S. Navy* as well as uncredited work on numerous military books. His short fiction has also appeared in the *First to Fight* military technothriller anthology series.

Prof. William Forstchen is the author of such works of nonfiction as *Honor Untarnished, Hot Shots—America's First Jet Aces*, novels such as *We Look Like Men of War*, numerous science fiction and fantasy novels, as well as several bestselling collaborations with Newt Gingrich.

Kevin Dockery has authored numerous books on the SEALs and on modern combat, including *Point Man; Hunters & Shooters*; and *Mercs*. He was the primary writer on a SEALs documentary which ran on the History Channel during the summer of 2000.

Harlan K. Ullman and James P. Wade Jr. Ullman was a former naval person and then served with the Center for Strategic and International Studies and the Center for Naval Analysis. Wade is a West Point graduate, former DOD head of Policy Planning and also of Defense Research and Engineering. The work included by them is where the term "Shock and Awe" was first used.

Brian M. Thomsen is an anthologist and award-nominated editor.